TEA OF THE SAGES

PICNIC-STYLE (NODATE) SENCHA SERVICE
At the semi-annual Issa-an Sencha School gathering at Manpukuji, May 1991. Photo: P. Graham.

TEA OF THE SAGES: The Art of Sencha

PATRICIA J. GRAHAM

Floating World Editions

Revised paperback edition, 2024
Published by Floating World Editions

Publication of this revised edition has been supported by funding from the Global Tea Institute of the University of California, Davis, and Dr. Stuart Katz. Publication of the original edition of this book by the University of Hawai'i Press was supported by grants from the Metropolitan Center for Far Eastern Art Studies and the Mary Livingston Griggs and Mary Griggs Burke Foundation.

Printed in China

Library of Congress Control Number: 2024939822

ISBN 978-1-953225-19-1

WOMEN PRACTICING LITERARY ARTS IN A GARDEN—1872
Noguchi Shōhin (1847–1917). Private collection, Japan. Photo courtesy Yamanashi Prefectural Museum of Art, see p. 144.

Contents

Acknowledgments

Over the course of many years, I have received numerous grants to support research for this book. Major sources have been the Fulbright Scholar Program, a faculty summer research grant from Hobart and William Smith Colleges, the Metropolitan Center for the Study of Far Eastern Art, the Northeast Asia Council of the Association for Asian Studies, and the Westport Fund of Kansas City. Moreover, my research could not have been accomplished without the enthusiastic support of the many sencha tea masters, pupils, and collectors I encountered in Japan.

I am especially indebted to the Tanaka family of the Kagetsuan *sencha* school in Osaka and my mentor there, Fujisawa Akiko, who helped me decipher numerous tea treatises. Ōtsuki Mikio, professor of Chinese studies at Hanazono University and researcher at Manpukuji's Bunkaden (museum/treasure house), generously provided his scrupulously researched and often unpublished references to sencha in Ōbaku primary sources as well as introductions to various curators and collectors. I also received invaluable assistance from others at Manpukuji: Tanaka Chisei, curator of the temple's Bunkaden, and Morimoto Nobumitsu, the late director of the National Japanese Sencha Association, and his staff, who invited me to numerous sencha gatherings, gave me free access to their private library, and photocopied for me numerous rare editions of premodern books on sencha. Tsukuda Ikki of the Issa-an sencha school in Osaka helped clarify my understanding of the historical development of sencha, loaned me old books, and assisted with preparation of the illustrated glossary of sencha utensils for this book. Ogawa Kōraku, headmaster of Kyoto's Ogawa sencha school, also gave generously of his time and resources.

Many museum curators, collectors, art dealers, and friends in Japan proved indispensable to my studies. I thank them all, especially Professor Yokoyama Tadashi of Tokyo University for his assistance with sencha architecture; Professor Ōba Osamu of Kansai University, a magnanimous and knowledgeable sponsor; Joseph Seubert of Geibundō, whose ability to procure obscure publications never ceases to amaze; and Taki Kozue and Mitsuo, and Matsumoto Toyoko, who helped and offered moral support during the arduous process of gathering the photos.

I also wish to acknowledge the assistance of many scholars, curators, and collectors in the West, especially Stephen Addiss, William Atwell, Paul Berry, Frank Chance, Christine Guth, Lawrence Marceau, Howard and Mary Ann Rogers, Melinda Takeuchi, and Richard Wilson. This book would not have been possible without their encouragement and constructive criticism at various stages of the project. Above all, David Dunfield deserves my deepest appreciation for his unwavering faith in this project, his insightful commentary on the text, and his drawings of sencha utensils for the glossary. Lastly, I must thank my colleagues in the Sino-Japanese Studies Group, especially Joshua Fogel, for inspiring me to search for broader cultural ramifications in my studies of Chinese-influenced Japanese art; and my editor at the University of Hawai'i Press, Patricia Crosby, who has guided development of this project from its formative stage.

Some translations and transcriptions of calligraphy from poems and other writings in *kanbun* (literary Chinese) have required assistance from Chinese friends. Joseph Tsenti Chang helped years ago with translations for my dissertation, which appear again here; Philip Wu and Du Zhong-gao transcribed and helped translate a lengthy painting inscription; and Yang Siliang assisted in translating poems by Ōbaku monks.

Despite all this expert advice and assistance, errors inevitably remain, for which I take full responsibility.

Preface to the New Edition

Having the opportunity to revisit and update a publication from 1998, twenty-six years ago now, is both a frightening and welcome experience. I am delighted that the original edition of this book sold out and that Floating World Editions, under the direction of Ray Furse, has agreed to republish it in a revised edition.

When considering how to create this new edition, we opted to leave the main text basically intact, since its narrative presenting the history of sencha remains accurate. But I did augment this revised edition with extensive updates to the secondary sources bibliography that post-date the original edition (new entries are marked with (*); these number sixty publications that focus on or contain significant discussion of sencha and its arts. The primary sources also now include two newly-discovered old books. These new sources are discussed further below. In addition, this new edition corrects small errors throughout the original text and character glossary, and updates the photos to higher quality digital images, most in color, that are placed adjacent to their relevant text, and not, as in the original edition, as an insert section (which only had 16 color plates). This new edition includes new photography for all but one of the images from the original edition (Ōtagaki Rengetsu's sencha tea cups, fig. 53, are now represented by a superb set recently donated to the Denver Art Museum).

In the remainder of this preface to the new edition, I want to comment on notable contributions to and new directions in the scholarship on sencha and broader studies with which it is discussed, in Japanese, Chinese, and Western languages. Of the new secondary sources I have included (which I fear are not exhaustive), thirty-two are in English, one is in Russian, one is in Chinese, and twenty-six are in Japanese.

Only a few exhibitions, collection catalogues, and scholarly studies in the West have addressed crafts created for use when preparing sencha. This is in spite of the rise in popularity of sencha as a beverage for everyday consumption. To date, there has been only one very recent exhibition in the U.S., at the Cleveland Museum of Art (Maezaki and Vilbar 2023), that has included a substantial number of sencha ceramics, within the context of discussing a lineage of potters, the Seifū Yohei studio, for whom the production of sencha utensils was central to their success beginning in the Meiji period.

Another significant outgrowth of the Japanese popularity of sencha in the Meiji era, briefly touched on in my book, was the proliferation of artists specializing in the production of bamboo basketry (fig. 83), a craft closely associated from its inception in Japan with sencha. In the decades since the original edition of this book was published, the collecting of Japanese bamboo arts, especially in the West, has become immensely popular. Initially baskets were inspired by and made in Chinese styles to harmonize with the Chinese atmosphere of sencha rooms, as I explored in an essay for a publication on the first major Western collection of bamboo arts assembled by Lloyd Cotsen (Graham 1999). Later, as reflected in the diverse scope of the Cotsen and other collections that include historic and contemporary basket arts, artists' forms, techniques, and styles diverged from the art's initial association with sencha, as the exhibitions of the Abbey collection at the Metropolitan Museum of Art in New York and several Japanese museums have demonstrated (Bincsik and Moroyama 2017 and 2019). Superb bamboo baskets, with many examples created for use in sencha gatherings or inspired by Chinese styles, are also featured in the catalogue of the private Naej collection in Europe (Earle 2017).

The Russian publication (Arapova 2015) is a catalogue for an exhibition of 116 sencha teapots in the Hermitage Collection, St. Petersburg, that were originally collected by a Russian statesman, Alexander Polovtsov (1832–1909). This collection is representative of the types of small sencha teapots that were enthusiastically collected by many Europeans and Americans in the second half of the nineteenth century and reside, unpublished and understudied, in many Western museums, including the Museum of Fine Arts Boston. Ai Fukunaga (Fukunaga 2021) wrote a dissertation on two such collections in the British Museum and the Maidstone Museum, and Princess Akiko of Mikasa also addressed the collecting of sencha tea wares in her dissertation (Mikasa 2009). These studies reflect an important and relatively recent direction in anthropological/art historical scholarship, that of the history of collecting.

Related to studies of collecting are those about tea generally, addressing its use in ceremonial preparations and as a national and global commodity—within Japan, between Asia and the West, and within Asia itself. Not surprisingly, some of these publications include discussions of sencha. William Farris writes about the historical commodification of tea in Japan (Farris 2019). A somewhat different focus is taken by Morgan Pitelka in his edited volume, *Japanese Tea Culture: Art, History, and Practice*, to which I contributed the only essay about sencha (Graham 2003). Lawrence Zhang (Zhang 2016) considers the recent rise in popularity of the Chinese practice of brewing *gongfucha* ("making tea with effort/skill") in modern China, and especially in Taiwan, as a kind of Chinese tea ceremony inspired in part by the way of sencha (Zhang 2016, 59). Several other Western publications include sencha in their macro-level studies of tea. Victor Mair and Erling Ho's book (Mair and Ho 2009) considers the history of tea worldwide, as does John Griffiths (Griffiths 2007), and I contributed a short historical essay on the sencha tea ceremony in Beatrice Hohenegger's exhibition catalogue, *Steeped in History: The Art of Tea*, for the Fowler Museum at UCLA (Graham 2009).

One of the most intriguing and insightful recent essays I found is by Yu-chih Lai (Lai 2012), a focused study of the participants who attended an illustrious sencha gathering in 1874 that was subsequently illustrated in the 1875 book *Seiwan meien zushi* (Pictorial record of famous utensils used at the Azure Sea Tea Gathering) which I very briefly discuss and illustrate in my book (fig. 72). Lai has identified many of the participants, who are both Chinese painters and calligraphers from Shanghai, and Japanese individuals, some well-known and others now obscure, Sinophile painters and calligraphers. Among the participants were the Japanese calligrapher Chō Sanshū (1833-1895) and the Shanghai artist Wang Dao. The antique dealer host (Yamanaka Kichirobei) and his descendants, who subsequently became prominent international antique dealers in the West, are discussed at length, particularly in relation to the presence of Japanese antique dealers in Shanghai. That this book highlights the objects featured in a sencha gathering seems a natural extension of the vocation of the host. It represents a new twist on records of sencha gatherings that had preceded it, although its inclusion of illustrations of *seki* (room arrangements) follows models of more traditional sencha gathering records. This essay, published the edited volume, *The Role of Japan in Modern Chinese Art*, reflects a new transnational emphasis in the study of Chinese and Japanese literati painters and calligraphers active during the second half of the nineteenth century (Graham and Chance 2021, section titled "Interchange Between Modern Era Chinese and Japanese Literati Painters and Scholars").

More conventional sencha tea ceremony accounts have also been the subject of recent publications. Fumoto, Hitsumoto, and Hamada 2019 is an annotated bibliography of fifty-one illustrated sencha tea ceremony records published between 1852 and 1926. The 1852 publication that they mention, *Meien hinmoku* (A list of items for a tea gathering), is of particular interest as its author is Yamamoto Baiitsu (1783-1856), about whom I wrote my dissertation (Graham 1983), and whose passion for sencha inspired my writing of this book. I did not know of its existence until that book's publication in 2015 (Bunjinga Kenkyūkai 2015). This and other recent publications about Baiitsu and sencha have only reinforced my assertion of his central role in literati culture centered around sencha in his day. These recent publications include the 2016 exhibition at the Aichi-ken Tōji Bijutsukan (Aichi 2016), the 2008 publication of an 1844 illustrated sencha gathering manuscript (Bunjinga Kenkyūkai 2008), and Ai Fukunaga's 2019 article in English in the journal *Andon* (Fukunaga 2019). The networks of Japanese literati who promoted and participated in sencha gatherings is further explored in the meticulously-researched book by Anna Beerens (Beerens 2006).

Broadly speaking, the Japanese language publications can generally be divided into four types: exhibitions featuring Edo and Meiji period utensils (for example, Seikadō Bunko Art Museum 2015, Aichi 2007, and Aichi 2000); exhibitions exploring, from written records, the sencha interests of notable Edo-period individuals; broad exhibitions on the origin and development of sencha; and essays in journals based on primary sources—documentary records about sencha gatherings compiled by various individuals (many essays of this type are featured in Nomura Bijutsukan 2007). A number of Japanese publications have also highlighted the involvement of Japanese literati with sencha and their inheritance of Chinese literati tea-drinking and related practices. These include Ogawa 2000, Ōtsuki 2004 (this is the late Ōtsuki Mikio's exhaustive study of Chinese and Japanese practitioners of sencha, which was originally published serially in the journal *Senchadō*, and now available as a stand-alone volume), Iruma 2001, Tsukuda 2013, and Shimamura 2022.

Another direction in recent scholarship on sencha is the role of monks of the Ōbaku school of Zen in its dissemination (Anjō 2007, Graham 2014, 2017, and 2023, and Komazawa 2023). For example, rather late in this process, the afore-mentioned 1875 book, *Seiwan meien zushi*, was illustrated by Tanomura Chokunyū, a leading literati painter who was also an Ōbaku monk. This is a direction I am currently investigating and sencha arts will be included in a major U.S. museum exhibition on Ōbaku now in the planning stages.

In conclusion, I want to briefly mention what other aspects of sencha studies have yet to be undertaken, particularly in the West, where it remains relatively unknown due to the predominance of *chanoyu* practice by foreigners and the collecting of its related historical and contemporary crafts, especially teabowls. Recently, I was asked to help a major U.S. museum find someone in this country to do a sencha tea ceremony demonstration in conjunction with a planned exhibition of literati arts. Unfortunately, I could not recommend anyone; I do not know of any sencha schools with branches and teachers here, although there are many *chanoyu* tea practitioners. Although a few English language publications mentioned above situate sencha within a broader, global tea history, there remains an overemphasis on chanoyu, especially as presented in museum exhibitions. This results partly from the consolidated nature of its schools in Japan and their wealth, and partly from the long-standing association of *chanoyu* with Japan's national identity (see Surak 2013). As a result, chanoyu is better known internationally and wields more influence than any of the many small sencha schools could. This skews our understanding of the continued presence of sencha in Japan and its importance to the country's cultural history.

Thus, I am very grateful to Ray Furse and his Floating World Press for keeping this book in print. I also want to thank my amazing colleague, Janet Chen, for undertaking and correcting errors in the transcribing of the characters for the glossary of this new edition, to Mary Mortensen for updating the index that she prepared for the initial edition in 1998, and to my husband, David Dunfield, and Stuart Katz, for reading page proofs.

TEA OF THE SAGES

Introduction

The numerous varieties of tea known in the world are generally classified into four types: white, green, semigreen, and red. White teas are rare, derived from buds only. The other three types utilize the leaves of the tea plant and are distinguished by the methods employed during the production processes. After picking, all tea leaves are generally steamed, then rolled and dried. Green teas retain their bright green coloring because they are unfermented (oxidation of enzymes that cause fermentation is prevented during the production process by the initial step of steaming), semigreen teas (oolong teas) are partially fermented (oxidation is begun then intentionally halted), and red teas (English-style black teas) are completely fermented (wholly oxidized). Within these categories are innumerable varieties of tea defined according to the type of tea plant, where the plant originated, the size of the leaves, and the time of year the leaves were harvested.

Powdered green tea (*matcha* or *tencha*), made from pulverized leaves, has been processed in Japan since the thirteenth century. In the Japanese tea ceremony of chanoyu, it is whisked together with hot water in a bowl. More widely available are three other types of green tea—*bancha*, sencha, and *gyokuro*—all leaf teas, prepared by steeping leaves in a pot of hot water (Ukers 1935, 1: 292–293, 309–323). Despite widespread popularity today, the drinking and domestic processing of leaf tea is a relatively recent development in Japan. First imported from China around the late sixteenth century, it was recorded as a beverage of frequent consumption only from the mid-eighteenth century, following the perfection of cultivating and refining techniques.

Bancha (common tea), comprised of mature leaves picked late in the season, is the most inexpensive leaf tea, consumed at all hours of the day. Finer, more expensive grades of green leaf tea utilize young and tender leaves harvested in the spring. The most widely propagated of these is known as sencha (literally translated in its broadest sense as "infused tea" or "boiled tea"). In addition to widespread domestic consumption, sencha became a major export product to the West, especially the United States, in the years between 1859 and 1941 (Ukers 1935, 2: 210–229). The most distinguished and costly green leaf tea manufactured in Japan is gyokuro (jade dew), whose delicate flavor stems from shading the leaves during a critical juncture in the growing season. While sencha can be consumed as a daily beverage, both it and gyokuro are often reserved for distinguished visitors, served on special occasions, or featured as the focus of a formal tea ceremony, the subject of this book. The ceremony is generally known as *senchadō* (the Way of sencha), regardless of whether sencha or gyokuro is served.

Sencha and gyokuro derive their extraordinary, delicately pungent flavor from a number of factors, foremost of which is the host's brewing techniques. If the tea maker is unskillful at this apparently simple procedure, the resulting flavor will be bitter. Additionally, taste is dependent on the age of the tea leaves (tea is best used within one year of picking, for there is much color and flavor loss over time); the selection and blend of teas; the source and type of water (from river, well, spring, stream, etc.); the temperature of both the coals and of the water; the amount of time the tea leaves are steeped; and the utensils in which tea is stored, prepared, and served (for example, porcelain tea cups are considered best because the flavor of past servings of tea does not permeate their vitreous surfaces). Aficionados today insist that the flavor of tea has declined in recent years due to impurities in the water, use of machinery to plant and harvest the tea, and factory production techniques. The preoccupation with producing the best flavor contributed to the standardization of preparation into a formal ritual, a sencha tea ceremony.

I first learned of this ceremony during the course of my dissertation research on the life and art of a Japanese painter, Yamamoto Baiitsu (1783–1856), who belonged to a movement alternately known as *bunjinga* (literati painting) or *nanga* (southern school painting).[1] This artist was well known in his day as a collector and connoisseur of Chinese paintings, calligraphies, and antiquities, but he was also celebrated as a sencha tea master. In the beginning, I simply sought to understand the role of sencha as a source of artistic inspiration for literati painters such as Baiitsu. I had no idea that it was still being practiced in contemporary Japan. I felt that investigation of the sencha tea ceremony in the Tokugawa period (1615–1867) would help me better understand the influential subculture of Sinophile intellectuals to which these artists belonged. Typically, studies of these artists have focused variously on their lives, Chinese-influenced theories, and painting styles. While specialists in the visual arts usually focus their researches on a single medium such as ceramics, architecture, or painting, I hoped that an exploration of various art forms, using sencha as a unifying factor, would allow for broader insights into the aesthetic influences and interrelationships among diverse arts and within the literati world.

For those who belonged to Japanese literati circles, the flavor of sencha was only part of its allure. Sencha was for them associated with the refined culture of China, especially that of the Ming dynasty (1368–1644), which they sought to emulate. Knowledge of this culture was gleaned only from Chinese visitors to Japan and from imported material culture, for overseas travel was proscribed by government edicts. Through the creation of a Way of sencha that elevated it as elixir of the sages, these intellectuals forged spiritual connections with the ancient Chinese literati who had idolized the beverage. As their preference for sencha spread throughout the general population, appreciation of Chinese literati values was conveyed as well, and these ideals irrevocably altered the basic nature of Japanese culture. This premise, that the sencha tea ceremony as practiced by the literati exerted great influence in the widespread assimilation of Chinese values, serves as a prevailing theme of this book. Invariably, absorption of Chinese literati values and tea-drinking customs resulted in the emergence of a new canon of aesthetic taste. Identifying this aesthetic is an important goal of this book.

Sencha, with its distinctive material culture—the tea treatises, utensils, assorted decorative accouterments, and consciously Chinese environments in which the beverage was, and still is, consumed—can be viewed as a symbol of "cultural trespass," as its association with Chinese learning, once the exclusive domain of elite classes, came to be appreciated by all. In its universal appeal, sencha both encouraged and reflected the breakdown of distinctions between the officially decreed social classes during Japan's transition from a feudal society to a modern nation in the eighteenth and nineteenth centuries.

This assimilation was complex but generally resulted in increased formalization of tea preparation procedures. Although sencha encouraged universal acceptance of Chinese values, as it increased in popularity, its material culture and ideals became altered in response to the varied interests and tastes of its proponents. Ritualistic sencha tea ceremonies gradually emerged that were, in many ways, contrary to the unpretentious environment in which the beverage had been enjoyed in China. This formalization of sencha is a trend that has continued up to the present and constitutes yet another major theme addressed in this study. Inadvertently, its initial codifiers were the literati themselves, who drank sencha at ostensibly informal gatherings during which they recreated an imagined Chinese world, surrounded by Chinese-style tea-making paraphernalia. While partaking of sencha, they wrote poetry in Chinese, painted literati-style pictures, and surrounded themselves with Chinese paintings, calligraphies, and antiquities. These activities were destined to become requisite elements of more formal sencha tea ceremonies that were devised as a means of appropriating the spirit of literati life through emulation of its outward forms.

For these first practitioners, sencha was a means of enjoying tea without the constraints imposed by chanoyu rules of etiquette. Ironically however, the growth in popularity of sencha among the general population resulted in part from incorporation of formalized procedures borrowed from chanoyu. The absorption of elements of chanoyu progressed to the extent that in its modern incarnation, sencha has come to be considered an offshoot of chanoyu. For anyone who has been exposed to chanoyu, sencha tea ceremony rituals would seem generally recognizable, although the exact procedures vary due to differences in the types of tea being prepared.

The assimilation, popularization, formalization, and absorption of chanoyu influences evolved concurrently in the history of sencha appreciation in Japan and are fundamental aspects of its historical development. Yet the evolution of sencha as a ritualized service of tea did not proceed in a linear manner; well into the twentieth century both self-consciously Chinese literati styles of sencha tea gatherings and more formalized, chanoyu-influenced sencha tea ceremonies coexisted within different social circles. Today, though the Sinified literati Way of sencha has largely vanished, vestiges can be found in some of the existing schools.

Sencha preparation now involves the use of a wide variety of utensils in numerous artistic styles. Individual schools and tea masters have devised personalized sencha ceremonies, and the atmosphere and activities at each sencha ceremony is distinct. Still, all sencha tea ceremonies share general similarities in form and have become relatively standardized according to the season, level of formality required by the occasion, location, and the like. I was introduced to these conventions at the first formal sencha tea ceremony I attended, an annual gathering for teachers and advanced pupils at the Kagetsuan sencha tea school in Osaka in 1987. A kimono-clad young woman guided me from the nearby subway station to the main entrance of the school. After signing the guest book, I was directed along with a number of other guests into a large tatami-matted waiting room where I was served *kōsen* (fragrant herb or flower tea) to cleanse my palate while I admired a flower arrangement and painting hanging in the *tokonoma* (alcove). Beside the flowers was an elegantly written record of the art on display and the utensils to be used in the ceremony.

Soon about fifteen of us were ushered into the main tearoom where sencha would be served. Adjacent to a mat upon which the utensils had been laid out for use sat the host for the occasion, the school's *iemoto* (headmaster), who chatted informally with us as we entered. After all were settled, the person who actually prepared the tea arrived with essential utensils in hand, and the ceremony began. Bowls with sweets were passed around as the tea was being prepared, coals in the clay brazier were stoked, and the kettle was filled and heated. The tea caddy was ceremoniously wiped with a silken cloth, and a measured quantity of tea leaves was placed in a teapot that was then filled with hot water from the kettle. As the tea was steeping, a tiny set of five matching porcelain cups and saucers, plus one plainer cup (from which the server later drank her serving of tea), was ritually washed and set out. Finally the tea was poured and served to the five most distinguished guests. Attendants appeared from the adjoining rooms with cups for the rest of us. A second round of tea followed; this time a small side-handled teapot (*kyūsu*) was passed around and we filled our own cups. During these preparations, we chatted with the host, sometimes jokingly, as we admired the tea utensils, the painting in the tokonoma, and the flower arrangement. All too soon the cups were cleared away and cleaned by the server as we watched. She then gathered together the smaller utensils and departed, returning briefly to refill the fresh water pot and kettle for the next round of guests. This signaled the end to this phase of the ceremony. After lingering to look more closely at the paintings, other decorative objects in the room, and remaining utensils, we gradually made our way up steep, dark stairs to the salonlike atmosphere of an expansive tatami-matted room that overlooked a large courtyard garden.

The atmosphere of this room was boisterous, filled with guests admiring treasures associated with the sencha luminary Ueda Akinari, a best-selling author in his day and sencha tea master who was the focus of this sensitively contrived exhibition. In the tokonoma were a number of teapots and braziers that Akinari had made himself. Laid out also were first editions of books authored by Akinari and examples of his calligraphy, in both hanging scroll and handscroll formats. All displays were accompanied by explanatory notes. Here I could stretch my legs and wander about, admiring the artworks at leisure, a welcome respite from the more formal ambiance of the tea ceremony I had just finished in the room below. Characteristic of sencha tea ceremonies in general, this gathering featured alternating periods of formal and informal activities, the climax of which was the tea ceremony itself.

Although the number of participants who could enter the tearoom at one time was limited, this gathering, like many I attended, had several hundred guests. In many of these events, to accommodate the crowds, guests would come and go all day. Guests often participate in more than one tea service. Upon entry, they receive an admittance ticket to a number of different sencha tea ceremonies that occur concurrently in different rooms or environments (some of these take place out-of-doors). Between ceremonies, guests sit in waiting areas consuming box lunches or admiring artworks and flower arrangements.

A very different sort of sencha gathering I attended was held at a Shinto shrine in Osaka in conjunction with a memorial service for Fujisawa Nangaku (1842–1920), a Confucian scholar and professor of Chinese studies at Kansai University whose family had close ties to the Kagetsuan sencha school (my tea teacher at Kagetsuan, Fujisawa Akiko, was his granddaughter). Guests numbered approximately three hundred—family, friends, Kansai University officials, and members of the family of Kagetsuan's headmaster. This gathering featured a spirited variation on the art appreciation portion of the tea ceremony and of the Chinese literati custom of painting for one's friends at parties. After participating in several services of tea, we entered a large room full of professional painters seated at tables with brush, ink, and paper at hand. We were instructed to select a painter whose style we admired, and, as we waited, the painter brushed a painting for us to keep as a memento.

Another smaller and more formal evening gathering to which I was invited took place at the Issa-an school in Osaka. With the exception of myself, the fifteen or so guests were prominent local businessmen and women, all fans of sencha, but some obviously more experienced and knowledgeable than others. The elegantly appointed tatami-matted waiting room was adorned with scholars' paraphernalia laid out on a Chinese writing table. Preceding the actual tea service was a meal served in a large salonlike tatami-matted room. Food was prepared according to Chinese-style Tokugawa-period recipes from a famous restaurant in Edo (Tokyo) that catered to the literati. Unlike the Chinese manner of dining for which the original restaurant was famous—with guests sitting on stools or chairs around a single table and helping themselves to food from serving bowls placed on it—we were seated Japanese style, on floor cushions, with individual trays before us. Yet food was served in the Chinese manner, being passed around in large dishes. After the meal we were ushered into the tiny tearoom to partake of sencha, and as we were a small group, the host prepared the tea for us himself.

While the present ritualization of sencha, as described above, owes a great deal to chanoyu, the patterns of development and institutional bases of these two tea ceremonies are different. Indeed, clarifying the complex relationship between chanoyu and sencha is a necessary and important task of this study. Unlike chanoyu, which today is dominated by several large national schools, numerous autonomous schools of sencha flourish throughout the country, though a few of the older, larger schools do have branches in different cities. Some of these schools are led by female iemoto, a situation unheard of within the chanoyu establishment.

One of the main reasons for sencha's relative obscurity is the perceived primacy of chanoyu as exemplifying pure Japanese aesthetic and cultural values. Modern exaltation of chanoyu first took place in the late nineteenth century when Japan sought to distance itself from many centuries of cultural domination by China. Scholars of chanoyu abound in Japan, although much of their research perpetuates carefully constructed myths designed to maintain the status of chanoyu, its luminaries, and their philosophical and aesthetic ideals (Kramer 1985). Meanwhile, few specialize in sencha. Except for a few recent exhibition catalogues, most books on the subject have been written by tea masters seeking to instruct their growing legions of followers. They inevitably perpetuate myths of their own through biases and omissions. Too often, important documentary materials are overlooked due to their inaccessibility; few premodern sencha texts have been reprinted in modern typeset editions. Also, typical of much of Japanese scholarship is the tendency to accept as genuine, publish, and thereby promote artworks and documents belonging to collections with which the author is affiliated. Many of the sencha teachers and collectors I encountered during my studies willingly assisted me because of my status as an outsider, and I was often told that such an unbiased study was badly needed. Still, maintaining a distanced perspective from which to distinguish the myths, their sources, and influences has been a formidable challenge.

Largely because it has been viewed as an exotic pastime of bourgeois dilettantes, sencha has typically been left out of discussions of Tokugawa-period aesthetic and intellectual history, except as a footnote. This study suggests rather that the place of sencha and its arts belongs among the central issues in a discourse on Tokugawa culture and society. Although sencha is not as familiar as chanoyu to Western scholars, or to the general public in Japan, it deserves similar attention.

This book is a first attempt to assess the importance of sencha in Japan and to identify the products associated with its distinct aesthetic and philosophy. Direct influence of sencha on Japanese arts can be found in the numerous craft traditions that it nurtured that still flourish today (for example, certain styles of metalwork, ceramics, basketry, and flower arranging) and the continued high regard for Chinese literati arts among Japanese scholars and an interested, well-educated public. I believe that it is not an overstatement to suggest that the contribution of sencha to Japanese culture is broader still. As sencha assisted in disseminating the understanding of Chinese literati culture on a popular level in Japan, the widespread acceptance of Chinese literati values that resulted became a critical component in the development of modern Japan's own national identity, as self-proclaimed preserver of East Asian (primarily Chinese) wisdom in the late nineteenth and early twentieth century. Furthermore, it was largely under the influence of sencha, especially the gatherings of the literati where connoisseurship of Chinese paintings and antiquities was most rigorous, that the modern appreciation and scholarship of Chinese arts in Japan originated. The Japanese collectors, scholars, and dealers of these arts in the early twentieth century not only influenced the perception and appreciation of Chinese art in Japan, but also in the West. This legacy is too often forgotten.

In the first three chapters of this book, I introduce various background materials essential to the formation of the sencha tea ceremony: a brief cultural history of tea in China and the transmission of its values and practices to Japan (chapter 1), the existence and reception of Chinese material culture in Tokugawa Japan (chapter 2), and the formation of a sencha aesthetic in Japan (chapter 3). I then deal with the creation and perpetuation of a tea ceremony for sencha in the context of the widespread assimilation of Chinese cultural values in the Tokugawa period: the emergence of a Way of sencha in the eighteenth century (chapter 4), sencha as practiced by the literati who mythologized the pastime (chapter 5), and the popularization of sencha in both mass and elite culture through the emergence of the first formalized schools and the proliferation of craft production for its preparation and service (chapter 6). I conclude with the efflorescence of sencha in modern Japan, a lasting testament to the presence of Chinese culture in an age of encroaching Westernization (chapter 7).

A Note on Translations, References, and Usage of Chinese and Japanese Names, Dates, and Terms

Unless otherwise noted, all translations are mine. Chinese words are rendered in pinyin romanization, indicated, where appropriate, with "C," but for words more generally known by the older Wade-Giles system of romanization, I have added that transcription with "WG." Important Chinese terms, names, and titles for books republished in Japan are transcribed in both Chinese and Japanese, as they frequently appear in Japanese sources indexed by their Japanese pronunciations. Where appropriate, Japanese pronunciation is indicated by "J." For the names of Chinese authors writing in English and for translations by others quoted in the text, I adhere to their preferred romanization system.

All Chinese and Japanese names, except for those of authors writing in English, appear with surnames first. As is customary, Japanese individuals born prior to the end of the Tokugawa period in 1868 are referred to by their given or artist names. Family names are used for reference to modern individuals and authors. I state ages according to Western calculation and have converted the traditional system of noting dates according to era names into their Western equivalents. Macrons are used over all long vowels in Japanese words except for those words that appear in Webster's dictionaries, which are not italicized, and commonly known proper nouns. Full citations for the references and notes appear in the bibliography.

CHAPTER ONE

The Transmission of Chinese Tea Culture to Japan

Prior to the introduction of sencha to Japan, tea, in the form of chanoyu rituals, had become an integral part of the fabric of elite Japanese culture. From the late sixteenth century, it exerted enormous impact on Japanese life. Chanoyu influenced not only the aesthetic taste of its participants, but also served as an agent of control, legitimization, and even social mobility. Appreciation of sencha developed as a route to recapture the spirit of the early days of chanoyu, before its transformation into an institution of the establishment. Sencha reflected renewed emphasis on the venerable legacy of tea in China—both tea lore and processing technology. Because they strove to assimilate and replicate the form and practice of Chinese tea, followers of sencha, more than practitioners of chanoyu, searched out the vast literature on Chinese tea history. Yet owing to restricted access to primary source materials and cultural differences, their understanding of these Chinese texts was limited. My study of sencha in Japan begins with a historical survey of Chinese tea culture and the sources by which it came to be transmitted.

Framing a Philosophy for Tea in Early China

Tea was originally cultivated in southwestern China some twenty-five hundred years ago when farmers first recognized its medicinal properties. The earliest reference to tea in Chinese prehistory tells of Shen Nong (the legendary founder of agriculture in China) drinking tea as an antidote to poison. Another often-repeated tale of this prehistoric age describes how Tong Jun, herbal adviser to legendary emperor Huangdi, recommended tea as a means of remaining alert. The first document to detail the role of tea in official life was the *Manual of Zhou Dynasty Rituals (Zhou li)*, generally thought to have been compiled in the second century B.C., during the Han dynasty (206 B.C.E.–C.E. 220). It described ceremonies, including those in which court officials presided over religious rituals involving tea, of the preceding eastern Zhou dynasty (794–221 B.C.E.). These three uses for tea in early China—as an herb that promotes health, as a means to achieve a heightened state of alertness, and as a beverage that, when ritually prepared, allowed communion with divinities—suggest the reasons for its continued appeal in later ages in both China and Japan.[1]

By the Tang dynasty (618–907), tea had become closely associated with Chan Buddhism, whose clergy used it as an aid to meditation. Fine quality tea-making utensils were donated to temples by the court, which recognized the value of tea in secular society and established an official Bureau of Tribute Tea in 770. Commoners also were then embracing tea, and the beverage was readily available in nationwide markets.

The most significant manifestation of a booming interest in tea was the appearance of the first serious and systematic treatise on the beverage, the mid-eighth-century *Classic of Tea* (C: *Cha jing*; J: *Chakyō*), by Lu Yu (J: Riku U; died 804).[2] Lu Yu was raised in a Chan temple where he learned how to cultivate and prepare tea. Later he became a scholar-recluse, absorbing influences of Confucianism and Daoism, which are evident in his writings. A Confucian predilection for order permeates his categorizations of tea and its paraphernalia, while Daoist influences abound in references to the medicinal and alchemical nature of the beverage and its spiritually regenerative properties. As he synthesized practical knowledge and philosophical associations then current about tea, Lu Yu elevated the status of the beverage through use of scholarly writing conventions.

Through his book, Lu Yu's influence was profound; he came to be considered the patron saint of tea. Even during his lifetime, Lu Yu was so revered that it was not uncommon for small statuettes of him to be displayed during tea or poetry gatherings and distributed to customers by tea sellers. Lu Yu came to be similarly revered in Japan by both chanoyu and sencha enthusiasts.

Lu Yu's *Classic of Tea* is divided into three volumes with separate sections on tea history, varieties of tea, methods of cultivation and manufacture, preparation for drinking, utensils, tea-producing regions, varieties of water for tea, and tea's physical and spiritual benefits. The high degree of specificity with which all information is recounted allowed readers to duplicate Lu Yu's methods, thereby encouraging codification. For example, many adhered to Lu Yu's dictum that white- or green-glazed tea bowls should be used because they were best for highlighting the amber color of the beverage. Not only does Lu Yu provide detailed information on the various aspects of tea he discusses, but he confers relative ranks within each category. This typically Chinese method of discrimination is characteristic of many later Chinese books, especially treatises on tea and the material culture of discerning consumers published during the Ming dynasty (Clunas 1991, 89–90). Lu Yu's cataloguing approach is perhaps most pronounced in his descriptions of the varieties of tea available and their preparation methods. He recorded four different types of processed tea: coarse tea; powdered tea (J: matcha); loose leaf tea (commonly referred to in Japanese as sencha), and caked or brick tea; the latter he described in greatest detail. He also recounted two distinct methods for preparing tea. In the first, powdered tea was added ("thrown in") to a pot of boiling water. In the second, tea was first prepared by roasting and pounding and then steeping in boiling water. In both procedures, tea was brewed by decoction or extracting its essence by boiling (J: sencha). A third method for preparing powdered tea was new in his day, though he did not discuss it. This was the whipped tea technique (J: tencha) in which mortar-ground compressed brick tea was placed in a bowl; hot water was then poured over it, and the mixture was whisked together.

Although the *Classic of Tea* is an important document, the original manuscript does not survive. The earliest recorded, but now lost, printed edition dates to the Xianshun era (1265–1274) of the Song dynasty (Nunome 1987, 1: 19). The *Classic of Tea* survives only in copies dating to the Ming dynasty, the earliest of which dates to the Hongzhi era (1488–1505). Japanese writers on tea from the thirteenth century mention the *Classic of Tea*, yet since early editions no longer exist it is difficult to ascertain the extent of their familiarity with the contents of this fundamental tea treatise. Documents listing titles of officially imported books survive from the Tokugawa period, however, and it is only from that time—when collections were systematically recorded and Chinese texts were first reprinted in Japan—that a better sense of the availability of Chinese books in Japan can be ascertained.

One of the most popular Chinese editions of the *Classic of Tea* contained explanatory notes by the editor, Lu Dingcan (active mid-eighteenth century), an eminent literatus from Jiading. This *Sequel to the Classic of Tea* (C: *Xu chajing*) was published in 1734 and already imported to Japan by 1739 (Ōba 1967, 689d). The basic text of the *Classic of Tea* was first printed in Japan in 1758, based on a different Ming edition that also included some Song tea treatises. The Japanese edition was faithful to the Ming version save for the addition of punctuation marks to facilitate reading. Several decades later, in 1774, a Japanese publication titled *Detailed Explanation of the Classic of Tea (Chakyō shōsetsu)* appeared as the first publication of the *Classic of Tea* with critical commentary by a Japanese scholar, the Kyoto Zen priest Daiten Kenjō, an early promoter of sencha.

Lu Yu was not the only proponent of tea in the Tang dynasty to become a luminary in the world of tea in China and Japan, though his position remained supreme. Another important figure was Lu Tong (J: Ro Dō; died 835), a reclusive Daoist poet and tea devotee from northern China, whose poem entitled "Thanks to the Imperial Censor Meng for His Gift of Freshly Picked Tea," alternately known simply as the "Tea Song," has become the most famous ode to tea in China and Japan, where it appears in virtually all books on sencha. In the central section of the poem, translated below, the poet recounts his growing spiritual exaltation after drinking seven successive cups of tea. He likens the experience to the flight of the Daoist immortals to their legendary paradise island (WG: P'eng-lai; C: Penglai; J: Hōrai). In his implication that tea has the ability to facilitate Daoist enlightement, Lu Tong elevates the status of the beverage from a mere drink to a mystical potion.

My bramble gate closed tight against vulgar visitors,
Wearing a cap of gauze, by myself I boil and taste the tea.
The blue smoke cloud, drawn by the wind, remains unbroken;
A white froth—floating luster—congeals in the bowl.
With bowl number one, my throat and lips are moistened;
With bowl number two, my lonely sadness is dispelled.
Bowl number three cleans out my withered bowels,
Leaving only five thousand volumes inside!
With bowl number four, I raise a light sweat
And all the worrisome affairs of my entire life evaporate through my pores.
With bowl number five, my skin and bones are purified;
With bowl number six, I commune with immortal spirits.
Bowl number seven I can barely get down:
I only feel pure wind blowing, swishing beneath my arms!
The mountains of the P'eng-lai paradise, where can they be found?
The Master of the Jade Stream wants to mount this pure wind and go there now.[3]

Lu Yu and Lu Tong were among the elite literati (C: *wenren*) of their time who, according to later chroniclers, spent their days in thoughtful seclusion, gathering together with like-minded friends to drink wine and tea, compose poems, and paint pictures. Their verses inspired an entire genre of writings on tea that was later to become a separate tradition from that of the more practical tea treatises. Knowledge of the Chinese literati tea culture was carried to Japan, where sencha texts described Tang literati gatherings at a place called the Gyokusentei (Jade Stream garden), after a reference in Lu Tong's poem. According to Japanese writers, the design of this garden followed the "shape of the immortals' path" (*tsusen shiki*), which consisted of a meandering clear stream and several large rocks, among them the "spirit hiding rock" and the "spirit calling rock."[4]

Because of extensive direct contacts between China and Japan during the Nara period (710–794), tea was likely to have then been imported. However, only later records chronicle its consumption at court ceremonies (Murai 1989, 5). The earliest document to mention contemporary tea drinking in Japan dates from the early Heian period

(794–1185), the *Later Chronicles of Japan (Nihon kōki)*, published in 840. The entry for the year 815 contains a reference to the emperor Saga (reigned 810–823) being served boiled tea (*senji cha*) by the priest Eichū (743–816) after the latter had returned from a thirty-year stay in China.

Emperor Saga was much enamored with Chinese literati culture, and he popularized tea drinking at his court as part of his emulation of Chinese civilization. He planted tea in his garden and served it at official functions. Although the boiled tea favored by Saga and his court was not prepared in the same manner as later sencha (it was the molded "brick tea" of Tang times), some later writers on sencha saw a spiritual connection between this first era of tea popularity in Japan and their own tradition. They equated these early tea drinkers with Tang dynasty literati, just as sencha became a symbol of their own spiritual communion with the Ming-period inheritors of literati tradition (Tsukuda I. 1981, 481). After Saga's time, though contacts with China and continental influences decreased, tea drinking did not completely die out. The custom was preserved at Buddhist temples, where priests appreciated tea's medicinal qualities and served it at banquets accompanying religious ceremonies (Murai 1989, 7). These functions were based on the use of tea at Chinese temples. In general though, until Zen priests reintroduced tea to Japan in the thirteenth century, tea drinking did not continue as a widespread custom as it had in China.

Maturation of the Art of Tea in China and Japan

During the Song dynasty (960–1279), the Jianzhou region of Fujian province became China's preeminent tea production center with the invention of a new processing technique for brick tea well suited to the whipped tea method (Takahashi T. 1992, 36). Although whipped tea preparation was efficient and simple, specialized techniques and appropriate utensils were still required. Most essential was the tea bowl. The most distinctive and popular of the new styles created in response to whipped tea's popularity was the black-glazed Jian ware tea bowl (J: *tenmoku*) from Fujian. Other wares, chiefly Ding and porcelains made at the newly opened ceramic complex at Jingdezhen in southern Jiangxi province, also became known for their tea utensils. The wide variety of tea utensils from this era includes tea bowls designed to sit atop lacquer or ceramic stands and tall metal or ceramic ewers that held boiling water. Such ewers were later adapted for use as a sencha utensil, a fresh water container for replenishing the kettle.

Tea remained important to the Chinese imperial court. Its production became highly regulated as it was a crop used as tribute tax. Cultivators and processors were therefore required to adhere to rigorous quality control standards. Tea also continued to hold a central position in intellectual life. Like their predecessors, the scholar-recluses of the Tang dynasty, Song dynasty literati appreciated the flavor and spiritual benefits of tea. They consumed it during painting and poetry gatherings and idolized it in their poems (Takahashi T. 1992, 39). Emulation of these men by later literati, including Sinophile scholars in Japan, assured that tea drinking remained integral to later literati lifestyles. The Japanese literati particularly admired Su Shi (J: Sō Shoku), alternately known as Su Dongpo (J: Sō Tōba; 1037–1101), whose tea poems they often copied.

By the twelfth century, Buddhist monastic rituals also routinely included elaborate tea rituals featuring whipped tea. Because of close relations between Chinese Chan monks and visiting Japanese Zen priests in the thirteenth century, this whipped tea was introduced to Japan. As visiting Chinese Chan monks and their Japanese Zen priest disciples gained favor among the Japanese rulers, their rituals paved the way for the creation of the chanoyu tea ceremony.

Credited with tea's reintroduction to Japan is the Zen priest Eisai (1141–1215), founder of the Rinzai school, who apparently returned from a journey to China in 1187 with tea seeds or plants. Eisai reputedly first grew tea at his temple in northern Kyushu and later gave some plants to his friend, the Kegon sect priest Myōe (1173–1232), who planted them at his temple, Kōzanji, in Kyoto's suburbs of Toganoo. Tea cultivation flourished there and resulted in Toganoo becoming one of the earliest tea-producing regions in Japan. In addition to being revered by chanoyu followers, both Eisai and Myōe were apotheosized in historiographic writings on sencha in the eighteenth century for the purity of their religious devotion and their initiation of the propagation of tea in Japan.

Eisai authored a small two-volume book on tea, Japan's first tea treatise, a *Record of Drinking Tea for Good Health (Kissa yōjō ki)*, which was published in 1211 and 1214.[5] It is modeled after and makes reference to Lu Yu's book, includes much information from Song encyclopedias, and also contains many original ideas such as suggestions on how tea promotes longevity and spiritual harmony (Murai 1989, 8–9). Eisai stimulated interest in tea among Japan's ruling samurai class by presenting his book to the shogun Minamoto Sanetomo (1192–1219) with the advice that tea would cure the shogun's illness, brought on by excessive drinking of alcohol, which it reportedly did (Plutschow 1986, 43).

Although Eisai was well aware of the medicinal value of tea, in practice he seems to have stressed the Chinese use of tea in religious rituals, for he wrote that he drank the beverage "not as a stimulant during meditation, but as an esoteric ritual conducive to the harmonious functioning of the bodily organs" (Collcutt 1981, 39).

Following Chinese Buddhist practices, Eisai initiated in Japan the ritual of offering tea to the Buddha (*kucha*) and created a similar offering to Shinto deities (*kencha*), claiming that these liturgies were essential to the establishment of an unbreakable bond between humankind and the gods. These services were perpetuated by later Japanese chanoyu and sencha tea masters as their most formal, dignified tea ceremonies. One Chan Buddhist tea ritual of the Song dynasty that has been maintained in Japan is based on the monastic rules outlined in the treatise *One Hundred Rules of Order* (C: *Baizhang qing gui*). This ceremony in Japan, known as the *Yotsugashira* (four hosts), is distinguished by the use of Chinese utensils and mannerisms. It is still performed annually at the three oldest Rinzai temples (Enkakuji in Kamakura and Kenninji and Tofukuji in Kyoto) to honor the deaths of each temple's founder. Kenninji's homage to Eisai on April 20, for example, has taken place almost every year since his death (Plutschow 1986, 44–48). As part of this event in recent years, prominent sencha and chanoyu tea schools have been invited to host tea ceremonies concurrently in subtemples, reinforcing the bonds between Chinese and Japanese tea liturgies.

In thirteenth-century Japan, as in Song China, the *hōjō* (abbot's quarters) functioned as a place where high-ranking patrons could mingle with the priests in various cultural pursuits (Collcutt 1981, 201). This permeation of secular influences into religious rites proliferated to the extent that by the early fourteenth century regulations warned monks to adhere to their austerities, demanding, for example, that only a single variety of cake should be served during temple tea ceremonies (Collcutt 1981, 75). Eventually, in response to the need for appeal to secular patrons, religious services grew into elaborate affairs that often incorporated lengthy tea ceremonies. At one initiation service in 1460 for an abbot of a *gozan* temple (a temple that enjoyed official patronage of the shogunate), the inauguration day of feasting was followed by an entire day devoted to the tea ceremony (Collcutt 1981, 233). By the mid-fifteenth century, nonreligious literary activities and more formalized secular tea ceremonies also regularly took place in the salon atmosphere of Zen temple hōjō (Collcutt 1981, 100).

Gatherings of secular patrons in the hōjō exposed them to various aspects of Zen culture, including the informal drinking of tea and the appreciation of *karamono* (Chinese things, usually referring to decorative arts and paintings), which had originally been imported both for ritual use in Zen Buddhist temples and for commercial profit (Murai 1989, 15). By the late thirteenth century, these patrons had begun to drink tea outside the environs of Zen temples. The first secular tea gatherings (*cha yoriai*) featured contests (*tōcha*) in which participants guessed the variety of tea served. This event was loosely based on the Chinese custom of judging the quality of the tea, an activity that in China continued as an elegant amusement of the literati (Murai 1989, 11). In chanoyu circles, these events developed into occasions to display prized collections of newly imported karamono. Throughout the history of chanoyu, karamono continued to play an important aesthetic role. Participating in tōcha and displaying karamono also became essential elements in the atmosphere of eighteenth- and nineteenth-century sencha gatherings.

Despite this emphasis on chanoyu and powdered tea in Muromachi society, the characters for the word "sencha" often appear in the poems of Zen monks. However, it is uncertain whether the writers consumed leaf tea that was steeped or were referring to the process of boiling tea in a more generic manner, as had been the customary usage of this term in China as early as the Tang dynasty. These poems may reflect the knowledge about steeped leaf tea (sencha) that reached Japan via Korea, which had also embraced Chinese tea customs. It has been suggested that owing to the close relations between Korean and Japanese monks, Japanese Zen monks may have learned of new Chinese tea procedures and terminology from these Korean contacts (Kumakura 1976).

References to tea that was steeped (*senji mono*) are also found in documents detailing customs of the lower classes during the Muromachi period. The 1403 *One Hundred Books of Tōdaiji (Tōdaiji hyakugō no sho)* records that tea—probably bancha or some kind of low-grade steamed leaf tea—was being made and sold for commoners' consumption in the courtyard in front of the temple. Such tea sellers are illustrated in Muromachi-period handscrolls such as the *Handscroll of Poetry Competition Matches of Seventy-one Different Occupations (Nanajūichi-ban shokunin uta-awase emaki).*[6]

Steeped Tea in the Literati Culture of Ming and Qing China

Although whipped tea was undeniably the most popular tea preparation method in the Song dynasty, as in the Tang dynasty, the particular preparation technique employed depended on one's status, occupation, geographic location, and wealth. The older method of boiling tea never completely disappeared during the Song dynasty, and a number of varieties of tea—particularly in southern and western China—were cultivated and processed as loose leaf tea for this purpose. Processing techniques for these leaf teas were further refined during the succeeding Yuan dynasty (1279–1368), when tea leaves were steamed, then dried to prevent fermentation. The result was unfermented green leaf tea. In the fifteenth and early sixteenth centuries, however, brewing leaf tea retained aspects of older, more complex procedures involving grinding the leaves into a powder, straining them into a serving bowl, adding boiling water, and whisking.

It was not until the end of the sixteenth century that a sophisticated method for steeping leaf tea (C: *paocha*; J: *hōcha*, but sometimes referred to in Japan as *dashicha* or more commonly as sencha) was perfected. The Chinese literati, China's consummate tea connoisseurs, recognized that the flavor of loose leaf tea could be enhanced by developing detailed specifications for water temperature, tea strength, and steeping duration. These procedures required the use of specialized utensils, primarily the teapot and teacup, the sizes of which gradually diminished as innovations in processing and brewing methods yielded stronger and more flavorful teas. Porcelain teapots, essentially variant forms of ewers, seem first to have been manufactured at Jingdezhen during the Xuande era (1426–1435). Both teapots and teacups are closely related in shape to utensils used for serving wine. Indeed, in the early days of production of wares for steeped tea, they were sometimes used interchangeably.

Among tea connoisseurs, Yixing stoneware teapots from Jiangsu province, first made in the early sixteenth century, were preferred for their iron-rich clay bodies that absorbed impurities in the water, accentuating the flavor of the tea. Crafted and signed by individual artisans for a small circle of patrons, they were the most expensive pottery produced at the time (Clunas 1991, 132). Much later, Yixing ware was to become esteemed in Japan among sencha fans and copied by native potters. Also imported to Japan for use with sencha were fine quality white porcelain tea wares now known as *blanc de chine*, a specialty of the Dehua kilns of Fujian province from the early seventeenth century.

By the early Qing dynasty (1644–1912), in order to more efficiently prepare large quantities of tea for expanding markets, further advances in processing led to the creation of a new type of tea. Recently harvested tea would be laid out to wither (instead of being immediately steamed) so that it would partially ferment before being roasted. This semifermented tea was called *wulongcha* (literally, black dragon tea; J: ūroncha; popularly known in the West as oolong tea) after the region in which it was produced, the Wuyi district of Fujian province. This tea became the most sought-after variety in the export trade with Europe. Oolong tea was soon infused by its own method, "laborious" or "leisurely" tea (C: *gongfucha*), which flourished in Fujian and Guangdong provinces.

For gongfucha, leaf tea is placed in a teapot that in turn is set in a large bowl filled with boiling water. This procedure helps maintain proper water temperature, a critical step for preserving the tea's flavor.[7] By the Kangxi era (1662–1722), a special covered teacup had been devised for oolong tea that allowed it to be brewed and kept warm in individual servings. Although oolong tea was not adapted by the Japanese until after World War II, the lidded teacup for gongfucha was known during the Tokugawa period. Japanese potters copied its form from around the 1830s, though it then functioned as a means of keeping green tea (sencha or bancha) warm after infusion in a conventional teapot.

From the late sixteenth century, tea and its paraphernalia became important commodities in the flourishing luxury products market geared to increasing numbers of upwardly mobile, sophisticated consumers. Fueling this market was a thriving publishing industry that advised readers who wished to achieve social parity with the admired scholar-elite that they should possess knowledge of appropriate etiquette, styles for residential architecture, food and drink, and suitable objects with which to surround themselves. One of the earliest and most important of these texts was the 1591 *Eight Discourses on the Art of Living* (C: *Zunsheng bajian*), by Gao Lian (active late sixteenth century) with a preface contributed by Tu Long (1542–1605). This book became a model for many later scholars' texts, including those on sencha in Japan, which commonly excerpted sections verbatim without citation. Such plagiarism can be found in the immensely popular *Treatise on Superfluous Things* (C: *Zhang wu zhi*) of circa 1615–1620, by Wen Zhenheng (1585–1645), who hailed from an exalted lineage as the great-grandson of Wen Zhengming (1470–1559), one of the leaders of the literati painting movement in the Ming dynasty.

The *Treatise on Superfluous Things* also included original commentary, advising on tea selection and preparation and defining suitable environments in which to consume it. It defined the eremitic retreats of the literati from the Tang and Song eras as models for these environments. Within this discussion the treatise provided the following recommendations for constructing a teahouse:

> *Build a structure of one column's span, adjacent to a mountain studio, and set therein the tea utensils. Train a boy to the exclusive service of tea, so that the whole day may be spent there in pure talk, the chilly night spent in sitting there in a dignified attitude. This is the first priority of a recluse, which cannot be dispensed with (Clunas 1991, 41).*

Ming writers on literati life invoked two concepts, elegance (C: *ya*; J: *ga*) and vulgarity (C: *su*; J: *zoku*) to distinguish cultured intellectuals and the things they enjoyed from the preferences of dilettantes. In ancient Chinese Confucian texts, ya was equated with proper conduct (*zheng*). Crafts appreciated by the literati became identified with elegance. Although contemporary writers acknowledged that certain types of objects inherently possessed elegance, they also asserted that even objects dismissed as vulgar, such as contemporary crafts admired by the disdained nouveau riche, might take on the aura of elegance when used appropriately (Watt 1987, 9). In this respect, the authors echo sentiments familiar to chanoyu tea connoisseurs in Japan who admired carefully selected assemblages of objects. Writers on sencha and other literati arts in Japan frequently referred to these concepts in their discourses with similar intent to distinguish the sophisticated consumer from the plebeian. Tea, as an elegant literati pastime, became the focus of an entire genre of books. Beginning with Lu Yu's treatise, some sixty-nine separate tea texts were published in China before 1912, with most dating to the Ming and Qing dynasties (Wu 1990, 66–68). These include compendia of annotated editions of famous tea books of the past, contemporary tea treatises, and related texts on various aspects of literati life that contain significant sections on tea.

Conveying the Culture of Steeped Tea to Japan

During the sixteenth century, when steeped leaf tea was displacing brick and powdered tea in China, Japanese tea drinkers still preferred the powdered tea of chanoyu. Chanoyu had become adopted by upper-class Japanese society as much more than a beverage to be served at ceremonies in Zen temples or at formal banquets in secular environs. Participation in chanoyu functioned as a form of required etiquette among high-ranking samurai as well as a means for merchants to elevate their status. Embracing its rituals was evidence of refinement and education. Some merchants escaped the confines of their class by serving the samurai leaders as tea masters. The most famous of these was Sen no Rikyū (1522–1591), who successfully elevated and popularized one style of chanoyu, that of *wabicha*, above others. Wabicha valued rusticity, restraint, and simplicity, the antithesis of Chinese aesthetic taste, though its emphasis on eremiticism grew out of many centuries of Japanese intellectuals' admiration for the Chinese sages (Brown 1997, 19–52, 69–70). *Wabi* ideals were manifested in a preference for humble Japanese-made tea wares and service of chanoyu in intimate, rustic tea huts.[8]

Despite the enormous influence of chanoyu on Japanese tea-drinking preferences, evidence for the consumption of steeped tea exists in late-sixteenth-century Japan. One controversial source that makes reference to it is the *Records of Nanpō (Nanpōroku)*, a text purportedly discovered in 1686 by Tachibana Jitsuzan (1655–1708) and published soon after on the one hundredth anniversary of the death of Sen no Rikyū in 1691 (Varley 1989, 166–168). It features comments on chanoyu by Rikyū as recorded by a disciple, the priest Nanbo Sokei, including the statement that Rikyū would sometimes go to the Sakai temple of Shukoin and drink "jade-colored" sencha (Tsukuda I. 1981, 482). Since Sakai was a major international port in the sixteenth and early seventeenth centuries and home to numerous Chinese immigrants, the appearance of sencha there is plausible enough.

A more reliable source is a record left by the Jesuit priest João Rodrigues, who arrived in Japan in 1577 and stayed for over thirty years. He commented extensively on tea and chanoyu etiquette from firsthand experience. While in residence in Nagasaki, he must have observed Chinese tea drinking, for he accurately remarked upon the Chinese method for brewing tea: "They [the Chinese] do not observe any particular ceremony, nor do they set aside a special place for the pastime. They boil the leaves in the water, and in fact this way is also practiced in Japan by peasants and lowly people" (Cooper 1989, 123).

This leaf tea—sencha—became more accessible and popular during the seventeenth century. By 1658 sencha was being sold by peddlers in Edo. The *Compendium of Food from Our Time (Honchō shokkan)*, published in 1692, informs us that among the women of that city it was common to drink a number of cups of sencha before breakfast. Contemporary scholars assume this was something like ordinary bancha (Kadoyama 1988, 23; Nishiyama 1984, 283). Similar observations about commoners drinking steeped leaf tea were made by the Dutch physician Engelbert Kaempfer (1651–1716), who included a section on tea in his voluminous writings about his stay in Japan between 1690 and 1692 (Kaempfer 1906, 3: 238–239). These sources all seem to refer to sencha as a general term for steeped leaf tea.

Chinese books on tea and the literati culture with which it was intimately connected began to be imported to Japan soon after the adoption of leaf tea drinking.[9] Ōeda Ryūhō, author of two of the earliest Japanese books on sencha and Chinese literati lifestyles, indiscriminately copied sections from assorted Chinese books in his 1756 *Chats on Tea by the Azure Harbor (Seiwan chawa)* and 1762 *Miscellaneous Records of Elegant Pastimes (Gayū manroku). The Eight Discourses on the Art of Living*, for example, served as a model for his discussion of places to drink tea in his *Chats on Tea by the Azure Harbor*. Ōeda's *Miscellaneous Records of Elegant Pastimes* opens with passages from two other Ming books, *A Pure Record from a Small Window* (C: *Xiaozhuang qingji*), by Wu Cong, which was known to have been imported in 1747 (Ōba 1967, 736c), and the *Five Miscellaneous Records* (C: *Wuzazu*), by Xia Zhaozhi, which was widely known in Japan in Ryūhō's day (Nunome 1987, 1: 10).

During the Tokugawa period, publications on literati ideals of the Qing dynasty were also being imported concurrent with earlier Ming texts. A favorite Chinese author among the Japanese was Li Yu (J: Riku Gyo; 1611–1679), celebrated as both a writer and a publisher. His *Casual Expressions of Idle Feelings* (C: *Jianqing ouji*) of 1671 was imported as early as 1711,[10] and his illustrated manual on literati-style painting, *Mustard Seed Garden Manual of Painting* (C: *Jieziyuan huajuan*; J: *Kashien gaden*), first published in 1679 and expanded in 1701, was known in Japan from the late seventeenth century. This latter text, first reprinted in Japan in 1748, was one of the most popular Chinese literati painting manuals, widely influential beyond the realm of artists alone. In passages such as "Avoiding Vulgarity," Li discussed literati life in the context of elegance and vulgarity, terms that became central to the discourse on defining refinement in eighteenth-century Japan (Nakano 1989, 128).

One important general Chinese volume on the material culture of the literati was the *Desultory Remarks on the Abode of the Retired Scholar* (C: *Kaopan yushi*), by Tu Long, author of the preface to the *Eight Discourses on the Art of Living*. Within a discussion of the essential material possessions of the scholar, it included a lengthy chapter on tea and its utensils, water, varieties, preparation, and growing. There was also a separate, short section describing a tea hut as a small retreat that contained little more than utensils for tea. Not only was the appearance of this place defined, so too was the nature of discussions (on pure matters only) that should take place therein. The ideas presented here were little different from other famous Ming texts, which it may indeed have copied (Clunas 1991, 28–31). *Desultory Remarks on the Abode of the Retired Scholar* was published in 1606 as part of the first edition of the famous Ming compendium *Secret Book Collection of the Treasured Writing Hall* (C: *Rao yan tang bi ji*). Yet it was probably not known in sencha circles in Japan until it appeared in the Qing compendium *Secret Book of the Majestic Dragon* (C: *Longwei mishu*), first published in 1794 and owned soon thereafter by the illustrious bibliophile and sencha master of Osaka, Kimura Kenkadō.

Works of Ming and Qing literature with tea as their primary subject were also available in Tokugawa Japan, where they were copied and circulated in Japanese editions to fans of sencha and chanoyu alike. Among the most important was an influential Ming text on tea in the context of literati culture, the *Tea Treatises* (C: *Chadong*; J: *Chatō*), by Xia Shufang (J: Ka Juhō), of circa 1610; the Japanese edition of 1758 was the first collection of Chinese tea books to be printed in Japan. It contained a preface by the Kyoto Confucian scholar Kiyota Tansō, who was close friends with early promoters of sencha.

Another influential set was the 1613 *Complete Collection of Tea Books* (C: *Chashu quanji*; J: *Chasho zenshū*), edited by Yu Zheng (J: Yusei), which included twenty-eight Chinese books on tea plus a number of tea poems. The edition of this book now in the National Diet Library in Tokyo was once owned by the Confucian scholar and shogunal adviser Hayashi Razan (1583–1657) (Nunome 1987, 1: 10). This compendium, which became required reading for all aspiring sencha aficionados, was not printed in Japan until 1804, however (Nunome 1987, 1: 74).

For the most part, Qing publications on tea were abridgments and summaries of older texts. It was these easily available contemporary publications with which the Japanese interested in sencha were most familiar. Many that were reprinted in Japan under the auspices of sencha devotees were liberally quoted in Japanese sencha texts. Among the earliest of the Qing compilations to be published in Japan was the *Secrets of Steeped Tea* (C: *Jiancha jue*; J: *Sencha ketsu*), by Ye Zhuan (J: Yōsen), first printed in 1764 under the direction of Daiten Kenjō and copied from a Chinese original owned by Kimura Kenkadō. Deemed an essential source, it was translated into Japanese and published as part of the *Detailed Record of Sencha* (J: *Sencha ryakusetsu*) in 1798. Another of these tea compendia, the *History of Tea* (C: *Cha shi*; J: *Cha shi*) of circa 1675, by Liu Yuanzhang (J: Ryū Genchō), was also copied from an edition owned by Kenkadō and reprinted in Japan in 1801 (Nunome 1987, 1: 60–61). Although it was comprised entirely of excerpts from earlier treatises, it also exerted significant influence.

Japanese writers on tea would freely crib from whatever Chinese sources they could find, for to mention Chinese sources conferred an air of authority. As already mentioned, Ōeda Ryūhō listed a large number of Chinese tea books from different eras as his sources, although it is doubtful he had access to the complete texts of them all; their names more probably came from some compilation that contained summaries of their contents. Another popular writer, Ueda Akinari, quoted liberally from the 1570 *Records of a Tea Hut* (C: *Cha liaoji*), by Lu Shusheng (1509–1605), in his famous sencha volume *Miscellaneous Comments on the Way of Pure Elegance (Seifū sagen)* of 1794, apparently from extracts in a Qing compendium.

It can be surmised that nearly any Chinese book on tea that found its way to Japan ultimately became a treasured item. Many, such as the *Pictorial Album of Tea Utensils* (C: *Chaju tupu*; J: *Chagu zufu*), abridged by Fu Shiran (J: Fu Shizen), came to exert influence out of proportion to their significance among the greater body of Chinese tea texts. This particular book had been presented to the literati painter and sencha tea master Tanomura Chikuden by an acquaintance in Nagasaki. He subsequently had it reprinted in 1829 so that its information could easily be disseminated.

This exploration of the transmission of Chinese tea-drinking practices to Japan and their subsequent reception has shown that Japan had extensive but not comprehensive or entirely contemporary access to continental developments. Although Japanese writers and tea drinkers embraced the heritage of Chinese tea as inheritors of a venerable tradition, they were continuously modifying it to suit their own purposes and their particular political and cultural environment. Only rather late in this transmission, from the eighteenth century on, did Japanese writers about tea use the Chinese sources as a means of asserting the supremacy of the Chinese tradition, with specific reference to admiration for literati values. This attitude shift is symptomatic of changing perceptions of China, closely tied to issues of self-identity within the Japanese intellectual community. As will be shown in the following chapter, these new attitudes were stimulated by growing numbers of consumers possessing the necessary education, wealth, and access to Chinese material goods to allow for appreciation of the complexities of elite Chinese culture, of which tea was an important part.

CHAPTER TWO

The Reception of Chinese Material Culture in Tokugawa Japan

To premodern Japanese, China embodied the highest civilized values. The ability to read and write in Chinese and possession of Chinese artifacts initially helped to distinguish those who belonged to elite Japanese society—the aristocrats, upper-ranking samurai, and Buddhist priests—from the lower classes. Only they had the time and wealth required for such endeavors. By the late sixteenth century, the Chinese philosophies of Confucianism and Daoism were well accepted among members of these various factions.

With the advent of the Tokugawa period, the new shogunal rulers mandated the propagation of Confucian doctrine throughout their realm. Although this promotion of Confucianism stimulated even greater curiosity about Chinese civilization, political instability in China and legal restrictions imposed by Japanese authorities on their citizens made it impossible for Japanese nationals to visit China for most of the Tokugawa period. Consequently, Chinese philosophy and customs were gleaned from imported books and from contact with Chinese residents in Japan, most of whom resided in Nagasaki. These residents were merchants, emigrant Chan Buddhist monk-scholars, and expatriates loyal to the Ming dynasty.

As ordinary citizens grew more affluent under the peaceful Tokugawa regime, their desire for Chinese material goods increased, prompting large quantities to be imported. The favorable reception of Chinese values and artifacts led directly to the emergence of the art of sencha, since tea drinking was an essential aspect of Chinese life, tied to both its philosophical ideals and its consumerism.

Shogunal Policies Regarding Trade and Diplomacy with China

Prior to the Tokugawa period, Japan's diplomatic relations with China were sporadic and largely unregulated. The Ashikaga shogun Yoshimitsu (1358–1408) first formalized an official policy on the large volume of international trade in 1401. He acquiesced to Chinese demands for Japanese subordination, however, a condition that later Japanese leaders refused to accept. Because of increasing political instability in both countries during the sixteenth century, clandestine trade increased. This encouraged the rise of Japanese pirates (*wakō*) who plundered the waterways, sometimes under the direction of local daimyo (military warlords). Ming traders were especially incensed at the success of the pirates, and in 1557 China officially terminated all trade with Japan. Toyotomi Hideyoshi (1536–1598), who planned to conquer China after first vanquishing Korea in the 1590s, further enraged the Chinese, who sent troops to aid the Korean effort. Until 1610, when the first Tokugawa shogun, Ieyasu (1542–1616), welcomed Chinese traders, trade continued unofficially, often indirectly via other nations' ports, from harbor towns such as Sakai south of Osaka, and smaller outposts along Japan's coasts as far west as the Kii Peninsula. Chinese merchants in Japan were so numerous in the sixteenth century that many coastal communities became small Chinatowns (Toby 1991, 24; Jansen 1992, 6–8).

The seventeenth-century Tokugawa shoguns modeled their authority on the strict and, in their minds, successful Confucian bureaucratic organization of China. They subscribed to Confucian precepts that their right to rule was validated by their unification of the country, their continued leadership for three generations, and acceptance of their authority by foreign powers who dispatched diplomatic missions to meet them (Toby 1991, 69–70). This diplomatic policy included extensive provisions for regulating international trade. Despite the chaotic political climate of the late Ming dynasty, China sought to reestablish official trade, a proposal that the Japanese rejected in 1621 (Toby 1991, 196). Meanwhile, private trade with China, largely with merchants from China's southern provinces of Nanjing and Fujian, was flourishing, with as many as twenty to thirty Chinese ships annually making the roundtrip journey in the 1620s.

During the 1630s, however, the *bakufu* (alternately known as the shogunate), Japan's military bureaucracy administered by the shogun, began cracking down on this unauthorized trade. The first step in implementing the restrictive trading policies, later known as the closing of the country (*sakoku*), occurred in 1633, with the banning of international travel by Japanese citizens in order better to control national security. For similar reasons, in 1635 the China trade was restricted to the port of Nagasaki, and in 1639 the government banned all European traders except the Dutch, whose commercial activities were thereafter confined to Hirado. In 1641 the Dutch were forced to move to the island of Dejima in Nagasaki harbor. From then until the forced opening of the port of Yokohama in 1859, Nagasaki served as Japan's sole international port. Nevertheless, independent international trade through other seacoast towns was not completely eliminated; it continued with Korea and the Ryukyu islands, the latter under the control of the daimyo of Satsuma, and with independent smugglers via various ports off the coast of Kyushu (Toby 1991, xxv).

In 1644, when the Manchus overran China and established the Qing dynasty, Japanese authorities had misgivings about diplomatic relations with these new Chinese leaders. They were concerned that the aggressive Manchus threatened the peace of the entire East Asian region. The Japanese were acutely aware of a thwarted Manchu invasion of Korea in 1627 and did not like the Manchu acceptance of the Jesuits, whom shoguns had attempted to ban from Japan since 1587. The Tokugawa rulers did not accept subordinate status with the Manchus. Their sympathies clearly lay with the overthrown Ming loyalists (C: *Ming yimin*), and they considered offering military support, but instead granted them sanctuary and gave preferential treatment in matters of trade (Toby 1991, 138).

Because the Tokugawa bakufu did not have diplomatic ties with China, Chinese traders—who, as merchants, occupied the bottom level of the Confucian social scale—were accorded the lowest status among the foreigners in Japan. Furthermore, the Chinese government provided little assistance in upgrading the status of their merchants, perhaps because encouraging trade as a source of revenue was taboo in traditional Chinese society (Clunas 1991, 142). Regulations on trade imposed by both countries continued to change throughout the Tokugawa period. Between 1661 and 1683 Qing rulers enacted and strictly enforced a ban on international shipping, resulting in a substantial decrease in the volume of Chinese trade in Nagasaki. The few Chinese ships that did manage to enter Japan circumvented this prohibition by embarking from Southeast Asia. When the ban was lifted in 1684, 102 Chinese ships entered Nagasaki, and this number increased annually until 1688 (the peak year), when the number of ships reached 194. Meanwhile, in 1685, the Japanese implemented ever more restrictive trade regulations, setting a maximum value on imports allowed per year. After 1688, restrictions were imposed by the Japanese that set an upper limit on arriving ships at 77 (Iwao 1976, 13; Totman 1993, 145). Throughout the eighteenth century the number of Chinese ships allowed to dock at Nagasaki was further restricted, so that by the year 1790 permission was granted to only 10 ships.

Predictably, ships turned away from Nagasaki after the yearly limit had been achieved became unauthorized smuggling vessels. Smugglers also set sail from China aboard other ships that had no intention of calling at the Nagasaki port, as they brought forbidden goods into Japan and needed to bypass censors in Nagasaki. These goods included books on banned subjects such as Christianity or heterodox Confucian teachings.[1] Although prohibitions against smuggling had been enacted beginning in 1670, it was not until smugglers were massacred in 1726 that this activity ceased to be a major problem.[2]

Detailed records of cargo exist only for authorized trading vessels from China that entered the official port of Nagasaki. They indicate the kinds of goods desired by the Japanese. These documents show Chinese ships carried raw materials as well as finished goods, generally luxury items and agricultural products. Among the products for one ship docking in 1645 were 2,750 catties of Chinese tea (about 3,644 pounds) and 433 teapots (Innes 1980, 474–503, 668–669).[3] Although not clearly indicated, this tea would likely have been leaf tea (sencha), which was most prevalent in China at that time. Evidence for the drinking of sencha in seventeenth-century Japan can be gleaned from sources such as this.

One of the paradoxes of the Tokugawa policy was that while official laws forbade Japanese citizens from traveling to China, the government unceasingly promoted the importance of Confucianism. By distancing their high regard for Confucianism from concerns they had about the barbarian-ruled Qing dynasty, the Japanese shoguns, in counsel with their Confucian advisers, began to reassess their nation's attitudes toward China, emphasizing the positive aspect of Confucianism's universal principles. Formerly they had grudgingly acknowledged China's superiority. Now, as foreigners ruled China, the Japanese government could legitimately claim parity with and even superiority over China. Ming loyalists who settled in Japan reinforced perceptions that China was no longer the "Middle Kingdom" and that the new center of Chinese Confucian culture had shifted to Japan (Toby 1991, 223–224). Japanese leaders felt that their country's superiority over China in the upholding of Confucian values was particularly evident in its political institutions, presentation of rituals, and preservation of old forms of music. By maintaining or reinstituting antique Japanese forms that were closely modeled on those of ancient China, Japanese authorities reasoned that they had perpetuated the authentic culture from which latter-day China had deviated (Nakai 1980, 173–179).

This respect for Confucianism, divorced from present-day Chinese politics, was promulgated among the samurai class through required schooling. Although Confucian learning was initially restricted to the samurai class, private academies of Confucian studies were soon opened for commoners (*chōnin*), resulting in the study of Chinese language and Confucian classics becoming the basis of all children's education (Dore 1965, 127–145). Samurai were first tutored privately, but by the late eighteenth century official domain-sponsored schools proliferated. Many of these contained separate structures for observation of Confucian rites. Teachers were most often *rōnin* (masterless samurai) or their sons, sons of scholars, or even intellectuals born into the chōnin class. Many independent scholars, such as Itō Jinsai

(1627–1705), founder of the *Kogaku* (ancient learning) school of Confucian studies, congregated in Kyoto, where most of the nation's approximately fourteen hundred autonomous Confucian academies came to be located. Some of the chōnin teachers at these private schools were so renowned that they attracted samurai pupils. Others were themselves elevated to the rank of samurai in order to teach at domain-al academies or to serve as advisers to daimyo.

The first and most influential of the government-sponsored Confucian academies, the Shōheikō (later known as the Shōheizaka Gakumonsho), was founded in Edo in 1630 to teach approved interpretations of Confucianism to the elite of the samurai class, with the shogun's chief Confucian adviser, Hayashi Razan, serving as head teacher. Tokugawa Yoshinao (1600–1650), daimyo of Owari and seventh son of Ieyasu, provided funds for an adjacent Confucian temple (Seidō or Kōshibyō) in 1632, where semiannual ceremonies in honor of Confucius (*sekiten*) would be held.[4]

In 1690, following increases in funding from the bakufu, the Shōheikō relocated to the Yushima district of Tokyo, where it was enlarged into a complex of some twenty structures. It was thereafter known as the Yushima Seidō and remains today, though in reconstructed form (the original was destroyed in the Great Kanto earthquake of 1923). Modeled after Confucian temples of China, the Yushima Seidō was the site of Confucian rites that took place in a self-consciously Chinese atmosphere over which statues of Confucius and other Chinese sages presided. Although Confucian temples and sekiten ceremonies had existed in Japan as early as A.D. 701, they increased in number from the late seventeenth century, when they were constructed throughout the country together with daimyo-sponsored Confucian academies.[5]

Ravaged by repeated fires and neglected by the shoguns for the greater part of the eighteenth century, the Shōheikō and its Confucian temple were refurbished in the late eighteenth century to become the symbolic centerpiece in the shogunate's promotion of the tenets of orthodox Confucianism. It was here that the sons of many high-ranking samurai received their primary education. Some of these men, such as Rai San'yō, a central figure in early-nineteenth century literati sencha circles, later turned to other interpretations of Confucian philosophy that were less supportive of the supremacy of shogunal authority.

The Japanese political structure, which was based on military might and inherited birthright, was basically at odds with the Confucian philosophy's dictate that the right to rule be mandated by moral conduct (Bodart-Bailey 1993, 313). Because the bakufu could not stifle unauthorized interpretations of Confucian doctrine, they inadvertently sowed the seeds of rebellion against their rule. Indeed, many of the most passionate Tokugawa-period Confucian scholars were idealistic men from the fringes of the samurai class, often rōnin, who found in Confucianism a means of bolstering their personal status while simultaneously employing the doctrine to urge the creation of an ethical Confucian society in Japan (Nakai 1980, 158). In this context, sencha demonstrated conscious rejection of the highly formalized protocol of chanoyu in which they, as members of the samurai class, were required to participate (Wilson 1989, 71–72).

Ming Loyalists in Japan

Japanese Confucian scholars and political leaders sought the guidance of Ming loyalists, admired for their wisdom and courage, who emigrated to Japan. Shogunal ordinances on the movement of foreigners within Japan permitted few Chinese to leave Nagasaki. Only several Ming loyalists at a time could accept daimyo invitations, authorized by the bakufu, to settle in various provinces where they served as advisers on Confucianism and other aspects of Chinese culture.

The most famous Ming loyalist in Japan was Zhu Shunshui (WG: Chu Shun-shui; J: Shu Shunsui; 1600–1682), one of two Chinese scholars to serve Tokugawa Mitsukuni (1628–1700), grandson of Ieyasu and daimyo of the Mito *han* (fief).[6] In 1659 Zhu settled in Nagasaki, where he taught Confucianism. He left for Edo in 1665 at the invitation of the Mito daimyo, whom he instructed in Confucian philosophy and its rituals, Chinese garden design, and Chinese methods of agriculture. Zhu also designed a Confucian temple, Hijiridō, for Mito City, which was completed in 1672. His plan for this temple formed the basis of the design of the Yushima Seidō in Edo (Ching 1975, 188). In order to ensure that proper utensils would be used in services for Confucius, Zhu designed copies of ancient Chinese bronzes and supervised Japanese artisans in their production. Such copies of ancient Chinese bronzes would later come to be utilized in sencha gatherings as flower containers and braziers. They continued to be widely manufactured throughout the Meiji period (1868–1912).

Zhu is perhaps most famous for his design of a garden of some sixty-three acres in Edo, the Kōrakuen (garden of the philosopher's pleasure), which was the prototype for the many daimyo estate gardens constructed during the Tokugawa period (Kuck 1980, 226–227; Ching 1979, 202). His legacy also includes a posthumous publication of 1713, *Master Zhu Shunshui's Illustrious Lectures* (*Shunsui Shushi danki*), a record of his public discussions on diverse aspects of China. The text includes sections on food and drink in which various types of tea are discussed, including sencha.[7] It was compiled and published by his disciple Asaka Tanpaku (1656–1737), a friend to influential sencha-drinking Confucian scholars of his day.

In Nagasaki, Zhu had become acquainted with fellow expatriates, including Tai Mangong (1596–1672) from Hangzhou, an excellent calligrapher, seal carver, poet, and student of Chinese medicine. After his arrival in Nagasaki, Tai became acquainted with the large community of Chinese Chan monks who founded the Ōbaku school of Zen in Japan (discussed further in the following chapter), and he took up the tonsure himself in 1654. He then assumed the name by which he is best known, Duli (J: Dokuryū), and is remembered as an influential Ōbaku monk admired in sencha circles and described as "in some ways the greatest literatus to come to Japan at that time" (Addiss 1978, commentary for pl. 14).

The second Chinese resident allowed to serve the Mito daimyo was Xinyue (J: Shin'etsu; 1639–1696). He was a Caodong Chan (J: Sōtō Zen) sect monk in China and a Ming loyalist who emigrated to Nagasaki in 1677. Although invited by a Chinese monk at Kōfukuji in Nagasaki, his position in the monastic hierarchy of Nagasaki was rather low because of his affiliation with the Sōtō sect rather than Ōbaku, the denomination of Kōfukuji. He accepted an invitation to establish a Sōtō Zen temple in Mito in 1683 and opened his temple there, Gionji, in 1692. Like most Chinese priests, Shin'etsu was a learned scholar. He is credited with spreading the arts of seal carving and the music of the Chinese *qin* (a seven-string zither, a favorite instrument of the literati) in Japan (Addiss 1989, 90–91). These were arts enjoyed by later fans of sencha.

Another Chinese scholar permitted to serve a prominent daimyo

1. PORTRAIT OF CHEN YUANBIN—1844
From volume 2 of *Famous Sites of Owari Province (Owari meisho zue)*. Woodblock-printed book; ink on paper. 25.5 x 32 cm, Kansai University Library, Osaka. Photo: P. Graham.

was Chen Yuanbin (J: Chin Genpin; 1587–1671) (fig. 1), whose imaginary portrait was included in the 1844 woodblock book *Famous Sites of Owari Province (Owari meisho zue)*. Seen through a round Chinese-style window of a thatched cottage surrounded by bamboo and potted plants in the Chinese manner, he is portrayed as a quintessential Chinese scholar-recluse, examining calligraphy together with two Japanese admirers.

Descended from a long line of literati, Chen was a poet, calligrapher, and painter in the Chinese literati tradition.[8] After failing the civil service examination, he trained in the martial art of *gongfu* (kung fu) and learned pottery at the Shaolin temple. He first visited Japan in 1621 and was at that time befriended by Hayashi Razan, among others. He then served in the influential position of translator to the Chinese ambassador to Japan. He returned in 1638 to escape from the tumultuous circumstances in China and was allowed to leave Nagasaki to serve as a retainer to the daimyo of Owari, Tokugawa Yoshinao.

Chen influenced the development of various Chinese-inspired arts in Japan, helping create the pottery style of the Ofuke kiln in Mino, introducing a new type of cuisine (a kind of fried cake), and becoming known as the father of Japan's martial art of judo, which he taught at a temple in Edo. He wrote extensively on the Daoist philosopher Laozi and published numerous original poems, of which a selection was published in collaboration with his Japanese friend, the Nichiren sect priest Gensei (1623–1668). Chen's service to the Owari Tokugawa lord may account for the later emergence of the seat of his domain, Nagoya, as a major center of Chinese learning and avocations, including Japanese literati painting and sencha.

The Chinese Community at Nagasaki

Foreigners in Japan congregated in Nagasaki owing to prohibitions restricting their movements. Most numerous were the Chinese residents—transient merchants, immigrants, and resident priests. They numbered between two thousand and three thousand persons by the 1620s, and their population increased to a peak of near ten thousand, approximately one-sixth of the city's total population, before the end of the century. These Chinese expatriates constructed for themselves an extensive enclave of Chinese culture encompassing all manner of religious and secular activities, including the drinking of sencha. Their habitats were specially constructed Chinese-style residences and temples complete with Chinese furniture, interior decoration, utensils for serving food and drink, and articles associated with common literati activities, such as writing implements.

As affluence and education increased during the Tokugawa period, Japanese interest in the Chinese culture of Nagasaki escalated. The city's Chinese community became famous through the writings of Japanese visitors and through widely circulated illustrated books and paintings. Eventually, many aspects of this culture became incorporated into Japanese high and popular culture.

Nagasaki's ideal natural harbor had first been noticed by Portuguese traders in 1571. In 1580 the local daimyo granted the city to the Jesuits for their headquarters, but Toyotomi Hideyoshi reclaimed the city in 1587 and designated it as an international port under his authority. By the end of the sixteenth century, despite the lack of formal trading agreements, the Chinese were so well established in Nagasaki that they received permission in 1598 to establish a mortuary temple, Goshinji, at the rear of the city's main cemetery on Mount Inasa. The temple initially served as the main gathering spot for the Chinese residents, mostly merchants from China's southern provinces. Beginning in 1654, Westerners buried their dead in its precincts as well (Yamamoto 1983, 181–186). In 1603, to monitor the growing Chinese presence and negotiate in matters of trade, the government created the hereditary position of official Chinese interpreter (*tōtsuji*), which eventually grew to over twenty-five subdivisions staffed by Chinese emigrants and their descendants who had become naturalized Japanese citizens.

As Nagasaki's Chinese community flourished, institutions catering to its cultural life emerged. The importance of religious worship in China, a necessity in matters of birth, burial, and spiritual enrichment, accounted for the establishment of four Chinese Buddhist temples during the seventeenth century: Kōfukuji (est. 1623); Fukusaiji, the largest (est. 1628); Sōfukuji, the best preserved (est. 1629); and Shōfukuji, popularly known as the Guangdong (Canton) Temple (est. 1678).

Their appearance, with upward-curving tile roofs and brightly painted exterior surfaces, resembled Ming temples and was markedly different from Japanese Buddhist structures. Although the intent was for each to serve expatriates from different regions of China, Japanese citizens could also attend services and take religious vows at these institutions. In fact, while the head priests of three of these temples were customarily of Chinese descent, at Shōfukuji they were always Japanese. Chinese residents also had a large Confucian temple constructed in 1647.[9] The Japanese government accepted these foreign religious institutions in its country because, like Japanese temples, they served as a means of keeping track of the populace and providing assurance that their parishioners were not secret Christians (Jansen 1992, 10). Both the Chinese Buddhist and Confucian temples allowed Japanese visitors a chance to experience at first hand the authentic customs of China.

Nagasaki's Chinese inhabitants resided throughout the city until 1689, when the government confined them to their own compound, the Tōjin Yashiki, located on a hilly parcel of land of 9,373 *tsubo* (7.65 acres). There were twenty general living quarters, shopping areas, offices and residences for officials, parklike open spaces, bathhouses, public meeting places (the large assembly hall completed in 1761 was modeled after a Chinese palace), a Buddhist temple, several ponds and wells, jails and guardhouses, warehouses, and a rice mill. The compound was well separated from the city proper by a river, mud walls, and a series of gates (Chang 1970, 142–151). After its creation, Chinese desiring to leave and Japanese seeking entry into this district needed official consent.

Those permitted entry included interpreters and inspectors of Chinese paintings, courtesans of the licensed quarter (for Chinese traders brought no women with them), and selected merchants. Yet other well-connected Japanese could enter the compound, while the Chinese were given permission to visit Japanese friends in other parts of the city on numerous occasions throughout the year. Chinese and Japanese residents of Nagasaki also celebrated together the numerous Chinese annual festivals, with rites taking place at the four large Chinese temples located outside the compound (Chang 1970, 158). Fires, such as an exceptionally large one in 1784, frequently displaced the Chinese and necessitated temporary accommodation elsewhere in the city, including at the Chinese temples. The Chinese compound was not officially disbanded until 1871, when the Japanese concluded a treaty with the Qing government (Yanai 1973, 191). However, the opening of Yokohama and Nagasaki as treaty ports in 1859 challenged its raison d'être, and from this time many Chinese lived openly beyond its confines.

For most Japanese, paintings, prints, and illustrated books were the main means of acquiring knowledge of Nagasaki's Chinese community. Among the earliest pictorial records of the Chinese compound are handscrolls by Watanabe Shūseki (1639–1707), an important artist of Nagasaki and pupil of the great Chinese émigré painter of Buddhist subjects, the Ōbaku Buddhist priest Yiran (hereafter referred to by his Japanese name, Itsunen; 1601–1668). From 1697 Shūseki served the bakufu as inspector of imported Chinese paintings (*kara-e mekiki*), a position later inherited by his descendants, who were also painters. Shūseki had painted his handscrolls of the Chinese compound by order of the magistrate of Nagasaki; later members of his school and others made copies and adaptations of them.[10] Because the later versions are largely based on Watanabe Shūseki's, they can be considered as records of the manners and customs of the Chinese during Shūseki's time rather than their own.

2. THE CHINESE COMMUNITY AT NAGASAKI
Watanabe Shūsen (1736–1824). Section of a handscroll; ink and colors on silk. H: 37 cm. Kobe Municipal Museum.

These paintings show the Chinese living in modified Japanese row houses with furnishings of Chinese manufacture. In the scrolls, the residents are frequently depicted eating and drinking. Although it is often difficult to distinguish the drinking of heated rice wine from that of tea because of the similarity and interchangeability of the utensils, some scenes almost certainly illustrate sencha. Typical of these scrolls is one by Watanabe Shūsen (1736–1824), adopted son of Shūseki's son Shūsai (died 1761). The braziers, cups, ewers, and teapots illustrated reveal the sorts of Chinese utensils available in Japan in the late seventeenth century (fig. 2). The unlidded cups and the lack of a bowl for holding the teapot identify the utensils as for sencha rather than oolong tea.

Most of these handscrolls featuring the Chinese residents of Nagasaki depict their subjects sporting the long pigtails required by the Manchus. This hairstyle had been banned in Japan prior to the late seventeenth century in tacit support of the Ming cause (Toby 1991, 139). By the late seventeenth or early eighteenth century, when Shūseki began painting these scrolls, the Ming supporters had been thoroughly suppressed in China and the Manchu pigtail could no longer be censured. The pictures thus accurately reflect contemporary Chinese customs. Nevertheless, not everyone depicted was Manchu and those who were not were clearly identified. Among these is an elder wearing the distinctive garb of a scholar, indicated by the inscription as "*Daiminjin*" (person of the great Ming dynasty).[11]

Elite patrons commissioned the Watanabe-school handscrolls. The vast quantities of woodblock prints that pictured the Chinese residents of Nagasaki were intended for popular consumption, however, and were generally known as "souvenirs of Nagasaki" (*Nagasaki miyage*). They were designed mostly for tourists and other commoners curious about these exotic foreigners, though they may also have been circulated among government officials who desired details about Chinese lifestyles (Hosono 1978, 35). The first prints depicting the Chinese community were created around 1700, although most date from the late eighteenth to the mid-nineteenth centuries. Circulated by commercial publishing houses, their largely anonymous designers seem to have based their work on that of artists such as the official painting inspectors who had access to the foreigners (Hosono 1978, 44).

The Yamato-ya, which began issuing prints in 1801, was one of the largest of the Nagasaki publishers. It specialized in close-up views of the Chinese in their residences, typically showing a figure or two engaged in some characteristic activity, such as playing musical instruments with a courtesan or, as in *A Chinese Scholar's Study* (fig. 3), the activities of Chinese scholars in their studies. The man in spectacles in this woodblock print appears to be painting a fan for a friend who holds before him a blank open page of a book, perhaps the painter's next

3. A CHINESE SCHOLAR'S STUDY
Published by Yamato-ya, Nagasaki, early nineteenth century. Single-sheet woodblock print; ink and colors on paper. 37 x 25 cm. Kobe Municipal Museum.

project. The floor is tiled in the Chinese manner, and the room is filled with Chinese furniture and decorations. Sencha objects—a brazier, a teacup on a saucer, and a diminutive teapot—are prominently displayed in the cupboard, which was, as here, generally made of red sandalwood (*shitan*) (Nagasaki 1923, 645). The appearance of these utensils would have reinforced, for the Japanese viewing public, associations between sencha and scholarly activities.

As travel became easier and more common during the eighteenth century, numerous Japanese scholars and artists journeyed to Nagasaki to see the foreign communities for themselves. Many of these visitors were well-known figures who penned travel diaries, some containing illustrations, for legions of avid readers. One of the earliest such journals was authored by Shiba Kōkan (1747—1818), a pioneering Western-style painter who spent a month in Nagasaki in 1788. Initially published in 1794 as *Journey to the West (Saiyū ryodan)*, it was republished in 1803 and finally revised, expanded, and retitled in an edition published in 1815 as *Diary of a Visit to the West (Saiyū nikki)*. Although he was primarily interested in Western culture, Kōkan did take time to observe Nagasaki's Chinese community.[12]

Among the many other illustrated woodblock books about Nagasaki that appeared soon after Kōkan's, the most informative and widely read was the *Record of Chinese Customs (Shinzoku kibun)* of 1799. Tea, prepared by both sencha and gongfucha methods, was but one of the many subjects addressed in its pages.[13] Although a number of volumes about Chinese daily life had already been imported to Japan, this book was the first specifically designed to interpret Chinese culture for a Japanese audience by describing activities and customs as actually observed. Its publication coincided with escalating appreciation of Chinese material culture and fueled further interest in China.

Other popular woodblock books about Nagasaki containing detailed descriptions and illustrations of the life of the Chinese residents included *Things Heard and Seen in Nagasaki (Nagasaki bunken roku)* of 1800, *Illustrated Guide to Famous Sites of Nagasaki (Nagasaki meisho zue)*[14] and *Collected Scenes of Famous Sites of Past and Present Nagasaki (Nagasaki kokon shūran meisho-e)* of 1841.

Among the scenes depicted in these books, all featured Chinese feasting together with courtesans from Nagasaki's Maruyama district. This licensed red light entertainment district had been established in 1642 and grew by the Enpō era (1673–1681) to contain over three hundred licensed courtesans. The women of this quarter served both the Chinese and Dutch residents of the city. From 1698 they were allowed free entry into the Chinese compound (Nagasaki 1923, 15). The Chinese also visited the women in Maruyama, first secretly, then openly, as restrictions on their movements were relaxed in the latter part of the eighteenth century. These women sought to please their Chinese clients by learning Chinese customs such as songs and dances. Proprietors of Maruyama's tearooms and restaurants where the geisha entertained also had their establishments decorated in Chinese taste and served Chinese cuisine. As the women also entertained Japanese citizens and treated them to new Chinese foods and beverages, such as steeped tea, the popularity of Chinese music, food and drink, and interior design spread to the Japanese populace. Maruyama's most famous restaurant was the Kagetsu (teahouse of flowers and moonlight), established in 1618. One of its rooms was the Kawara no Ma (spring rain room), which was originally constructed in 1642 and restored during the 1870s (fig. 4). A hybrid Western-Chinese aesthetic dominated this room furnished with tables and chairs, a novelty in Japan but common to both Chinese and Western domestic interiors. Like Chinese residences, it featured a tiled rather than tatami-matted floor and windows covered with geometric latticed patterns. Japanese visitors admired the exoticism of the ambiance and borrowed elements of it for their own residences and for the upper-class teahouses and restaurants in the entertainment districts of other cities.

Restaurants of Maruyama, and the Nagasaki area as a whole, became nationally famous for *shippoku ryōri*, Chinese cuisine served Chinese style.[15] "Shippoku" is the Japanese approximation of the word for "table" in one of the regional Chinese dialects spoken by Chinese

4. THE KAWARA NO MA (SPRING RAIN ROOM)
At the Kagetsu teahouse, originally constructed in 1642, restored in the 1870s. Maruyama district, Nagasaki. Photo: courtesy Kagetsu and Motomura Futoshi, Kyushu Kokoku Company.

residents of Nagasaki (Nagasaki 1923, 628). Guests sat on chairs or stools around a single table and ate from large platters of food placed upon it. The seating arrangement for *shippoku ryōri* became popular among Japanese diners, for it encouraged boisterous conviviality. One type of shippoku ryōri in which local Nagasaki restaurants specialized was known as *fucha ryōri* (food to accompany tea). It originated in the Buddhist vegetarian cuisine served along with tea as part of a religious rite in Nagasaki's Chinese Buddhist temples. The eventual popularity of fucha ryōri in restaurants of other Japanese cities by the late eighteenth century helped to spread the popularity of sencha as well, which was served along with the food.

A number of the Chinese who went to Nagasaki possessed detailed knowledge of Chinese medicine or literati philosophy and arts, although most had initially traveled to Nagasaki as merchants. As their fame spread, Japanese from all parts of the country made pilgrimages to Nagasaki to study with them, and the Maruyama district became a popular meeting site. Approximately 130 of these learned visitors were skilled painters (Yamamoto 1983, 368–383). Some were amateurs, merchants whose education included acquiring proficiency in the literati arts of painting and calligraphy. Others had come to Japan as freelance professionals. The smallest group of these were illustrious painters in their home country, such as Shen Nanpin (J: Chin [Shin] Nanpin; 1682–after 1760), who was in Japan from 1731 to 1733 in response to official invitations (Rogers 1985, 24, 35).

Altogether these Chinese painters fostered innovations in Japanese painting by encouraging the birth of new artistic traditions and by influencing those already well established.[16] Artists of the literati painting movement that emerged in the eighteenth century profoundly benefited from contacts with Chinese artists in Nagasaki. Many literati painters were Confucian scholars, and all helped to popularize the ideals and pastimes of the Chinese literati through their Chinese-style paintings. Many of their paintings, which were modeled after Chinese prototypes, included scenes of Chinese scholars or their servants steeping tea and/or rice wine in a brazier while admiring antiquities or composing poetry or painting. Japanese artists in Nagasaki were themselves able to participate in such activities, known as *bunjin asobi* (amusements of the literati), during visits with their Chinese mentors in Nagasaki. In this way the drinking of sencha became closely linked with the art of literati painters and with literati activities.

The impact of these visiting Chinese artists on the art world of Japan was immense; their Japanese pupils and admirers not only assimilated their artistic styles but also helped to popularize the relaxed and informal Chinese literati manner of learning and socialization that often took place in the restaurants of Maruyama. One such gathering was portrayed by a Japanese artist of Nagasaki, Araki Kunsen (1781–1819). He illustrates a farewell party for fourteen guests that took place in 1815 in honor of the nanga painter Sugai Baikan (1784–1844), who was leaving the city after studying for ten years with the Chinese painter Jiang Jiapu (1744–after 1839) (fig. 5). Kunsen painted the scene for his friend, the Confucian scholar Kanai Shason (1791–1821), who visited Nagasaki in 1818. Shason's inscription at the top of the scroll describes the event (Sendai 1994, 132). Textual references confirm that sencha was indeed served at gatherings such as this, although here Chinese and Japanese figures are only shown mingling in a parody (*mitate*) of the requisite four scholarly arts of *go* (Chinese chess), calligraphy, painting, and music.[17]

5. FAREWELL GATHERING FOR SUGAI BAIKAN—1818
Araki Kunsen (1781–1819), inscription by Kanai Shason (1791–1821). Hanging scroll; ink and light colors on paper. 168.4 x 84 cm. Sendai City Museum.

The Japanese Political Elite and Their Taste for Chinese Art

The shogunate's emphasis on Confucian learning for its feudal retainers helped transform its military bureaucracy into a civil one. Although Tokugawa doctrine stressed that samurai should learn discipline through continued training in the martial arts (*bu*), they were also urged to explore the literary arts (*bun*) for their spiritual and moral enrichment, as espoused in Confucian texts on benevolent leadership. Because of the importance given to literary arts, samurai received practical instruction in painting and calligraphy, which supplemented their studies of the Confucian classics and the arts and history of their own country. They also became enthusiastic collectors of Chinese books, paintings and calligraphies, antiquities, and accouterments for the scholar's study (*bunbōgu*). These avocations served as models for activities and displays associated with later sencha tea ceremonies: exhibitions of Chinese art came to be held in conjunction with sencha gatherings, and the ambiance of sencha tearooms included displays of arrangements of scholars' objects (*bunbō kazari*).

Responding to official encouragement, many of the Tokugawa-era daimyo began amassing prestigious collections of Chinese art by acquiring famous objects (*meibutsu*) that had been owned by notable shogun and daimyo of the past. Many of these earlier collections had been formed out of a passion for the chanoyu tea ceremony, in which the samurai were also obliged to participate. Although most of these daimyo collections have now been dispersed, several remain intact. Each reflects the personal taste of its collector while providing invaluable documentation on the sorts of objects favored by high-ranking, wealthy samurai in general. Although sencha followers considered these collectors models for their own pursuits, in some respects the aesthetic preferences of the daimyo for Chinese arts differed from that of later sencha fans. The former, for example, favored earlier academic Chinese paintings, while the latter admired Ming literati paintings.[18]

The source most influential on the aesthetic preferences of the Tokugawa daimyo was the Ashikaga shogunal collection, the most famous and discriminating of all the early collections of Chinese art. Much of the collection and documents pertaining to its history entered the holdings of the powerful Owari Tokugawa daimyo, who continued to collect Chinese art throughout the Tokugawa period. This superb collection must have initially benefited from the advice of the Owari daimyo's resident Ming loyalist, Chen Yuanbin. Artwork in the Ashikaga shogunal collection is well documented in catalogues kept by successive generations of advisers. The most complete of these records is the well-illustrated *Connoisseurship Manual on Chinese Art (Kundaikan sayū chōki)*, the earliest edition of which dates to 1476.[19]

As appreciation of Chinese art and antiques spread among the samurai, knowledge of their proper selection and arrangement for display grew in importance during the seventeenth century. Documents such as the *Kundaikan* served as authoritative writings on the subject. The first part of the *Kundaikan* is the earliest critical evaluation of Chinese painters by a Japanese authority; the second section contains instructions on the proper hanging of Chinese paintings in a *shoin*-style room, a space in upper-class Japanese residences designed specifically for entertainment of important guests.[20] The latter section also describes the Chinese decorative arts—lacquers, ceramics, writing and incense utensils, and bronzes—that should be arranged for display on the built-in shelves and writing desks of shoin interiors. Later, similar Chinese arts would decorate the shoin-style interiors where sencha gatherings most commonly occurred. In fact, collectors interested in Chinese arts because of a fondness for sencha could well have been influenced by this text. The most widely known of fourteen extant editions of the *Kundaikan* was included in a compendium, *The Classified Collections of Japanese Classics (Gunsho ruijū)*, published between 1779 and 1819, the peak era for interest in sencha. The type of information and its organization found in this text also came to influence the appearance of later sencha tea ceremony records, which routinely included detailed information on all the utensils, decorative objects, and artworks displayed.

Although their taste in Chinese art was influenced by that of past collectors, samurai of the Tokugawa period developed an appreciation for more newly created Chinese artifacts due largely to the changes in tea ceremony aesthetics that took place in the seventeenth century. Foremost among tea masters under whom newly made karamono came into prominence was the daimyo Kobori Enshū (1579–1647), chief construction magistrate for the Tokugawa bakufu and official chanoyu tea master to the third shogun, Tokugawa Iemitsu (1604–1651), from around 1637. Although he expressed great appreciation for the courtly elegance of Heian-period aesthetics and admired antique objects of refined beauty, he is also credited with expanding the range of Chinese utensils appropriate for chanoyu (Guth 1993, 52–53).

A number of factors contributed to this change in taste. Enshū and other contemporary samurai tea masters may have used Chinese articles of contemporary manufacture because they developed appreciation of them from their association with emigrant Ming loyalists, who undoubtedly brought their favorite possessions with them to Japan. Production, and hence availability, of these luxury goods also increased due to the growth in affluent, appreciative Chinese consumers. Finally, accessibility to the Japanese market was assured as both nations' political situations stabilized and trade restrictions eased throughout the seventeenth century.

Ironically, although the samurai were avidly absorbing the tenets of Confucianism and Chinese literati culture in the seventeenth century, the newly imported Chinese ceramics that they so admired were not in orthodox Chinese literati taste. Rather, they were largely commercial products designed specifically as export wares, some made to specifications of Japanese chanoyu tea masters. Among these were porcelains from the kilns at Jingdezhen, including *kinrande* (gold brocades), which feature overglaze enamel and gold-leaf decoration, exported to Japan from the mid-sixteenth century; *kosometsuke* (old underglaze blue), the modern term for sparsely decorated Ming dynasty blue-and-white export wares for Japan; and *shonzui*-style underglaze blue and overglaze enamel wares, named from an inscription found on some of the vessels, all of which bear a distinctive style of decoration featuring pictorial designs together with geometric motifs. Regional kilns supplied the Japanese markets with *fahua* (ruled design), a multicolored, low-fired enameled ware that the Japanese called *kōchi* because they erroneously thought it came from Cochin (their name for Vietnam), although it actually came from export ware kilns in Fujian province; and Swatow porcelains (J: *gosu*), both Swatow blue-and-white (J: *gosu sometsuke*) and Swatow overglaze enameled (J: *gosu aka-e*) wares.[21] Shonzui- and kōchi-style wares were those for which Kobori Enshū had expressed particular preference.

During the seventeenth century, Japanese potters established porcelain manufacturing centers in Kyushu, under the patronage of the local daimyo, where they perfected these Chinese styles. Artisans were stimulated to adopt these new styles and techniques to compete with the influx of Chinese goods to their markets. They based their products on ideas culled from imported Chinese books, advice from emigrant Chinese scholars, and knowledge of Chinese craft technology learned from emigrant Korean and Chinese artisans. Porcelain was an especially demanding and expensive craft. Therefore at first the kilns mainly produced chanoyu utensils and elegant tableware for wealthy and elite samurai. Soon porcelains developed as both luxury goods and everyday wares for discerning commoners who adopted these new porcelain styles for sencha utensils.

Mass Consumption of Chinese Goods

The government's endorsement of Chinese learning for the masses and encouragement of trade, both domestic and international, led to far-reaching social changes, some of which the bakufu may not have foreseen or approved. Excelling at learning became a means of moving beyond restrictions imposed by birth into a lower class, for education allowed commoners access to knowledge of the higher culture of China to which they had previously been denied. Similarly, growth in trade resulted in increased wealth for merchants, allowing them to acquire the material goods that were associated with this higher culture. Wealthy merchants and townspeople aspiring to parity with the samurai class sought the material trappings of that class, including Chinese luxury products or Japanese substitutes in similar styles. Samurai taste for Chinese art grew out of their heritage; for the commoners it was an appropriation of modes of consumption that were not their own.

Similar considerations have been attributed to changes in patterns of consumption in Western societies. As noted by the cultural historian Pierre Bourdieu (1984, 76–77):

> *Every material inheritance is, strictly speaking, also a cultural inheritance. Family heirlooms not only bear material witness to the age and continuity of the lineage and so consecrate its social identity, which is inseparable from permanence over time; they also contribute in a practical way to its spiritual reproduction, that is, to transmitting the values, virtues, and competences which are the basis of legitimate membership in bourgeois dynasties.*

As the popularity of Chinese material culture grew among the masses, merchants and artisans sought to take advantage of its increasing profitability. This situation has also been remarked upon by Bourdieu: "The more legitimate a given area the more necessary and profitable it is to be competent in it, and the more damaging and 'costly' to be incompetent" (1984, 86).

By the early eighteenth century, attitudes held by the bakufu on Chinese politics and philosophy were well entrenched in popular culture. For example, the most celebrated play by the puppet theater (*bunraku*) dramatist Chikamatsu Monzaemon (1653–1725) was *The Battles of Coxinga* (J: *Kokusenya gassett*), which debuted in Osaka in 1715. It featured a hero loosely based on an actual person, Zheng Jenggong (1614–1662), the son of a Ming loyalist turned pirate, and a Japanese woman, who together with his father attempted to overthrow the Manchus. Zheng unsuccessfully petitioned the Japanese government for assistance between 1645 and 1647 and finally fled to Taiwan Island in defeat in 1661.[22] In the play, abstract notions of Confucian ethics and diplomatic policy have been reinterpreted for mass appeal by focusing on the exciting exploits of its protagonists. Sencha underwent a similar transformation as its tenets became subsumed by the apotheosis of its luminaries, its ritual forms, and its related objects.

This glorification of China in popular culture encouraged appreciation of Chinese arts and crafts among diverse consumers in major Japanese cities throughout the eighteenth century. Chinese merchandise, such as that seen in an illustration of a store in Osaka from the book *Famous Places of Settsu Province (Settsu meisho zue)*, published in 1792 (fig. 6), became procurable in shops specializing in luxury items of foreign manufacture. The major imports of Chinese luxury products included furniture, lacquer, metalwork, textiles, and ceramics, which, by the latter part of the eighteenth century, came to include Chinese teapots and teacups for sencha. Although it appears that most of the items in the Osaka shop are Chinese in origin, the illustration highlights an exotic Western import, a device for creating static electricity, which is being demonstrated for the benefit of passersby. The presence of these incongruous foreign goods in a single shop reflects then prevalent Japanese attitudes toward foreigners, who were indiscriminately classified together as "people of China" (*Tōjin*), a designation that defined all who were not Japanese (Jansen 1992, 86). Similarly, all foreign-made products came to be categorized as exotic, an aesthetic cultivated by sencha aficionados that allowed for the inclusion of non-Chinese foreign elements in ostensibly Sinophile sencha environments.

The entertainment areas of the major cities also reflected the Chinese preferences of the general population. Typically, the finer teahouses and restaurants in these districts would appear as ordinary

6. A FOREIGN GOODS STORE IN OSAKA—1792
From volume 6 of *Famous Places of Settsu Province (Settsu meisho zue)*. Woodblock-printed book; ink on paper. 25.5 x 32 cm. Kansai University Library, Osaka. Photo: P. Graham.

townhouses from the exterior, but inside they would resemble *sukiya* shoin-style structures of the sort designed originally to suit the personal taste of the wealthy samurai for whom they served as private retreats. Sukiya (literally, "abode of refinement") architecture originated in the design of tearooms for chanoyu and was the antithesis of the more formal shoin style. However, as sukiya aesthetics became integrated into shoin interiors, a new hybrid architectural style emerged, sukiya shoin, which merged aspects of both traditions. This sukiya shoin style retains the elegance of shoin interior design within a more relaxed, self-consciously rustic and idiosyncratic ambiance (Nishi and Hozumi 1983, 80–81). The sumptuous interior decoration in these teahouses created an aura of luxury in sharp contrast with the atmosphere of their patrons' own residences or places of work. With the growing fashion for Chinese culture in the second half of the eighteenth century, these teahouses often incorporated exotic Chinese design features.

Although most of the teahouses and restaurants of the

7. THE MAIN ALCOVE OF THE AOGAI NO MA (MOTHER-OF-PEARL ROOM)
At the Sumiya teahouse, constructed in 1641. Shimabara district, Kyoto.

entertainment areas have long since vanished, the finest of these structures, the Sumiya (four-cornered house) of Kyoto's Shimabara district, has survived. It opened in 1641 and underwent several stages of expansion prior to its final renovation in 1787, which its present appearance reflects. In its heyday during the middle to late eighteenth century, as the highest category of teahouse (*ageya*), it functioned as a salon where Kyoto's literati entertained in spacious rooms for parties, intimate private chambers, and chanoyu tearooms and gardens.[23] Although almost every room includes some features associated with Chinese-style design, these dominate one room in particular, the Aogai no Ma (mother-of-pearl room), whose overall interior scheme is resplendent with Chinese atmosphere (fig. 7). The wall of the alcove, its cabinets, and the adjacent staggered shelves are covered with Chinese landscape and bird-and-flower designs in inlaid mother-of-pearl. There is even a special spot on the floor for a mat, upon which was once placed a Chinese chair (Nakagawa T. 1989, 15). This sort of elegant and sumptuous decor came to represent Chinese aesthetics to the wealthy and cultured Japanese citizens who patronized the entertainment areas. As these patrons began to enjoy sencha, they incorporated elements of this aesthetic into the design of rooms where they drank sencha.

From shogunal policy extolling Chinese Confucian philosophy and its close monitoring of international trade, to the presence of Chinese citizens in Japan, to the quantities of Chinese material goods available to the Japanese consumer, China came to figure prominently in the minds of Japanese citizens. How this preoccupation with Chinese culture became channeled into the development of a Way of sencha is the subject of the following chapter.

CHAPTER THREE

Chinese Literati Ideals in the Formation of Appreciation for Sencha

Appreciation of sencha in Japan has, from its inception, been intimately tied to the embracing of Chinese literati ideals and lifestyles by Japanese students of Confucianism. Yet, as we have already seen, these literati ideals were not synonymous with the Confucian values espoused by the bakufu. They encompassed the inherently conflicting yet complementary philosophies of Daoism and Confucianism. On the one hand, Chinese literati ideals promoted a Daoist appreciation for nature manifested in a quest for reclusion from worldly affairs, and on the other, they mandated a Confucian sense of moral obligation to help better society through government service or teaching.

Many Japanese intellectuals professed affinity with the eremitic proclivities of the Chinese literati, whom they sought to emulate. Although reclusion had long been an accepted means of escaping the problems of society, in times past it had meant adhering to the ascetic disciplines practiced by Buddhist monks, as epitomized by the poets Saigyō (1118–1190) and Kamo no Chōmei (1153–1216). From the seventeenth century on, the scholar-recluse model became increasingly popular.

From the middle of the seventeenth century, imported editions and Japanese reprints of Chinese texts on Daoism and Confucianism enabled literati ideals to become more widely understood and admired. Of greater influence were the Chinese scholars in Japan, especially the Ōbaku monks who were free to interact with the populace at their widely scattered temples. As they drank sencha, the custom spread to their admirers, who later identified the Chinese Ōbaku patriarch Yinyuan as the founder of their tradition.

Many of the Japanese scholars who embraced literati ideals settled in or near Kyoto, close to the Ōbaku-sect headquarters of Manpukuji, where they established independent schools or inspired others by their conduct. While many contributed to a deepening of appreciation for Chinese literati culture, one scholar in particular, Ishikawa Jōzan, came to be revered as the founder of the literati tradition in Japan. Later, sencha followers considered him their spiritual progenitor as well.

Sencha and the Literati Culture of Ōbaku Zen Monks

The most influential Chinese literati in Japan were emigrant Linxi-school (J: Rinzai) Chan monks from the temple Wanfusi, on Mount Huangbo (C: Huangboshan) in Fujian province. The painter Itsunen, third abbot of Nagasaki's Kōfukuji, arrived first in 1644. He convinced Yinyuan (hereafter referred to by his Japanese name of Ingen; 1592–1673), abbot of Wanfusi, to emigrate also. Because Ingen was the highest ranking Chinese monk to come to Japan in centuries, the Chinese community in Nagasaki and monks associated with the powerful Japanese Rinzai Zen establishment in Kyoto eagerly anticipated his arrival. Due to Ingen's importance as a prelate, even the Japanese public knew of his writings, which were available in woodblock-printed editions in Kyoto bookstores (Baroni 1993, 37–38). His life story eventually entered into the realm of popular myth, as the Ming loyalist Coxinga, hero of Chikamatsu's bunraku play, was said to have aided his safe passage (Baroni 1993,42).

Ingen journeyed to Nagasaki in 1654 together with twenty monks and ten artisans and helpers in anticipation of an eager reception from numerous Buddhist believers seeking his spiritual guidance. He discovered instead that many Rinzai monks did not approve of his teachings. Rinzai doctrine differed significantly from his own school's beliefs, as Rinzai had remained largely unaffected by doctrinal changes in late

Ming China. Nevertheless, until 1876, when the government approved its designation as an independent sect, Ōbaku remained a branch of Rinzai Zen (Baroni 1993, 15–18). Not all Rinzai monks rejected Ingen. One who befriended him was Ryōkei Shōsen (1602–1670), from Kyoto's powerful temple of Myōshinji, through whom Ingen gained introductions into elite Kyoto society. There, Ingen found some of his staunchest supporters, including the retired emperor Gomizunoo (1596–1680), who became a powerful patron. The two never met, however, due to taboos against the divine imperial sovereign meeting foreigners (Baroni 1993, 149–152).

In keeping with their support of Ming loyalists, the bakufu granted favors to Ingen and his disciples. Ryōkei arranged for Ingen to travel to Edo in 1658 to meet with the fourth shogun, Ietsuna (1641–1680). During this audience, Ingen presented the shogun with Chinese tea and petitioned for permission to found his own temples. Because Ingen's presence gave the government an excuse to reform the contentious Rinzai school, his request was granted (Baroni 1993, 160). The following year construction began on a temple headquarters for his monks in Uji, near Kyoto, on land donated by the Konoe family of courtiers.

Ingen named the site Mount Ōbaku (Ōbakusan), the Japanese pronunciation of Huangposhan, the mountain location of his home temple in China, and designated his new Zen school as "Ōbaku." He named his headquarters temple Manpukuji, the Japanese pronunciation for the name of his home temple, Wanfusi. The temple complex officially opened in 1663, though construction was not completed until 1693. Like the Chinese temples in Nagasaki, Manpukuji was designed in emulation of Chinese Ming temples of the late sixteenth and early seventeenth centuries. With the approval of the fifth shogun, Tokugawa Tsunayoshi (1646–1709), Ingen established numerous other Ōbaku temples. One of these was Rakanji in Edo, founded with Tsunayoshi's direct patronage in 1696 (Screech 1993). Its celebrated exotic appearance helped further the popularity of Ōbaku Zen. During the heyday of Ōbaku in the eighteenth century, there were approximately five hundred Ōbaku temples scattered throughout Japan, and one account indicates as many as 1,240 subtemples existed as late as 1822 (Harada 1993, 26).

Beyond the novelty of their temples' appearance and the persuasiveness of the religious doctrine, visiting Ōbaku temples became popular because they functioned as repositories of knowledge concerning broader aspects of Chinese intellectual culture. Following Ingen's admonitions, the newly arriving Chinese monks were well versed in classical Chinese literature and philosophy (Graham 2017). Supplementing necessary religious texts, Ingen had brought a large number of secular works from China—books of poetry, philosophy, religion, and history—as well as numerous Chinese paintings and calligraphies.[1] These possessions, as well as the spiritual guidance of the learned monks themselves, attracted the attention of Japanese intellectuals and artists, who regularly visited Manpukuji. Among those who frequented Ōbaku temples in the seventeenth and eighteenth centuries, and to whom we will later return, were Confucian scholars and literati painters such as Itō Jinsai, Ogyū Sorai, Yanagisawa Kien, Gion Nankai, and Ike Taiga.

Japanese visitors to Manpukuji especially admired the temple's imported Chinese paintings. Among these were scrolls depicting a gathering of scholars at the Orchid Pavilion (C: *Lanting*; J: *Rantei*; hereafter referred to as the Lanting Gathering), the earliest recorded and most famous literati congregation in Chinese history, and a subject that became a favorite of Japanese artists in the eighteenth and nineteenth centuries, though it had occasionally been portrayed earlier.[2] In the year 353, the illustrious calligrapher Wang Xizhi (307–365) hosted a party for forty-two friends at this site in Shanyin, Zhejiang province, on the occasion of the spring purification festival. Servants filled cups with wine and set them on lotus leaves to float downstream to guests sitting along the banks of a meandering stream. As they drank the wine from cups floating by, each guest was obliged to compose a poem. The gathering has been immortalized in a compilation of the verses by each participant with a preface by Wang. That text has been described as the quintessential expression of literati values in China:

> *...an implicit manifesto for retreat or even dissent from the rat race of politics and bureaucracy. It thus belongs to the dialogue, ever present in Chinese life, between the official endorsement of order and hierarchy and the individual's wish to escape from such constraints to seek a deeper spiritual meaning in the natural world* (Rawson 1992, 100).[3]

8. PURIFICATION AT THE ORCHARD PAVILION—1671
Fanyi (Chinese; active ca. 1658–1671). Detail of a handscroll; ink and color on silk. H: 28.1 cm. Cleveland Museum of Art: Gift of the Junior Council of Cleveland Museum of Art and of Mrs. Wai-kam Ho in the name of the Junior Council, 1977.47.

The appeal of this subject for Ming loyalists such as the Ōbaku monks is obvious. As we will see later, the subject became closely associated with sencha.

While many artworks imported by the Ōbaku monks remain today in the possession of Manpukuji and other Ōbaku temples, some eventually entered private collections. One, a handscroll of the Lanting Gathering, *Purification at the Orchid Pavilion*, dated 1671, by the Nanjing painter Fanyi (active ca. 1658–1671) (fig. 8), has an interesting history. Now in the collection of the Cleveland Museum of Art, it contains a frontispiece and colophon by its owner in 1707, the Ōbaku monk Yueshan (J: Gensan; 1629–1709), who had emigrated to Japan in 1657. Seals affixed to the painting by Tomioka Tessai, the greatest literati painter and sencha master of the early twentieth century, indicate the painting also was once owned by him (Ho 1980, 287–288).

Japanese visitors to Manpukuji observed and participated in many Chinese literati customs, including the drinking of sencha. By Ming times, Chan temples had replaced their use of powdered tea with that of steeped tea, a custom followed at Ōbaku temples in Japan. Japanese Rinzai temples, however, continued to use powdered tea. Although the

Japanese public knew of and consumed Chinese leaf tea prior to the establishment of Ōbaku in Japan, the association of sencha with these highly respected Chinese Buddhist monks helped to increase its status and popularity during the latter part of the seventeenth century.

In accordance with Chinese Chan liturgical practices, many Ōbaku religious rites, such as the dedication of an ancestral hall to a deceased master, included the service of sencha. These rites are outlined in the official Ōbaku monastic code for Manpukuji, the 1673 *Ōbaku School Monastic Rules of Order (Ōbaku shingi)* (Takakusa and Watanabe 1924–1935, 82: 766–785, no. 2606). Sencha was also served at less formal assemblies for all the monks of the temple and at larger gatherings that included members of the lay public. In these cases, the ritual service of tea was known as fucha.[4] Sometimes a meal, fucha ryōri, would be served after the tea. This is the cuisine that became a specialty of Nagasaki restaurants. In the context of monastic life, fucha ryōri has always been festival cuisine and not the regular diet of the monks (Baroni 1993, 57, 88). Today fucha ryōri is considered the sencha ceremony's counterpart to the *kaiseki* meal served at formal chanoyu gatherings, and it is still served at Ōbaku temples.

One outspoken critic of Ōbaku was Mujaku Dōchū (1653–1745), a powerful abbot of Myōshinji, who circulated his opinions in an unpublished manuscript, *An Outsider's View of Ōbaku (Ōbaku geki)*, written around 1720.[5] Elsewhere, Mujaku criticized the current state of tea rituals, which included disparaging remarks on the use of tea in Ōbaku temples, in a general section about tea in his Zen dictionary, *Zen Notes on Objects in the World (Zemin shōkisen)* (Mujaku 1909, 672–679). His comments there provide a revealing look at the differing attitudes toward tea in Rinzai Zen and secular chanoyu circles of his day, while situating Ōbaku tea usage within this milieu. In particular, he derided the secular influences from chanoyu that permeated Zen tea rituals and considered the tea preparation methods and function of tea at Ōbaku temples as a further debasement of the religious significance of tea. Mujaku desired to return to the ways of the monk tea masters of the distant past for whom he believed tea drinking was a purely ecclesiastical event. In his entry for *senten* (boiling tea [for the tea ceremony]), Mujaku described what he considered to be the true meaning of the tea ceremony. He indicated that in ancient times the expression "senten" referred to the boiling of tea by itself, and that the current Japanese custom of eating sweets (or a light meal) as part of a tea ceremony was wrong because it shifted emphasis away from tea as the essential component of the ceremony. He noted that this custom originated in the misguided notion that drinking tea without first partaking of a meal was too simplistic.

Mujaku also commented on contemporary tea preparation techniques in the section on tencha (preparation of tea), an expression used interchangeably with chanoyu, but also possessing a secondary meaning of a formal Buddhist ritual serving of tea to the Buddha, to the general public, or to the spirit of a deceased person as part of a memorial service (Nihon Daijiten Kankōkai 1975, 14: 355). Mujaku contrasted the ancient usage of the term tencha with the modern one. In the past, he wrote, powdered tea was simply placed in a bowl, hot water was added, then a little cold water, and finally the mixture was whisked. In recent times, he lamented that people who put tea leaves in a pot of boiling water call themselves *tenchamono* (tea masters). He clearly implied that people of his time, not knowing the ancient method and context for preparing tencha, corrupted the tradition. Elsewhere, he identified the source of this problem as Ōbaku. In a section titled "fucha," he indicated that tencha had spread in popularity and was called fucha. By way of clarification, he added that the Ōbaku shingi recorded that the monks should hold fucha. He thus places blame for the popularity of this heterodox religious ceremony featuring leaf, not powdered, tea on the Ōbaku rituals.

Ōbaku monks did not confine the use of tea to formal rituals. Tea functioned as an important stimulus to their spiritual quest. It was a subject for meditation in *kōan* (Zen riddles), the main means of instruction for Ōbaku monks, and inspiration for *kanshi* (poems in Chinese), literati-style poems the monks wrote to express their personal feelings.

Ingen and his followers depended on the writings of Ingen's master at Wanfusi, Feiyin Tongrong (J: Hiin Tsūyō; 1593–1661), for spiritual guidance. Feiyin, who was second in the line of abbots to revive a famous old Tang dynasty Chan temple on Mount Huangbo (founded 789), wished to present himself to the greater Chinese Chan community as the true dharma heir of the Linxi sect. He sought to achieve this through reference to the wisdom of distinguished monks who had studied at Mount Huangbo during its heyday in the Tang dynasty. He especially admired Zhao Zhou (J: Joshu; 778–897), many of whose famous kōan were included in a woodblock-printed compilation of Feiyin's teachings preserved at Manpukuji, *Sayings of the Zen master Feiyin (Hiin Zenshi goroku)*, published in two editions, in 1639 and 1643. Among the kōan of Zhao Zhou are some, such as the following example, on the theme of tea:

> *One day Zhao Zhou visited his master, who asked why he had come. Saying nothing, he left and returned later to find the master drinking tea with another disciple. Zhao Zhou asked: "What is the meaning of drinking tea?" The master answered: "Three bowls and two bowls." Holding a new cup of tea, the master demanded Zhao Zhou tell him the meaning of drinking tea. Zhao Zhou responded: "I'm drinking rice gruel now."*[6]

Although the mention of tea serves here merely as a means of focusing the mind in order to achieve enlightenment, the kōan suggests the informal manner of drinking tea, which, in the spirit of the literati, was integral to Chinese Chan Buddhist life. Ingen's secular writings in the literati mode record this inclination. Particularly eloquent are a group of five poems he composed on the theme of brewing tea with melted snow, which are included in volume 3 of his *Miscellaneous Record of the Old Man of the Secluded Pines (Shōin rōjin zuiroku)*.[7] Two of these read:

> *In my leisure time I idly brew white snow tea.*
> *This method has been passed down to me alone.*
> *The heavenly old men have kindly bestowed upon me this piece of poor land.*
> *And yet day after day, jade flowers [tea] come scattering down like snow.*

> *It is pleasurable to spend quiet leisure time brewing snow tea.*
> *Reflecting upon the writings of old Zhao Zhou,*
> *Sitting by my gate I await famous visitors.*
> *Then I sip the cup to bring forth poems and literary grace.*
> *My activity incites the competition of heavenly deities who send down heavenly flowers [snow].*

The Ōbaku monks gained some notoriety for their habitual, informal consumption of tea in Japan. The custom must not have prevailed in other Japanese temples, for the Japanese monk Kyorei Ryōkaku (1600–1691), reflecting on an Ōbaku religious retreat in which he participated at Kōfukuji in Nagasaki in the winter of 1654–1655, made special mention of the tea (sencha) and cakes that were served at "odd hours," between meals and in the evenings. He also noted that the monks were fatter than those at other Japanese temples because they ate more frequently (Baroni 1993, 97).

By the early eighteenth century, leaf tea or sencha had become closely identified with Ōbaku in general and Ingen in particular. The samurai Morikawa Kyoroku (1656–1715), a *haikai* poetry disciple of Matsuo Bashō, mentioned "Ingen tea" (*Ingen cha*) in his *Anthology of Customs (Fūzoku monzen)* of 1706, a collection of haikai prose of the Bashō school (Ōtsuki 1996, 110). Apart from the obvious differences in preparation techniques, leaf tea drinking represented a different ideological orientation from that associated with the powdered tea utilized in chanoyu and Rinzai tea rituals. One of Ingen's disciples, the priest Gettan Dōchō (1636–1713), was the first to articulate these differences in the lengthy prose poem *Ode to Sencha (Sencha uta)*, of circa 1694, included in volume one (pp. 15–16) of his 1703 book, *Manuscript of the Rock Dweller (Gankyokō)*:

Tea from Jiangnan is excellent,
Better than other teas, it has a wonderful flavor.
Not only can it drive away the devil of sleep
But because it also dispels heat and thirst it is the elixir of immortals.
Ever since Lu Yu loved tea,
It was planted everywhere throughout the Tang dynasty.
Mengding and Jiangxi are two of the best varieties of tea;
Wuyi and Guzhu are also famous.
I only regret that it is not grown in Jugan,
And not a single word has been written about it there.
In Sangyu and Zhenggu people appreciate tea.
A festival of processing tea has taken place there since the time of emperor Ehuang.
Eisai brought the famous tea seeds and shared them with the monk Koben [Myōe] at Umeoka [Takao].
There, the valleys are deep, the dew is pure, and the tea leaves grow in profusion.
They are both bitter and sweet and make the tongue feel cool.
Akamatsu Enshin liked the taste,[8] *the great monk [and painter] Sesson composed lengthy poems praising tea.*
When mountain tea was measured out as a treat to official lay guests,
Visitors on horseback stirred the dust up to the white clouds.
Then the shogun living at Rokuonji appeared[9]
And ordered his official Yoshihiro to plant tea at Uji.
The fertile land stretches up to my home.
Field after field of tea create broad green spaces.
The locals trade it to make a living and care for the tea plants as if they are precious jade.
They cultivate them and trim them diligently, and fear the possibility of frost coming at night.

When the time of the Qingming festival approaches [early March],
the weather is warm.
Spring thunder awakens the insects and the tea shoots emerge.
Crowds gather, picking tea to the beating of drums.
The tender leaves fill the baskets and are selected, roasted, and
prepared with great care.
The first cup is offered to the shogun.
Who can resist the famous teas, "Sparrow's Tongue" and
"Dragon's Body"?
The teas "Falling Mortar" and "Jade Dust" appear light gold.
The fire roars in the brazier signaling that springtime is filling
the room.
In the iron kettle, the water boils into bubbles shaped like
duck eyes.
The green tea fills up the Korean teacup.
Guests drink in turn and exclaim that the taste is like nectar.
The calligraphy and painting on the walls are precious works by
the monks Xigeng and Muxi.
They have been studied and imitated for eons.
Notable among the followers of wabi are Jōō and Shukō.[10]
Samurai in fine clothing crowd into the tearoom.
Yet rural recluses also appreciate tea.
These humble men do not approve of attending expensive
tea gatherings;
They prefer simplicity and dwell in mountain huts.
By Lake Biwa, someone is brewing sencha.
The aroma of the brewing leaves seeps out of the pot.
Neither tea scoops nor whisks are needed.
Tea is brewed strong and drunk to moisten the bowels.
After three cups his spirits are elevated,
And he leans on the windowsill to listen to the reed flute.
Zen monk friends pass by and inquire about what is taking
place there.
They are shown teacups as an answer.
Zhaozhou liked to test his visitors.
They understood his bluntness and accepted the consequences.
Other people can compete for entry into the immortal land
of Lu Tong,
I am content to brag about my own fine home.[11]

Gettan Dōchō has here sketched out the first polemical stance on sencha in opposition to chanoyu. His comments reveal that by the late seventeenth century the Ōbaku monks had recognized differences between these two methods of tea preparation and were asserting the superiority of their tradition. According to Gettan, the early Japanese Zen monks understood the spiritual benefits derived from the taste of superb quality tea, but as chanoyu became formalized and adopted as an avocation by wealthy samurai and others, the emphasis shifted from the tea itself to an ostentatious display of material possessions. He implies that only Ōbaku monks and reclusive proponents of sencha remained true to the lofty ideals of their predecessors in their preference for fine-tasting tea brewed simply in a kettle in their humble homes.

The first treatises on sencha in the middle of the eighteenth century brought Ingen into the historiography of the tradition as patriarch although he had not actually attempted to popularize the drink.[12] He did, however, have his monks cultivate tea plants for production of sencha for their own use, perhaps for the first time in Japan. His tea-making paraphernalia also became famous, having been reverently preserved along with all his possessions. Among these were a lacquered wooden stand for holding utensils, a pottery brazier, and several large Yixing ware teapots, including one that to this day contains remains of his last brewing of tea (fig. 9).[13] Later sencha tea masters collected and sometimes duplicated some of these utensils and used them in special ceremonies in his honor.

Although the introduction of sencha in Japan was closely tied to Ōbaku at its inception, its institutional development did not parallel that of chanoyu, which had always been closely associated with Rinzai temples. Ōbaku temples did not become centers for sencha tea gatherings and contained no special chambers designed for that purpose, like the tearooms of the Rinzai temples. Sencha remained a private pastime of individuals seeking solace in the elegant pleasures of the world of the Chinese literati. Among those credited as such a literati pioneer was the samurai recluse Ishikawa Jōzan.

9. LARGE YIXING WARE TEAPOT
Formerly owned by Ōbaku Ingen, Chinese, seventeenth century. Burnished brown unglazed stoneware. H: 15 cm. Manpukuji, Uji, on extended loan to the Kyoto National Museum. Photo: courtesy Kyoto National Museum.

Ishikawa Jōzan and the Emulation of the Chinese Literati in Kyoto

Ishikawa Jōzan (1583–1672) came from a family of samurai in service to the Tokugawa clan. He carried on the tradition by serving valiantly as a warrior for Tokugawa Ieyasu during the latter's struggles for supremacy between 1600 and 1615.[14] Yet Jōzan's dissatisfaction with military life became apparent when he attempted to enter the Zen priesthood at Myōshinji. After being ordered back to duty, Jōzan violated orders and was thereupon expelled from service. Finally able to follow his inclination toward religious devotion, Jōzan joined Myōshinji and, with that temple's vast repository of Chinese texts at his disposal, began to study classical Chinese philosophy and poetry. In 1623, however, in order to support his aged mother, Jōzan left the clergy to serve the Asano daimyo of Hiroshima. He held that position until shortly after his mother's death in 1635.

The following year, 1636, Jōzan retired to a life of self-imposed isolation in the northeastern outskirts of Kyoto, in the village of Ichijōji. To fund construction of his residence, completed in 1641, Jōzan sold his book collection (Watson 1990, 6–7). How he supported his retirement thereafter is a matter of much speculation, but he seems to have pieced together income from a variety of sources, including proceeds from crops grown on his property's arable land, financial support from devoted disciples, and occasional writing commissions. Only after his death did Jōzan's home become known as the Shisendō (abode of the poetry immortals), its popular name today. The name derives from Jōzan's study chamber, which contained portraits of his favorite thirty-six poets of China brushed by the most important Kanō-school painter in service to the bakufu, Kanō Tan'yū (1602–1674). The two evidently had a long relationship, for around 1670, Tan'yū produced a formal portrait of Jōzan inscribed by the sitter.

Jōzan's retreat is a sukiya shoin-style villa embellished with a variety of details borrowed from Chinese architectural design.[15] Windows, for example, have cloud-shaped curves in the Chinese style. There is a small second-story room, the Tower for Whistling at the Moon, which was based on similar projecting structures in Chinese scholars' residences (fig. 10).[16] Shisendō became an important prototype for sencha architecture, and it remains today a tangible symbol of Jōzan's life in seclusion, a synthesis of Japanese and Chinese aesthetic ideals.

10. SHISENDŌ (ABODE OF THE POETRY IMMORTALS)
Ishikawa Jōzan's home, constructed in 1641. Kyoto. Photo: P. Graham.

The hermitage is enveloped in a lush landscape containing an upper garden, originally conceived by Jōzan though extensively renovated in 1825, and an expansive lower garden added after World War II (Bring and Wayembergh 1981, 116). The early garden, located adjacent to the main building, is similar in conception to others of its time, featuring a broad expanse of raked gravel, azalea bushes, and bamboo groves. More original, however, is the small stream on the south side of the original garden, which is bordered by clipped azalea bushes interspersed with other plants, Chinese-style rocks with pitted and twisted surfaces, and a small stone pagoda.

Jōzan counted many important artists and intellectuals of Kyoto as his closest friends and mentors. These acquaintances included the influential Confucian scholars Hayashi Razan, Razan's Chinese scholar friend Chen Yuanbin, and Fujiwara Seika (1561–1619), whose disciple he became. Unlike Razan, who stressed the political and social values of Confucian doctrines, Seika, and Jōzan after him, placed greatest emphasis on a personal quest for sagehood through self-cultivation (Brown 1997, 168–171). Jōzan also fraternized with Kyoto's cultural elite, including the Shingon monk Shōkadō Shōjō (ca. 1584–1639), a celebrated calligrapher and painter of Zen subjects (Anjo 1991, pls. 29–33). Although no records substantiate Jōzan's contacts with Ōbaku monks, he certainly must have been aware of their presence and have come under their influence through various mutual acquaintances, including the painter Kanō Tan'yū, who brushed numerous Buddhist icon paintings for Manpukuji during the period the two were acquainted (Graham 1991–1992, 51: 283–284).

During his retirement, Jōzan sought to recreate the life of a scholar-recluse of China by immersing himself in various literati pastimes, including composing kanshi, writing calligraphy, and playing the qin (zither). He is most famous today for reviving interest in Chinese clerical script (C: *lishu*; J: *reisho*) calligraphy and for his kanshi. Jōzan's poetry and other writings describe his emotional state as he occupied his days in seclusion. They are permeated by the spirit of *furyu*, a concept most closely associated with the haikai poet Matsuo Bashō (1644–1694), but retroactively associated with Jōzan as well (Rimer 1991a, 22–24). Fūryū, as applied to both Jōzan and Bashō, implied a deep understanding of Chinese literati culture, advocating an eremitic withdrawal from the world, and devotion to simple pleasures. A letter that Jōzan wrote to Hayashi Razan conveys this sense of fūryū:

> *Sometimes I pick flowers in the garden and make them companions of my heart. Or I listen to the first wild geese and treat them as my guests. Sometimes I open my brushwood gate and sweep out the leaves, or I look into the old garden and plant chrysanthemums. Sometimes I climb the eastern hill and sing to the moon, or I draw my chair to the northern window and read books and recite poetry. Apart from these pursuits I do nothing* (Keene 1978 , 539).

Previously, this word had been used to describe aesthetics associated with chanoyu, but in that context its essence was very different. Fūryū (literally, floating with the wind) was a Chinese term (*fengliu*) that had entered the Japanese vocabulary by the eighth century where it carried associations with courtly elegance and refinement, indicative of one's good deportment and manner. As the wabi atmosphere of chanoyu gained ascendance, especially from the time of Sen no Rikyū, the meaning of fūryū shifted to conform with wabi ideals. Jōzan and Bashō's conception of fūryū was closer to the original Chinese meaning of the term. It was this sense of the word that became the guiding principle and dominating aesthetic in the cult of sencha. However, variant meanings of the word "fūryū" remained in use in other circles. Some writers still applied it to chanoyu aesthetics, while others, following alternate Chinese interpretations, associated it with the flamboyant and dissipated lifestyle of the new urban townsmen.[17]

From Bashō's time fūryū became closely linked with those who emulated the Chinese literati, whom he described with the term "*bunjin*" (C: *wenren*), a word used to describe Jōzan as well. Bashō's use of this term to describe a scholar or literatus familiar with Chinese learning and culture became the standard meaning for the word in the Japanese language. The term first appeared in Japan in a kanbun (literary Chinese) text, the *Later Compilation of the Chronicles of Japan (Shoku Nihongi)*, in an entry for the year 721. The famous early Heian kanshi poet Sugawara Michizane (845–903) also used it. Bashō is credited with reviving its use during the Tokugawa period (Nihon Daijiten Kankōkai 1975, 17: 567).

Owing to admiration for his reclusive lifestyle with its self-imposed privations, Jōzan became a celebrity. His biography first appeared during his lifetime in the *Records of Japanese Hermits (Fusō in'itsu den)*, published in 1664 by Gensei (1623–1668), a Nichiren monk of Kyoto famous also as a kanshi poet. Although no documents corroborate an acquaintance between Gensei and Jōzan, the two had friends in common, such as the aforementioned Chen Yuanbin (whom Gensei met in Nagoya in 1659), and shared similar interests (Watson 1983, x-xxii). It seems inconceivable that their paths did not cross in the limited Chinese literary circles of that city. Soon after his death, another publication on recluses (*inja*) also included Jōzan's biography. This was the *Recent Stylish Recluses (Kindai yasa inja)*, published in 1686 by an Ōbaku monk, Seiroken Kyōsen (active second half of the seventeenth century), who was also a disciple of the popular novelist Ihara Saikaku (1642–1693) (Marceau 1989, 15).

After his death, Jōzan's followers turned his home into a memorial shrine. In 1716, under the care of a Shingon-sect priest, it was transformed into a Buddhist temple. By the mid-eighteenth century, when it was turned into an Ōbaku temple affiliated with Manpukuji, it had become a well-known tourist destination featured in popular guidebooks to the city, including the 1787 *Pictorial Guide to Famous Places of the Capital (Miyako meisho zue)*. During the late Meiji period (late nineteenth century), it came under the jurisdiction of the Kyoto National Museum. After 1958 the Shisendō was again independent, and since 1966 it has been a temple affiliated with the Sōtō Zen sect.

One of the many visitors to the Shisendō in the years immediately following Jōzan's death was Ogata Kenzan (1663–1743), painter and pottery designer working in the Rinpa painting tradition popularized by his elder brother, Kōrin (1658–1716). Kenzan's record of his visit in 1692 provides a thumbnail sketch of Jōzan's life and the appearance of his hermitage, while poignantly conveying the charm of its rural environs.[18] Despite his status as an artisan, Kenzan was a serious student of both literati ideals and Ōbaku Zen who also lived, between 1689 and 1712, in a rural retreat outside Kyoto. During this period Kenzan informally studied Ōbaku Zen with Ōbaku monks Gettan Dōchō and Dokushō Shōen (1617–1694), both disciples of Ingen, who visited his home on several occasions and with whom he corresponded. Gettan Dōchō, whose *Ode to Sencha* appeared in his book *Manuscript of the*

Rock Dweller, included in the same volume three poems composed in honor of his visit to Kenzan's home in 1690.[19] Kenzan also associated with prominent monks of the Rinzai school and had a familial relationship with Itō Jinsai, the first significant Confucian scholar to emerge from the merchant class (Wilson 1991, 51).

Kenzan has come to be esteemed as one of the first of the many Kyoto merchant-artists to effect the assimilation of the aesthetic values of the Chinese literati into popular Japanese taste and fuse them with Kyoto's celebrated craft traditions. By the late seventeenth century Kyoto was not only Japan's haven for intellectuals but it was well established as the center of the nation's most sophisticated, technically proficient, and commercially successful craft industries. Kyoto crafts, including pottery, had long embodied the native aesthetic preferences of the aristocrats who dominated Kyoto society.

In Kenzan's time, under the influence of chanoyu tea masters such as Kobori Enshū and encouraged by a burgeoning interest in Chinese literati culture, aesthetic taste began to change. The first Kyoto potter to experiment with the production of porcelain, Kenzan also attempted to copy Chinese Swatow ware. Both techniques were perfected by later Kyoto potters, who specialized in wares for sencha. Through influential artists like Kenzan, who admired both Jōzan's ideals and the material culture of China, Jōzan's fame increased and became closely identified with Chinese literati culture.

Because he was one of the earliest celebrated recluses whose life and art embodied the spirit of fūryū, Jōzan was accorded a place in the lineage of sencha masters as a founder of the tradition. The fact that the Ōbaku monk and renowned sencha master Monchū Jōfuku lived at Jōzan's estate for several years late in his life may have contributed to Jōzan's association with sencha. Circumstantial evidence also suggests that Jōzan did drink sencha. He probably learned about it from his friend Hayashi Razan, whose knowledge came from the influential Ming tea compendium *Complete Collection of Tea Books*, which was in his collection. Jōzan's home also seems once to have contained a room for informal service of tea in the manner of the Chinese literati. Located adjacent to his study, it was decorated in a manner different from tearooms for chanoyu (Suzuki H. 1991, 98). Additionally, some of Jōzan's poems focus on the theme of tea drunk in the informal manner associated with Chinese literati.[20] In that the monk Gensei also wrote several poems about drinking sencha,[21] the beverage may well have been popular among Sinophile scholars and artists in late-seventeenth-century Kyoto.[22]

The earliest-known document to link Jōzan with the sencha tradition is the treatise *Elegant Sayings about Sencha (Sencha kigen)*, of 1857 and 1858, by Tōgyū Baisa (1791–1879), which identifies him as the first in a long lineage of sencha tea masters. Tōgyū Baisa wrote that his inclusion of Jōzan was based on a lost letter by an obscure physician and sencha master, Ogawa Shin'an, with a postscript by a later sencha master, Yatsuhashi Baisa. This letter was said to have been passed down from Shin'an to the great popularizer of sencha, Kō Yūgai (the focus of the next chapter), and then to Yatsuhashi Baisa, who made it famous (Hasegawa 1965, 85).

Although the veracity of Tōgyū Baisa's lineage of sencha tea masters is questionable, later Japanese literati scholars (virtually all of whom drank sencha) did admire Jōzan as a pioneer of their tradition. He cannot actually be considered as a sencha tea master for he did not participate in any formal sencha ritual; none existed in his day apart from Ōbaku religious rites. In the seventeenth century tea for sencha was not processed in Japan, nor were there Japanese artisans manufacturing utensils for its service. Jōzan's consumption of the beverage, if he indeed drank it, was an informal, non-structured aspect of his lifestyle. Nevertheless, Jōzan's assumed propensity for tea drinking in connection with his literati pursuits must be recognized as a model for later sencha masters who turned his avocations into rituals.

By the early eighteenth century, there existed all the elements necessary to the formation of a formalized ritual for sencha. Chinese culture provided the aesthetic and philosophical framework for the sencha tradition. Japanese citizens, both samurai and commoners alike, learned of these through their education in Chinese literature and Confucian studies, through access to Chinese books on tea and material culture, via contacts with immigrant Chinese, and as a result of increased access to Chinese luxury goods and Chinese architectural styles in Japan.

The Ōbaku monks furnished an established source of moral authority, recognized by the court and bakufu as exemplars of the Chinese literati tradition. Thus they contributed spiritual legitimacy to sencha, in direct competition with the Rinzai monks who had enjoyed long association with chanoyu.

Ishikawa Jōzan, considered the first Japanese person to assimilate Chinese literati values, was idealized by sencha tea masters. They admired him as an eremitic eccentric whose life was imbued with the spirit of fūryū and were inspired by his abilities in the highly esteemed arts of Chinese calligraphy and poetry. The Chinese elements in the architecture of his home also created a precedent for an appropriate setting for sencha gatherings.

The final step necessary to the process of creating a sencha tea ceremony was for someone actively to promote it as an alternative avocation to chanoyu among the general population. This was accomplished by Baisaō Kō Yūgai, who championed sencha on the streets of Kyoto.

CHAPTER FOUR

Sencha in the Eighteenth Century, under the Spell of Baisaō and Beyond

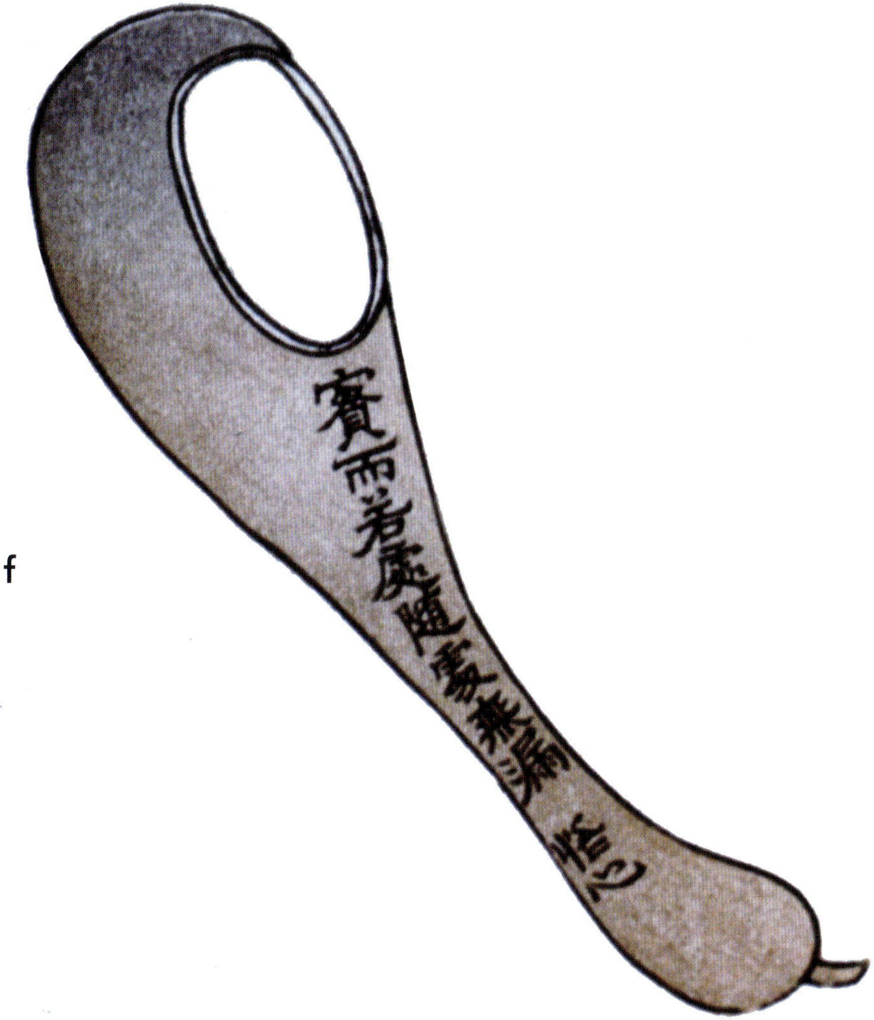

The high point of commoner culture during the Tokugawa period, when accumulations of wealth and increased levels of education contributed to widespread conspicuous consumption, began with the advent of the Genroku era (1688–1704) and lasted to the end of the Kyōhō era (1716–1736). A new fashion for Chinese arts accounted for a significant amount of this consumption. Concurrently, these eras were dominated by serious intellectual inquiry that resulted in the emergence of several independent schools of Sinophile studies. As these innovative philosophies became intertwined with appreciation for Chinese material culture, an environment conducive to fostering a tea ceremony for sencha developed.

Searching for the Spirit of the Sages

Soon after the Tokugawa bakufu adopted Confucianism as a basis for their legitimacy, diverse schools began to emerge whose tenets departed from interpretations taught by the shogunate's official school. Some were modeled after established Confucian lineages in China, while others reflected variant interpretations of the doctrine by creative Japanese scholars.

The bakufu's official Confucian academy followed the Chinese *Chengzhu*-school (J: *Shushigaku*) metaphysical philosophy that had been developed by the Chinese philosopher Zhu Xi (1130–1200) during the Song dynasty. Among other things, this philosophy emphasized logic and empiricism, stressing the need to understand the inherent order of the universe and humanity's place within it, manifested in a meticulous "investigation of things." In this mode of thinking, "real or practical learning was a process of self-realization through an active effort to integrate the internal and external, the ideal and the actual, principle in man and in things" (de Bary 1979, 173). Because this was the earliest, most influential school of Confucianism in Japan, many scholars received their primary education at Shushigaku academies. However, this philosophy tended to uphold the status quo; those scholars dissatisfied with its rigid intellectual parameters explored alternative interpretations of the doctrine and other aspects of Chinese literati culture, such as literature, painting and calligraphy, Daoist studies, and sencha.

One of the alternative Confucian philosophies influential in seventeenth-century Japan had reached maturity during the Ming dynasty under the leadership of Wang Yangming (1472–1529). Known as *Yōmeigaku* in Japan, its tenets emphasized the subjective and humanistic qualities of the individual. In this sense it was a more intuitive and idealistic philosophy than Shushigaku. Followers cherished a spirit of *kyō* (madness), which they felt characterized the passionate resolve of the ancient Chinese sages, allowing for integration of Daoist and Buddhist notions of sage-hood within a Confucian code of ethics. Followers of this philosophy in both China and Japan embraced a belief in the "unity of the three creeds," stressing the underlying similarities of the Confucian concept of self-cultivation and the Buddhist and Daoist preferences for renouncing involvement with worldly affairs (Brown 1997, 9–10). Consequently, many Buddhists, including those associated with the Japanese Ōbaku tradition, espoused Yōmeigaku.

A third influential Confucian school in Tokugawa Japan was a newly created Japanese school that departed significantly from Chinese Confucian teachings. It synthesized Shushigaku practicality and Yōmeigaku humanism in its emphasis on self-cultivation as a means of benefiting society. Furthermore, its scholars studied the earliest Chinese Confucian texts without relying on later interpretations, so their school came to be called Kogaku (ancient learning). This movement culminated in the philosophy of Ogyū Sorai (1666–1728), which fulfilled a need for a doctrine less dogmatic than Shushigaku during a time of economic and social instability (Maruyama 1974, 281). Sorai invited followers to develop their own interpretations of Confucianism, which encouraged further proliferation of Confucian academies. Under Sorai's influence, such independent thinking began to be encouraged even at the daimyo-sponsored academies. By the late eighteenth century though, authorities had become alarmed enough to ban this and other non-Shushigaku teaching at official schools. Yet these alternative philosophies were too popular to suppress completely. Although Sorai's teachings were already in decline by the 1780s, other unofficial schools remained a significant presence, and their supporters were among the most avid participants in sencha.

Partly as a result of having studied on his own in the countryside during his early years, Sorai developed original interpretations of Confucianism, influenced by his concurrent study of diverse aspects of Chinese literature, history, and colloquial Chinese language. In his later life, Sorai became acquainted with pupils of such Chinese scholars as Asaka Tanpaku, a disciple of Zhu Shunsui, and developed friendships with immigrant Chinese themselves, such as the eighth Chinese abbot of Manpukuji, Yuefeng Daozhang (J: Eppō Dōshō; 1655–1734). Sorai had such passion for things Chinese that he was said to have worn Chinese clothing and to have filled his home with Chinese furniture. Although no documents indicate that he partook of sencha, many of his followers became well known as its promoters.

Sorai aspired to emulate the reclusionist tendencies of ancient Chinese Confucian sages who lived simply in the countryside but served their governments in times of need (Yoshikawa 1983, 219–220). This interpretation of Confucianism as an introspective and intuitive creed had more parallels with Daoist thought than other Japanese Confucian schools, so it is not surprising that it was Sorai's followers—such as Dazai Shundai (1680–1747), to whom we will return later as an outspoken critic of chanoyu—who helped promote Daoism in Japan (Takeuchi 1992, 122–123). Sorai and his followers believed the Daoists possessed a spirit of *ki* (marvelousness, strangeness, or eccentricity), a concept first discussed in association with the ideals of the literati by a contemporary of Sorai, Gion Nankai (1676–1751), a gifted kanshi poet, Confucian scholar, and pioneering painter in the literati mode. Although Nankai is listed in Confucian genealogies as an adherent of the Shushigaku school, because he studied at their academies, like many of the creative thinkers of his era, his ideas were actually an eclectic mixture of various philosophies.

Nankai identified those who followed the Way of the sages with the spirit of ki and distinguished their spiritual path from ordinary existence within the common, vulgar (zoku) world. He also articulated the importance of elegance (ga) in literati pursuits, especially poetry, in opposition to zoku, and associated this aesthetic ideal with a quiet appreciation of nature.[1] Nankai derived the use of these words from Ming texts where they characterized aesthetic distinctions between the taste of the true literati from that of the nouveau riche (Clunas 1991, 82–83; Nakano 1989,128). Yet his understanding of these tenets was also indebted to the writings of the haikai poet Bashō, who had applied these Ming concepts to his definition of elegance with the terms "fūryū" and "*fūga*" (C: *fengya*; graceful and cultured) (Nakano 1989 , 128–129 ; Pollack 1986, 212).

Sorai also connected the concepts of ki and ga. He promoted ki in his belief that personal spiritual cultivation should be stressed. He felt that no particular path for proper conduct was supreme and that everyone should strive for goodness in their own way by developing their innate talents and inclinations. However, he qualified this individualism with the assertion that these activities should be elegant. His followers consequently engaged in various cultural pursuits that adhered to the ideals of ga or fūryū. These activities included composition of poetry and prose in Chinese, painting in the manner of the Chinese literati, and playing Chinese musical instruments.[2] Individuals with similar interests banded together in coteries often centering around a pivotal figure who served as a teacher or an elder statesman (Takeuchi 1992, 116). Sencha became one of the avocations that first flourished in this manner, initially through the guiding spirit of Baisaō.

Baisaō, the Old Tea Peddler

Baisaō (1675–1763), later apotheosized as the first true sencha tea master, was a native of the castle town of Hasuike in Hizen province (present-day Saga prefecture) in northern Kyushu.[3] Like many of his day, Baisaō went by various names during the course of his life. Baisaō (old tea peddler) was his nickname in his later years and the name by which he is most generally known. As a child, the third son of a physician who served the Nabeshima clan, he was called Shibayama Kikusen. When Baisaō was nine his father died. Three years later he entered the priesthood at Ryūshinji, an Ōbaku temple near his home, and took the clerical name of Gekkai Genshō. Baisaō's Ōbaku teacher was Kerin Dōryō (1634–1720), a Japanese monk who had received training directly from three Chinese abbots of Manpukuji, including Ingen. Accompanied by his teacher, Baisaō made his first visit to Manpukuji in 1687–1688 to attend a birthday celebration for the fourth abbot, Dokutan Shokei, his teacher's spiritual mentor.

In 1696, at the age of twenty-two, despite suffering from the effects of a debilitating intestinal ailment, Baisaō set off on a journey to seek spiritual guidance from eminent monks throughout the country. His wanderings led him to the northern city of Sendai, where he studied at an Ōbaku temple for several years, and back again to Manpukuji in 1703. Some later accounts indicate that prior to returning to his home temple, Ryushinji, in 1707, Baisaō may have stopped off in Nagasaki, where he may have observed and learned about sencha from local Chinese inhabitants. Yet as sencha was commonly drunk at Manpukuji, he would have learned of the custom there.

Upon his return, Baisaō served as his temple's steward until events in 1723 allowed him to move on. In that year his aged mother died and his master's senior disciple, Daichō Genkō (1678–1768), returned from Ōbaku and Confucian studies in Kyoto to assume the position of abbot. The following year Baisaō departed for Kyoto, where, except for a brief return to Hasuike in 1741 to renew his travel permit, valid for only ten years, he remained until his death.

Baisaō entered Kyoto armed with introductions from Daichō to the city's most influential Sinophile scholars and artists. Daichō, a disciple of Ogyū Sorai, had taught Confucianism to Uno Meika (also known as Shishin; 1698–1745) and the Shokokuji priest Daiten Kenjō (1719–1801). Daichō was also friends with the literati painter Ike Taiga

(1723–1776), a creative genius at the nucleus of an impressive coterie of scholars and artists (Takeuchi 1983, 166–167, and Fischer 2007). Daichō also knew Taiga's friend the Tendai priest and kanshi poet Rikunyo (or Rokunyo; 1737–1803), who was a frequent traveler to Edo, where he helped to foster interest in literati culture, as practiced in Osaka and Kyoto, among intellectuals there.[4]

Baisaō quickly gained the respect of these men who, together with their friends, became Baisaō's most ardent supporters. Among them were monks, scholars, and poets: Kinryū Dōjin (1712–1782), a Tendai priest and respected kanshi poet; Goshin Genmyō (1713–1785), an Ōbaku monk from Ise and a friend of Taiga; Katayama Hokkai (1723–1790), a kanshi poet and Confucian studies pupil of Uno Meika, who subsequently founded a Confucian academy in Osaka; and the Ōbaku monk Monchū Jōfuku (1739–1829), another of Taiga's friends and a Zen disciple of Daiten prior to switching sectarian affiliation. Baisaō's admirers also included artists, many of whom were members of Taiga's circle: Itō Jakuchū (1716–1800), a celebrated painter and lay practitioner of Ōbaku who specialized in Chinese-derived subjects and styles and who was patronized by the priest Daiten; Kō Fuyō (1722–1784), yet another friend of Taiga who was a seal carver, literati painter, and calligrapher; and Taiga's patron and painting pupil, Kimura Kenkadō (1736–1802), who was to play a central role in the subsequent dissemination of sencha.

Originally a successful Osaka sake brewer, Kenkadō had his fortune confiscated for exceeding allowable production quotas. After a period of exile from Osaka, he returned to become a major figure in Kansai (the Osaka-Kyoto region of Japan's main island of Honshu) literati circles as proprietor of a stationery shop patronized by intellectual and artistic luminaries from throughout the country. He was renowned for his vast collection of Chinese books and botanical curiosities.

Baisaō changed his residence numerous times during the course of his thirty-three years in Kyoto. He first resided at Manpukuji, but by 1730 he had moved to the city proper. Although he did not formally give up the tonsure until many years later, he did not live or evangelize as a conventional priest. Around 1735 he began selling sencha, his main occupation for the duration of his life, from a small portable stall he called Tsusentei (the pavilion along the pathway to the immortals), carting his utensils on his back in a bamboo basket he named Senka (den of the sages) to Kyoto's celebrated scenic locales. Baisaō wrote that despite its lowly status in society, peddling tea was for him an honorable profession that substituted for his unobtainable aspiration of living like the virtuous sages of China's distant past (Tanimura 1983,
89). Although he disclaimed allegiance to Buddhism, Confucianism, or Daoism, his poetic musings and untrammeled spirit reveal obvious indebtedness to the reclusive strains within all three philosophies.

Despite his many illustrious friends, Baisaō seems to have lived in impoverishment, though happily, throughout his life. He charged customers no fixed price, but asked them to pay what they could by dropping coins into a hollow bamboo tube (*sentō* or *zeni zutsu*) that he placed beside his stall. Nearby, a sign proclaimed that he was sorry for his inability to charge less than nothing, but urged patrons not to grudge him "one paltry *sen*" (Waddell 1984, 94). Many of his poems describe his difficult circumstances, but some also convey the essence of what he was really propagating in the guise of tea, such as one titled "Setting Up Shop at the Rengeoin [Sanjūsangendō]":

This place of mine, so poor
I'm often even out of water;
But I offer you an elixir
To change your very marrow.
You'll find me in the pines,
By the Hall of a Thousand Buddhas,
Come take a drink—who knows?
You may reach Sage-hood yourself.[5]

Like the Kogaku scholars who were intent on recreating the spirit of the earliest Confucian sages, Baisaō aimed to rekindle interest in the original spiritual benefits of tea. His poems make frequent reference to the early literati and Chan masters who had praised the beverage, especially Zhao Zhou, Lu Yu, and Lu Tong.

Alongside his tea stall Baisaō hung a banner inscribed with the characters "*seifū*" which expressed the essential philosophical and aesthetic qualities he felt sencha embodied. He used the term "seifū," an abbreviation of the term "*seifūryū*" (pure elegance), interchangeably with "fūryū." As his friend Daiten wrote:

> *He would set up his brazier, then ladle the pure stream water into the teapot with his gourd dipper, and before long the steam from the simmering tea would begin to rise curling and billowing into the skies. As he fanned the fire in the brazier, a wonderful aroma filled the air. Those who came to partake of his tea marvelled at its exquisite sweetness.*[6]

Although leaf tea had been consumed in Japan prior to Baisaō's time, his was renowned for its flavor. Whether this was due to the sagely aura surrounding the old tea seller, his preparation technique, the water he used, or the variety of tea that he brewed is unclear. Baisaō's poem "Infusing Tea under the Pine Trees on a Summer Day" suggests that his tea may have been imported from China:

I alone love the idleness
Of long summer days
Beside a fragrant brazier
Under ten thousand pines;
The sweltering heat
Of the human world
Cannot reach here;
Nor need I seek
The rare landscapes
Of the Sages' realm.
I ladle my water
From pure Otowa springs;
My tea is grown in China
(I have it sent from home).
Life's greatest joy
Is to be free from care,
Yet still the world laughs
At my mind's crazy turns.[7]

Baisaō may well have been able to acquire imported Chinese tea through hometown contacts that were close to the source of the China trade. Still, Baisaō might instead have been referring metaphorically to the original source for tea in ancient Japan. Since he was not independently wealthy and charged customers little, it is difficult to believe that expensive imported varieties could be his source. One scholar has suggested that he made use of the fine quality tea grown for matcha at Uji and Shigaraki, which could retain its flavor when prepared by the method he employed, called sencha, throwing leaves directly into a pot of boiling water and briefly simmering them (Hasegawa 1965, 93).

By 1738 sencha had become so popular that Nagatani Sōen, a tea grower in Uji who was acquainted with Baisaō, initiated specialized methods to produce a bright jade green-colored leaf tea, known as sencha, whose sweet-tasting flavor was particularly praised by Baisaō (Kyoto 1973, 535). Nagatani selected the finest of the young leaves and, as is still done today, soaked them in water, steamed them to curtail their fermentation, and dried them over a grill. This new process replaced the older practice of oven roasting a mixture of tough twigs and old leaves.

In 1745, when he reached the age of seventy, Baisaō renounced ties with the priesthood and changed his formal name to Kō Yūgai. Several years later, in 1748, some of his writings on tea were published in the book *A Collection of Tea Documents from the Plum Mountain (Baisanshu chafu ryaku)*, an allusion to Toganoo, whose ancient name was Baisan (plum mountain), the site of Myōe's temple, Kōzanji, where Kyoto's first tea fields were located. The contents of Baisaō's book reveal that he was not as innocent or aloof from worldly affairs as his persona suggested. His publication is distinguished as the first Japanese book to possess an agenda that extolled the superiority of sencha over that of chanoyu. In comments disdainful of both chanoyu priests and secular followers, Baisaō effectively linked sencha with the moral supremacy of Chinese literati values, thereby aligning preferences for tea with divisive political and social issues.

In the book's preface, Baisaō made explicit reference to the Ōbaku priest Gettan Dōchō's *Ode to Sencha*, by comparing Lu Yu and Lu Tong of China with Eisai and Myōe of Japan, stating that those two Japanese priests utilized tea to aid their quest for enlightenment, but that dissipated priests of the present only imitated their devotion to the beverage and participated in tea ceremonies as a means of escape from society. Their resemblance to the ancients, he wrote, is as distant as heaven from earth. He also included a short history of the transmission of tea from China to Japan. In it, the centuries between the Kamakura period (1185–1333) and Ingen's presentation of Chinese tea to the shogun were given only brief treatment, harshly critical of the formalized development of chanoyu that characterized those centuries. Baisaō was apparently successful in his alignment of sencha with the early Japanese monk-tea masters, for monks at Kōzanji published a second edition of his book in 1838 and supplemented it with a number of important early documents relating to tea propagation in the Toganoo area.

In 1755 Baisaō finally gave up his itinerant profession, succumbing to the infirmities of old age. He died in the seventh month of 1763 at the age of eighty-eight, the same month that a more complete compilation of his writings, *Verses of the Old Tea Peddler (Baisaō gego)*, was published by his admirers. Kinryū Dōjin was one of the compilers and the author of the preface; Itō Jakuchū brushed a bust portrait of Baisaō opposite the title page, which contained calligraphy by Ike Taiga; Daiten wrote the biography; and Daichō Genkō composed an afterword.[8]

Shortly before he died, Baisaō ceremoniously cast his tea utensils into a fire to prevent their becoming the cherished possessions of others, an act that consciously defied the chanoyu tradition of revering and placing great monetary value on the utensils made and owned by celebrated tea masters. Most utensils that Baisaō destroyed seem to have been made of rather common materials, however, and were ones he used exclusively at his portable tea stall.[9] Baisaō apparently saved some precious tea accouterments as mementos designated as gifts for his closest friends.

Although celebrated for his tea, Baisaō was equally renowned for his simple yet articulate writings in Chinese, both prose and poetry, written for amusement or as gifts for his friends. These appear

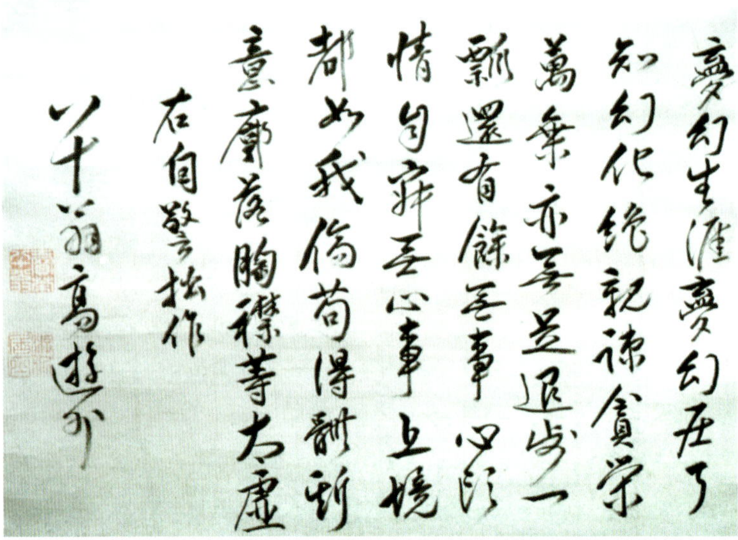

11. A VERSE TO ADMONISH MYSELF—1754
Baisaō Kō Yūgai (1675–1763). Hanging scroll; ink on paper. 27.5 x 42.3 cm. Private collection, Japan. Photo: P. Graham.

occasionally as inscriptions on paintings by his friends, primarily Jakuchū and Taiga.[10] His strong and deliberate calligraphy, most often brushed in semicursive (*gyōsho*) script, is much indebted stylistically to the calligraphy of the Ming literati. He brushed the poem “A Verse to Admonish Myself,” a fine example of his calligraphy, in 1754 (fig. 11). The poem reveals the Zen influences on Baisaō's philosophical approach to life:

Your life is a shadow
Lived inside a dream.
When you know it's unreal
You transcend “self” and “other.
“If you pursue fame, the glory
Of a prince won't suffice;
If you take a backward step,
A gourd of water is all you need.
When no matter is in the mind
Emotions quiet of themselves;
When mind is not involved in matters
You find suchness everywhere.
When each person can grasp
These truths for himself
His mind is pure and clear
Like heaven's empty void.[11]

Fascination with Baisaō must also have stemmed from his eccentric appearance. Kinryū Dōjin commented in his preface to the *Verses of the Old Tea Peddler*: “He has white hair and a beard, and is a bright-faced person of extremely calm temperament. The clothes on his body are modest and disheveled. From his tendency to drink too much sake, at one glance, you can discern his character" (Hasegawa 1965, 91). These physical traits are apparent in contemporaneous portraits by artist-friends such as Jakuchū and Taiga, who portrayed him in his old age either seated or standing alongside his carrying cases for tea utensils, always wearing a crane robe (kakushō-e; a white robe with black borders, reminiscent of the coloring of Japanese cranes), the traditional garment of Daoists. In a formal, saintlike portrait by Jakuchū, his long hair and beard appear unkempt, his chin is jutting forward, and his mouth is open in a semitoothless grin (fig. 12).[12]

Baisaō's talents at poetry and calligraphy, the perceived purity of his spirit, and his unorthodox means of searching for spiritual fulfillment through the medium of sencha impressed his friends as well as the Kyoto public at large. He became an inspiration to those seeking freedom and individuality within Japan's hierarchical and increasingly materialistic society. Baisaō consequently joined the ranks of individuals idolized as *kijin* (eccentrics), people distinguished for their precocity, strangeness, intellectual ability, or perceived spirituality, which set them apart from the common folk and deemed them worthy of admiration.

At the height of this fascination with kijin in the late eighteenth century, numerous individuals from various eras came to be so identified in two wildly popular publications by Ban Kokei (1733–1806), the *Biographies of Eccentrics of Recent Times (Kinsei kijin den)*, published in 1790 with a preface by Baisaō's friend Rikunyo, and its sequel, the *Second Series of Biographies of Eccentrics of Recent Times (Zoku kinsei kijin den)*, published in 1798.[13] Prominent Confucian scholars were

12. PORTRAIT OF BAISAŌ
Itō Jakuchū (1716–1800). Hanging scroll; ink on paper. 112.3 x 43.8 cm. Private collection, Japan. Photo: courtesy Kyoto National Museum.

included, as were others from diverse professions and social standings. There were chapters, for example, on Baisaō and Taiga, as well as on Ishikawa Jōzan, whose inclusion stemmed from his mastery of Chinese literary arts and his status as one of Kyoto's exalted recluses.

The World of Chanoyu in Baisaō's Day

Baisaō's ability to attract interest to his artless method of preparing steeped tea was due to more than his status as a venerated kijin, although this undoubtedly helped focus attention on him. Sencha could not have grown so popular if people were not already dissatisfied with chanoyu. By the late seventeenth century, chanoyu had entered an age of fragmentation, as various tea schools competed for preeminent status, each claiming that its protocol and ideology represented the correct interpretation of the tradition. These feuds and the increasingly rigid nature of chanoyu etiquette resulted in much criticism of chanoyu practices. Some opponents of chanoyu abandoned it altogether in favor of sencha, while others searched for new definitions of orthodoxy within an increasingly divided lineage.

Foremost among the critics was the Sorai-school Confucian scholar Dazai Shundai (1680–1747), who wrote scathing comments on chanoyu in his 1738 text *Soliloquy (Dokugo)*. His remarks are simultaneously politically elitist and aesthetically dismissive. He considered chanoyu a threat to the officially mandated social order, which he thought should be maintained. He felt chanoyu encouraged the blurring of distinctions between classes in its celebration of poverty in both the aesthetics of the utensils and the design of the tearoom, and he objected to the practice of inviting commoners to tea gatherings together with samurai. More pertinent to an understanding of the appeal of sencha, Shundai decried chanoyu gatherings as pretentious, its utensils as filthy and overpriced, the custom of crawling through a low door as insulting, and the tearoom atmosphere dark and suffocating (Varley 1989, 174–176).

Chanoyu ceremonies in this view were formal affairs that took place in the constrained and artificial atmosphere of a tearoom and focused on the correct use of expensive utensils. Sencha was, in contrast, informally prepared, sometimes for one's individual pleasure. Following customs of the Chinese literati, it would sometimes be consumed out-of-doors, often on outings to favorite scenic locales. Savoring the flavor of the tea while enjoying the beauty of the natural scenery was considered especially conducive to heightening the spiritual awareness of participants. Kimura Kenkadō is credited with initiating the first true sencha chakai (sencha tea ceremonies), which accompanied meetings of his Seifūsha (Elegant Society) in an environment that was a conscious rejection of formal chanoyu ceremonies.[14]

Such an atmosphere pervades an illustration showing Taiga's pupil, the priest Geppō Shinryō (1760–1839), preparing sencha on the veranda of his home, the Chokian at Sorinji, from the 1799 woodblock-printed book *Views of Celebrated Gardens of Kyoto (Miyako rinsen meisho zue)* (fig. 13). The accompanying poem by the kanshi poet Ryū Kobi (1714–1792), a disciple of Uno Meika, further explicates the mood:

When it rains the mountains become verdant hills,
fragrant with flowers when the snow has gone.
Lost in spiritual discussions, we forget to return,
finally, drunk with the golden cup [sencha] we end the day.

13. THE MONK GEPPŌ SHINRYŌ ON THE VERANDA OF HIS HOME, THE CHOKIAN, AT SORINJI IN KYOTO
From volume 2 of *Views of Celebrated Gardens of Kyoto (Miyako rinsen meisho zue)*, 1799. Woodblock-printed book; ink on paper. 25.5 x 32 cm. Kansai University Library, Osaka. Photo: P. Graham.

As identification with the highly respected Chinese literati tradition began to propel sencha into the limelight, chanoyu followers sought to acknowledge the equal importance of the literati to their tradition through emphasis on the spirituality of tea as described in Chinese sources. The first writer to allow for the inclusion of Chinese texts in the chanoyu tradition was Kaibara Ekken (1630–1714), an influential Confucian scholar near Fukuoka who taught commoners ethical values and practical knowledge as a means of improving the quality of their lives. In his 1713 *Precepts on Health Care (Yōjōkun)*, however, he recommended the drinking of sencha merely for its stimulating effect on the body and as an aid to digestion.[15] This interest in the medicinal value of sencha accorded with his educational mission and did not conflict with his personal devotion to chanoyu. Yet as he instructed readers to brew the tea in a manner derived from Lu Yu's treatise, he may have inadvertently helped to popularize sencha.

From Ekken's time on, references to Chinese tea texts in writings on chanoyu increased. In 1728 another chanoyu devotee and Confucian scholar, Mitani Sōchin (1665–1741), published *Documents on Tea in China and Japan (Wakan chashi)*, the first Japanese tea book to embrace both Chinese and Japanese tea history as a single continuum. This book, written in kanbun, ushered in a new age of writings on tea in Japan. The author affirmed the superiority of Chinese tea masters and practices over those from Japan, thereby shifting discussion away from the previous emphasis on schools and lineages within chanoyu (Kramer 1985, 67–69).

Another to incorporate the history of Chinese tea into a text on the history of chanoyu was Yabunouchi Chikushin (1678–1745), a Shushigaku-lineage Confucian scholar and the fifth-generation iemoto of the Yabunouchi chanoyu tea school. His treatise *Talks on the Origin of Tea (Genryū chawa)*, published in 1745,[16] elevated above all else the contribution of the Chinese literati to the formation of the Way of tea. Yet while he admitted the importance of the Chinese tea treatises, he criticized the indiscriminate borrowings from Chinese sources of authors such as Sōchin (Kramer 1985, 66). Obviously, it was not for fans of sencha alone that Kyoto booksellers began the reprinting of Chinese tea books in 1758, with Japanese editions of Lu Yu's *Classic of Tea* and Xia Shufang's *Tea Treatises*, although the publication of Xia's text was more closely associated with sencha, as the preface to the new Japanese edition was written by Kiyota Tansō (1719–1785), a friend of Ike Taiga.

Baisaō's Followers and the Formalizing of a Way of Sencha

Baisaō's friends Kimura Kenkadō and the priest Daiten Kenjō were largely responsible for creating a Way of sencha by providing detailed instructions on techniques for brewing fine-tasting leaf tea and by promoting the veneration of Baisaō and the tea utensils he used as the locus of the tradition. They accomplished this in two ways: first, by disseminating information about sencha to a broader audience through the publication, translation into Japanese, and annotation of a variety of Chinese tea treatises, and second, by publicizing Baisaō's tea-making paraphernalia.

In 1764 Kenkadō published a Japanese edition of the Chinese tea treatise *Secrets of Steeped Tea*, by Ye Zhuan, based on a copy from his own collection. Daiten edited the text and added commentary about two different Chinese methods for brewing leaf tea. One method he described, which was then generally known as sencha, was essentially Baisaō's technique of throwing leaves into a pot of boiling water so they could steep while simmering. The second method, later known as *encha*, was called by Daiten hōcha (literally, infused tea) and elsewhere dashicha, which is also a more general term for offering tea ceremoniously. In this technique, tea leaves were first placed in a teapot and hot water was poured over them. The brew subsequently steeped for a few minutes. Daiten deemed this second method most appropriate for preparing the more delicate Chinese tea leaves, which he indicated should not be boiled, for exposure to high temperatures would ruin their flavor.[17]

Because the average Japanese citizen, while literate, had only a limited command of written Chinese, reprints of Chinese texts could not be used to popularize the beverage outside of scholarly circles. Thus, Daiten and Kenkadō began to translate essential Chinese sencha texts into vernacular Japanese. Their initial effort, in 1774, was the *Detailed Explanation of the Classic of Tea*, the first Japanese-language edition of

Lu Yu's treatise. Daiten explained in straightforward language that he wrote the book to help people understand how to prepare tea properly. He explained the two main Chinese procedures of sencha and encha for steeping leaf tea. In conclusion, he acknowledged that the ancient Chinese methods would need to be adapted to contemporary Japanese conditions, and he added a section on tea utensils and their appropriate use in Japan. Although he claimed to be merely supplying this information to offer practical advice, with these remarks Daiten inadvertently initiated the process of formalizing sencha preparation procedures and establishing hierarchies for the selection of utensils.

In his enumeration of appropriate utensils, Daiten singled out types similar to those that Baisaō had used. Although Baisaō had himself counseled his friends against such infatuation with material possessions, he wrote that his twelve essential tea implements were his "teachers."[18] This attitude must have encouraged his followers to revere them as well. Consequently, the appearance of these utensils began to influence the aesthetic preferences of those who drank sencha, helping to create markets for imported Chinese and Japanese crafts in similar styles. Despite the fact that Baisaō had burned some of his utensils shortly before he died, nineteen of his utensils were listed and described in an appendix to the *Verses of the Old Tea Peddler*.

Subsequently, Kimura Kenkadō produced an even more detailed, illustrated record of Baisaō's utensils, complete with dimensions, in an accordion-folded sketchbook known as *Illustrations of Baisaō's Tea Utensils (Baisaō chagu zu)*.[19] Kenkadō's son, Kōyō (died 1838), had his father's book adapted for posthumous publication in 1823 in an accordion-folded printed album (fig. 14). His father's friend and fellow student in Taiga's painting studio, Aoki Shukuya (ca. 1737–1802), did the drawings. This *Pictorial Record of Baisaō's Tea Utensils (Baisaō chaki zufu)* included thirty-six objects, five more than in Kenkadō's original 71

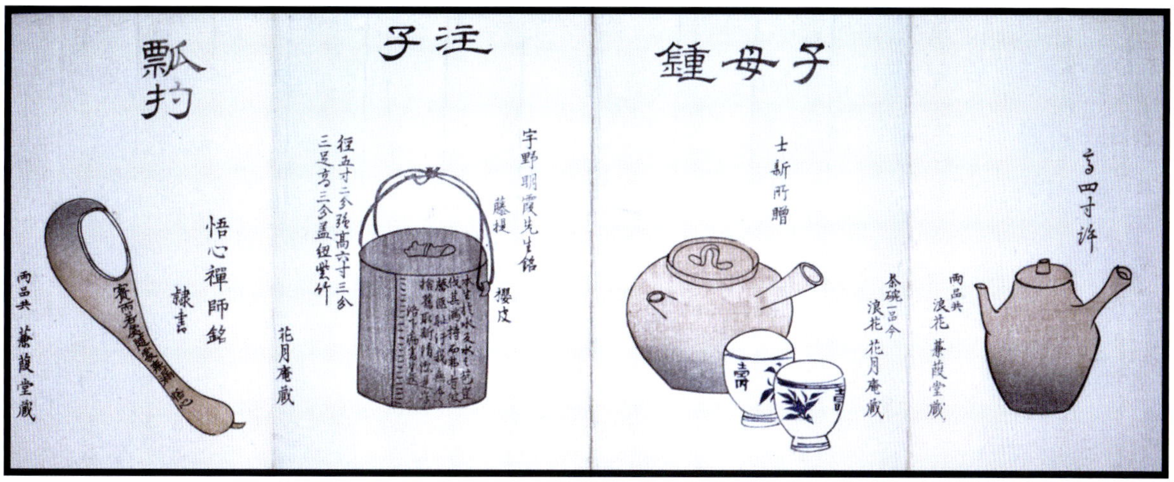

14. PICTORIAL RECORD OF BAISAŌ'S TEA UTENSILS (BAISAŌ CHAKI ZUFU)—1823
Aoki Shukuya (ca. 1737–1802). Section of an accordion-folded, woodblock-printed album; ink and light colors on paper. 20.6 x 50.4 cm (section shown). Private collection, Japan. Photo: P. Graham.

sketch, to encompass utensils only recently identified as Baisaō's. This printed book also named the owners of eleven of the illustrated utensils, most in the possession of Kenkadō's descendants or Kagetsuan (Tanaka Kakuō, founder of the Kagetsuan sencha school).

Kenkadō also had Japanese crafts makers copy his favorite Baisaō utensils, including some that Baisaō had burned. Some of these copies, as well as actual examples of utensils purported to have been owned by Baisaō but not included in Kenkadō's book and printed album, still exist, though it is difficult to distinguish authentic examples from the copies.[20] The authenticity of these pieces can be corroborated by comparison with illustrations in Kenkadō's sketchbook or printed album, supplemented with supporting documentation and information on provenance found in inscriptions by Baisaō's associates on the objects themselves or on the accompanying boxes.

Among the most famous and best accepted of this group is a seventeenth-century Ming stoneware teapot that Baisaō presented to Ike Taiga just before his death in 1763, known erroneously as *Gikōkan*, meaning a product of the Yixing kilns near Lake Tai in Jiangsu province (fig. 15).[21] Identification of this pot as a product of the Yixing kilns was based on information supplied by Kō Fuyō, who also noted that the vessel functioned as a kettle (*bofura*) for heating water atop the brazier (Hasegawa 1965, 113–114). In Ming China, the burnished and unglazed stoneware vessels of Yixing were the most expensive wares of their day, consumer products for the literati, and not readily available as export wares for Japan (Clunas 1991, 132). In the mid-eighteenth century, the Japanese had only limited exposure to Yixing wares; some had been imported by immigrant Chinese Ming loyalists, Ōbaku priests such as Ingen, and cultivated Chinese merchants of Nagasaki for their own use. Imported books on Ming material culture also lauded them and enumerated the names of their illustrious makers.

15. HOT WATER SIDE-HANDLED KETTLE TOGETHER WITH FIVE TEACUPS FROM A SET OF TEN POPULARLY KNOWN AS "SHIMOSHO" (CHILD AND MOTHER BELLS) WITH DESIGNS OF FLOWERING TEA PLANTS AND THE CHARACTER "JU" DENOTING FELICITY
Chinese, 17th-early 18th century. Kettle: unglazed buff colored stoneware, h. 9.9 cm; cups: Jingdezhen porcelain with underglaze blue, h. 4.5 cm, diam. 6.1 cm. Private collection, Japan. Photo: courtesy of the Osaka Municipal Museum of Art.

Also pictured in these books and widely accepted as genuine is a set of ten seventeenth-century Ming Jingdezhen-ware porcelain underglaze blue (kosometsuke) bell-shaped teacups. Records indicate that Baisaō gave them to Uno Meika (Shufunotomosha 1975, 24), from whom Kenkadō probably acquired them. Baisaō called these *Shimoshō* (child and mother bells), as their bell-shaped forms allowed for compact stacking, like the natural closeness between mothers and their children. They are decorated with flowering tea (camellia) plants and the character "*ju*," denoting felicity (also pictured in fig. 15).

By placing emphasis on Baisaō's utensils and their subsequent owners, Kenkadō and his followers injected their personal proclivities for collecting, influenced by similar practices in chanoyu, and imposed these on the developing custom of sencha. They thus began the transformation of it from an unpretentious activity in which anyone could participate into a formalized pastime accessible to a privileged few. In the process, they also created a lineage for sencha that began with Baisaō.

Osaka Writers and the Promotion of Sencha

Baisaō's particularly zealous and unorthodox means of proselytizing sencha in Kyoto made him its foremost early advocate. Yet a number of his contemporaries, generally well-educated and affluent merchants and samurai, also drank the beverage. Some of these individuals, such as Taiga's painting teacher, the samurai-scholar and literati painter Yanagisawa Kien (1706–1758), were more renowned for other avocations. Others, like the physician Ogawa Shin'an (1649–1743) and his medical teacher in Kyoto, Funaya Ichimu (dates unknown), are obscure figures whose names have been handed down only in sencha genealogies (Hasegawa 1965, 85; Tsukuda 1972, 36). Though all early sencha fans shared an interest in Chinese leaf tea and pursued it as a private pastime, their differing personalities and tastes precluded establishment of an orthodoxy for sencha etiquette.

By the 1750s, under the spell of Baisaō, the situation began to change. The second half of the eighteenth century is marked by an increasing accessibility of Chinese tea treatises, the first appearance of Japanese instructional texts about sencha etiquette, increased availability of imported Chinese utensils, and the initial production of Japanese sencha utensils.

Baisaō's intuitive approach to promulgation of sencha and the literati spirit through his witticisms and poetry was complemented by that of his contemporary Ōeda Ryūhō (died ca. 1756), who provided practical information on literati culture in clearly organized texts. The son of a wealthy Osaka merchant, he wrote books about the incense ceremony, shell collecting, and flower arranging in addition to sencha and Chinese-style literati accomplishments. Although he was not a member of Baisaō's intimate circle, their paths crossed at least once. The evidence is a poem that Baisaō wrote for Ryūhō, included in his *Verses of the Old Tea Peddler* (Waddell 1984, 109).

Ryūhō's book, *Miscellaneous Records of Elegant Pastimes*, published in 1762,[22] served as a primer for the Japanese public on the creation of a proper literati environment. In the preface, his friend Tsuga Teishō described how in his youth, Ryūhō pursued the reclusive life of Chinese Daoist sages, living in a secluded thatched hut north of Kyoto. He described Ryūhō's home as surrounded by bamboo and pines, and having only a bright window and a plain table. Yet after many years, he said, Ryūhō returned to live in Naniwa (Osaka), settling by a bend in the river known alternately as *Aminoshima* (island of nets) or Seiwan (azure harbor). He adopted the latter term as one of his art names. Calling himself and his friends eccentric hermits of the mountains, Ryūhō spent his time in scholarly pursuits: chatting with friends while drinking sencha, playing the qin, and surrounding himself with refined objects in literati taste.

Within his book's seven volumes, Ryūhō lovingly describes assorted literati objects in a Japanese vernacular text liberally sprinkled with kanbun quotations from Chinese tea treatises that he probably had read only in excerpts included in later compendia. After a general overview of the various treasures of the Chinese scholars' studio, he moves to sections on topics as diverse as providing instructions on twenty-seven different methods for decorative knotting; descriptions of utensils for incense, tea, wine, and flowers; appropriate traveling gear (including picnic supplies); descriptions of different painting formats; evaluations of the merits of assorted embroidered brocade patterns; introductions to musical instruments, including a section on musical notation; and explanations of literati games such as the arrow-toss game, tea competitions, rhyming games, the shell game, and go. He justifies the moral value of these pastimes and the objects used therein based on ideas derived from Ming texts, stating that "one could behold the nature of a person's heart from the things they possess, and that looking at things that are vulgar (zoku) and not elegant (ga) is annoying."[23] Because Ryūhō was the first to acknowledge the intimate relationship between participation in sencha and appreciation of Chinese literati arts, this book should be considered the first guide to the correct selection and use of objects for elegant activities in which to engage while drinking sencha. To clarify his ideas, Ryūhō included numerous detailed illustrations, such as a view of the interior of a Chinese scholar's study (fig. 16).

16. VIEW OF A CHINESE SCHOLAR'S STUDY—1762
Ōeda Ryūhō (died ca. 1756), from volume 1 of *Miscellaneous Records of Elegant Pastimes (Gayū manroku)*. Woodblock-printed book; ink on paper. 21 x 16 cm. Private collection, Japan. Photo: P. Graham.

With his *Chats on Tea by the Azure Harbor* of 1756, the first true treatise on sencha in Japan, Ryūhō moved from general discussion about literati taste to detailing the specifics of what was to him a particularly important literati activity. Tsuga Teishō (1718–ca. 1794), an Osaka physician, Confucian scholar, and writer of popular (*yomihon*) fiction based on Chinese historical events, contributed the preface to this book too in which he explained that Ryūhō wrote the book in response to the rapid growth in popularity of sencha among ordinary people, who needed assistance understanding its spiritual associations.[24]

To define the atmosphere for sencha appreciation, Teishō described the Chinese custom of intermittently drinking fragrant tea and wine, although he erroneously connected it with the celebrated Lanting Gathering. Teishō described the otherworldly feelings (seifū) of the participants at the Lanting Gathering by stating that they must have felt as if they had arrived at the Daoist isle of Mount Hōrai. With this pronouncement, he neatly connected Lanting with the famous poem about drinking seven bowls of tea by Lu Tong. Although occasionally brushed earlier, the Lanting Gathering became a favorite subject for Japanese artists in the second half of the eighteenth and first half of the nineteenth centuries as a result of increasing enchantment with Chinese literati culture. Sencha enthusiasts appropriated its imagery because of its literati connotations, and the most creative interpretations of the theme were brushed by literati artists such as Ike Taiga who were avid fans of sencha. Taiga's colorful screen dating to circa 1760 captures the inebriated, lively spirit of the participants (fig. 17).

Following Teishō's philosophical preface, Ryūhō's introduction intersperses comments about sencha's relationship to chanoyu (which

17. ORCHID PAVILION GATHERING—CA.1763

Ike Taiga (1723–1776). Right side of a pair of six-fold screens; ink and colors on paper. 162.8 x 359.1 cm. Metropolitan Museum of Art, Mary Griggs Burke Collection, Gift of the Mary and Jackson Burke Foundation, 2015.

he identifies with the term "matcha") with descriptions of the book's contents and an explanation of why he chose not to include certain aspects of the subject:

> *This book is written mainly for explaining sencha and has nothing to do with matcha. Books about tea discuss nothing but its medicinal value, but this book will also discuss its origins. Tea is an extremely famous product of China and Japan, and I have written this book in order to enumerate its benefits for those with free time to investigate such things. Despite its being a famous product, people are ignorant of it. Although there are famous tea-growing regions in both China and Japan, I will not enumerate these here. Also, there is no benefit just to knowing the source for obtaining excellent water for brewing tea, especially if the fine water is found in far-away places in China that we cannot reach. Thus I will not discuss water in this book. As for utensils, most of them are not considered treasures and only a few are truly fine. Thus 1 will not discuss these here either. Those utensils that have been recorded in books on tea are already well known. However, other types of tea utensils that have not been recorded in books have appeared, and these I think it is useful to know about, so for the readers' convenience, I have discussed them.*

In the body of the text, chapters focus on topics including instructions on the proper use of utensils, the charm of tea, places appropriate for drinking tea, and the various procedures for preparing tea, one of which was the Chinese custom of brewing flower petals or fragrant leaves (kōsen). The book of teachings by the immigrant Chinese scholar Zhu Shunsui, *Master Zhu Shunshui's Illustrious Lectures*, had earlier mentioned this custom of the drinking of such teas derived from shisō (beefsteak plant leaves), bitter orange, lotus flower, gardenia, chrysanthemum, orchid, plum blossoms, or some other aromatic flower. These were thought to cleanse one's palate and assist in purifying the spirit. Kōsen was subsequently included in virtually all the premodern treatises on sencha and remains an integral part of a formal sencha ceremony today. It is not unique to sencha, however. Some chanoyu ceremonies, particularly those that are held in winter months, also feature it as a beverage to serve prior to the formal presentation of matcha.

An appendix to the *Chats on Tea* describes some tea competitions (tōcha), pastimes that originated in China but were transformed by chanoyu followers into popular parlor games. As adapted again for sencha, these games involved guessing the type of tea being served. Although Ryūhō's sincerity of intent in appropriating the manners of the Chinese literati is clear, his inclusion of tōcha as a suitable activity for sencha enthusiasts reveals his connection to the world of amateur dilettantes who must have enjoyed the beverage as one of many fashionable leisure pursuits (Tsukuda I. 1981, 484). This context for appreciation of the beverage was vastly different from the simple environment that Baisaō preferred. Ryūhō felt it was not enough to embrace the literati spirit through the ingestion of Chinese tea alone; it was necessary to surround oneself with the material trappings of the Chinese literati as well. This attitude exerted great influence on later sencha followers.

Despite acknowledging differences in their perspectives, Ryūhō identified Baisaō and his Ōbaku tradition as central to the appreciation of sencha. The utensils he illustrated as appropriate for sencha resembled those Baisaō had used, including some of Baisaō's own pieces. Elsewhere he credited Ingen as the first in Japan to prepare tea in the manner later popularized by Baisaō. In general, the topics Ryūhō discussed, as well as his book's organization, served as a model for the numerous treatises on sencha that were soon to follow in the late eighteenth and early nineteenth centuries.

Among the next generation of sencha's many fans in Osaka, Kenkadō and Ueda Akinari (1734–1809) became its greatest promoters. As we have already seen, Kenkadō's fame rested on his connoisseurship of Baisaō's utensils and his knowledge of Chinese books on tea. Praise for Akinari was derived primarily from his writings, the *Miscellaneous Comments on the Way of Pure Elegance*, a popular guide to sencha published in 1794, and the *Drunken Words of a Tea Addict (Chaka suigen)*, completed around 1807.[25] Akinari first trained as a physician and later became a celebrated writer in the stylish *ukiyo zoshi* (stories of the floating world) genre and in haikai, and he was a Kokugaku (national learning) scholar.[26] He knew of Ōeda Ryūhō through his medical teacher and mentor in Chinese literary studies, Tsuga Teishō, who had contributed the prefaces to Ryūhō's books, and he admired Ryūhō as second only to Baisaō in selecting tea and water for sencha (Waddell 1984, 109). Akinari also developed a close friendship with Kimura Kenkadō, with whom he shared a common interest in medicinal plants—tea, of course, being prominent among them.

Like Kenkadō, Akinari made frequent visits to Kyoto to participate in literati activities with illustrious intellectuals there. He was particularly close with the haikai poetry group centered around Yosa Buson (1716–1783), a prominent literati painter. Their gatherings would frequently take place in the finer houses of the entertainment areas

18. PORTRAIT OF UEDA AKINARI BREWING SENCHA
Matsumura Goshun (1752–1811), section of a handscroll of annual activities (*Nenjū gyōji*); ink and light colors on paper. H: 19 cm. Fukuoka City Museum. Photo: P. Graham.

such as Kyoto's Sumiya. One of Akinari's friends in Buson's group was Matsumura Goshun (1752–1811), Buson's star painting pupil who brushed an intimate portrait of Akinari quietly seated before a brazier preparing sencha (fig. 18). Other friends from Kyoto included prominent Confucian scholars associated with the Kogaku schools, such as Minagawa Kien (1734–1807), an important teacher who is also known for his literati-style paintings, and Murase Kōtei (1746–1818), who wrote the preface to Akinari's *Miscellaneous Comments on the Way of Pure Elegance*.

Akinari's interest in Chinese studies might have precluded involvement with Kokugaku had he not been such an independent-minded scholar with broad-ranging interests. Many Kokugaku scholars maintained an outwardly antagonistic relationship with Sinophile Confucian scholars, for they sought to preserve the purity of Japan's national heritage through study of ancient Japanese sources, while the followers of Confucianism stressed China's superior learning. Yet the emphasis on study of original texts, which preoccupied the scholars of the Kogaku schools with whom Akinari associated, reveals some sharing of values with Kokugaku. Participation in sencha became a point of commonality, as followers of both philosophies sought to recapture the spirit of ancient times. Sencha followers admired the Tang dynasty founders of the art of tea in China, rejecting as decadent the tea traditions of the Song dynasty upon which chanoyu was based (Kumakura 1980, 62).

Although criticism of chanoyu abounded from the middle of the eighteenth century, Ueda Akinari's *Miscellaneous Comments* was the first book to state that sencha was superior to chanoyu.[27] His book provided a historical sketch of the art of tea in China and Japan and included a selection of Chinese tea poems. Following Baisaō's paradigm, Akinari defined the essential appeal of sencha as its ability to facilitate spiritual fulfillment in the manner of the Chinese sages. He likewise portrayed chanoyu as emphasizing superficiality, having degenerated into little more than a complicated ritual with innumerable rules required of participants. Murase Kōtei implied as much in his preface, where he defined the differences between the two traditions with the succinct statement: "chanoyu is about knowledge, sencha is about purity of spirit."[28] This search for purity or nobility of spirit was of paramount concern to Akinari, and immersing himself in sencha became one of his main means of escaping from a degenerate world, sentiments he expressed in his poetry:

Though I cannot flee
From the world of corruption,
I can prepare tea
with water from a mountain stream
And put my heart to rest.[29]

As a physician, the high value Akinari placed on purifying the spirit with sencha must have had a great deal to do with the physiological benefits, including clarity of thought, that resulted from drinking tea. He felt that the physical and spiritual benefits of tea were interdependent, indicating that tea could be either purifying or poisonous depending on its preparation methods. Matcha, he said, weakened the spirit, for the desired flavor poisoned the body (Kumakura 1980, 63). A concern for purity led Akinari and like-minded sencha fans to seek out the purest sources of water and the best varieties of tea. It also accounted for sencha followers' meticulous attention to procedures for cultivating, processing, and brewing the tea. Akinari discussed all these points in detail in his *Miscellaneous Comments*.

In addition to laying out the philosophy, the book also contained illustrations of utensils appropriate for the sencha tea service, of both Chinese and Japanese manufacture. Akinari included some owned by Baisaō, a teapot from Kenkadō's collection, for example, but his selections were culled from more diverse sources. He listed a wide assortment of braziers, including an ancient Chinese cast-bronze example from the collection of Hōryūji; a tall, simple, cylindrical Chinese-made pottery one; and a distinctive large-mouthed brazier of pottery that he identified as being made in Akita. He categorized teacups and teapots into standardized types, illustrating teacups of three distinct shapes

19. TEACUPS AND A NANBAN-STYLE TEAPOT—1794
Ueda Akinari (1734–1809), from volume 1 of *Miscellaneous Comments on the Way of Pure Elegance (Seifū sagen)*. Woodblock-printed book; ink on paper. 12.2 x 15.8 cm. National Japanese Sencha Association Library, Manpukuji, Uji. Photo: P. Graham.

(basin, bell, and bowl), and distinguished a specific kind of teapot, *Nanbansei* (southern barbarian style), imported from southern China (fig. 19).

Although *Nanban* was also the name given to Spanish and Portuguese traders, the teapot had no direct connection with Europe, but was so named because it had been imported from southern China following the same sea route taken by the Europeans. Baisaō had also owned a teapot of this type (it appears in both Kenkadō's sketchbook and its later printed version), and this line drawing from Akinari's book must have been based on Baisaō's original. Nanban teapots later became the most popular style of sencha teapots crafted by Japanese artisans. Typically made of dark brown, unglazed, roughly textured clay, they were light in weight and small in proportion, with tiny, crudely attached side handles and spouts. Although these teapots were dearly admired in Japan, in China they were inexpensive wares that actually functioned as pots for brewing medicinal herbs. In this reverence for such humble vessels, Japanese sencha enthusiasts may have been betraying a subconscious attraction to Chinese styles reminiscent of chanoyu wabi taste.

Akinari became so enthralled with the accouterments of sencha that he began designing them himself with the assistance of Kyoto potters in whose workshops the pieces were probably finished and fired. A number of his rough and unglazed stoneware braziers and teapots are extant (fig. 20), similar in appearance to the coarse Nanban-style wares used by Baisaō. Yet Akinari's occasional whimsically shaped sculptural forms—a brazier in the shape of a crab or a teapot lid with an animal-shaped knob, for example—and exaggerated textural patterns reveal the imprint of his idiosyncratic personality.

The Further Dissemination of Sencha

Popular acclaim for Akinari's *Miscellaneous Comments* created a veritable boom in the publishing of books about sencha that lasted for the next several decades. These new publications stimulated the inception of widespread popularization of sencha and catered to an audience desirous of, on the one hand, simpler and more instructive texts on the subject and, on the other, reprints of Chinese tea treatises. The first two Japanese reprints of major Chinese tea compendia were published in

20. HOT WATER KETTLE AND CRAB-SHAPED BRAZIER
Ueda Akinari (1734–1809). Brazier: unglazed, buff-colored stoneware. H: 8 cm. Kettle: brown stoneware with ash glaze, repaired with gold lacquer. H: 7.6 cm. Idemitsu Museum of Arts, Tokyo.

this climate. Both included prefaces, actually endorsements, by prominent Kansai-area Confucian scholars. The 1801 edition of the circa 1675 *History of Tea* contained a preface by Kenkadō's friend, a fellow native of Osaka and Taiga's painting pupil, Totoki Baigai (1749–1804). Another of Akinari's friends, and Baigai's teacher in Confucian studies, Minagawa Kien, contributed a preface to the 1804 Japanese edition of the *Complete Collection of Tea Books.*

Concurrently, other popular sencha books appeared geared to a more general audience. The first of these was the *Detailed Record of Sencha (Sencha ryakusetsu)*, written by Nakajima Rakusui (active late eighteenth century), and published in 1798 by a prominent Osaka publisher, Maekawa Zenbei. Its first part was a translation into Japanese of the Qing treatise *Secrets of Steeped Tea*, which Daiten and Kenkadō had published in 1764. Rakusui added his own commentary in the second section. Kenkadō, who owned the original Chinese edition, lent his name to the project by brushing the title calligraphy. Another of Kenkadō's many friends, Kikuchi Gozan (1769?-1855), a kanshi poet from Edo who has been described as "an opportunistic advocate of poetry for the masses" (Markus 1993, 147), contributed a preface, a lengthy biographical poem about the author. Gozan's description of Rakusui's lifestyle reveals that he aspired to lead a life similar in spirit to Ōeda Ryūhō's:

> *Even though his body is old, he is only as old as he feels,*
> *As he dwells in the mountains every day, brewing sencha with fresh spring water.*
> *He makes a pillow of stone and blocks out the moonlight,*
> *The bamboo stand for the brazier rests in the shade of the banana leaves.*
> *A soft breeze causes the flowers to flutter like wisps of smoke*
> *As he drinks up his tea, absorbed completely with the task.*
> *Then he awakens as if from a dream and reads a hundred Chinese poems,*
> *Laughing at himself like an impoverished drunkard.*
> *He cares not if many or few guests call in a year,*
> *For he has entirely abandoned material pursuits.*

Like Ryūhō and Akinari before him, Rakusui provided detailed information on how to brew fine-tasting tea. On the source of the water, for example, he deemed well water bad, but praised water from fast-moving streams—identifiable by the smooth, rounded rocks under the current. He also noted that Japanese and Chinese tea differed in flavor because the composition of the soil in which the plants grew was different.

Rakusui enumerated utensils for sencha more completely than any previous author, although curiously, his book contained no illustrations. In one section he distinguished seven different types of side-handled teapots that are generally known as kyūsu, but which he identified with the more archaic moniker of "*kibishō*." Rakusui considered Chinese teapots the best, the first acknowledgment of the existence of Japanese-made ones. Yet he noted that among the Chinese varieties some were good and others bad. He wrote that the best of the Chinese teapots were similar in shape to Baisaō's Gikōkan kettle that he called *Baisaō gata* (Baisaō shape) (fig. 15), and noted that the Kyoto potter Kiyomizu Rokubei I (1733?–1799) copied this form. Rokubei, the only Japanese potter named by Rakusui, was later acknowledged as the first Japanese potter to produce wares for sencha. His utensils, primarily braziers and teapots, appear to be faithful copies of Chinese originals (Kawahara 1985, 26, pl. 8).

Rakusui also included two sections on braziers in his book, titled "*fūro*" and "*ryōro*" respectively, in which he pointed out that Lu Yu had indicated that ancient Chinese bronzes in tripod (*ding*) shape had been used as braziers. Because these were similar in shape to braziers used to heat water for chanoyu, Rakusui acknowledged that chanoyu braziers could also be used for sencha. This is the first reference to the appropriation of chanoyu utensils for sencha and indicates a dramatic shift from attitudes held by earlier sencha enthusiasts whose enmity toward chanoyu was famous. This indebtedness to chanoyu increased as the assimilation and popularization of sencha continued.

Although sencha remained predominantly in the Kansai region, as fans socialized with friends from domains to the east (primarily Ise, Nagoya, and Edo), it soon gained followers and commentators from those regions. Generally eschewing philosophical discussions, these authors emphasized utensils and procedures for preparing the tea, often with terminology borrowed from the more familiar chanoyu. Among the earliest of such publications was the *Quick Guide to Sencha (Sencha hayashi nan)* of 1802, written by an obscure monk from Nagoya, Ryukatei Ransui (dates unknown).[30] Although Ransui only briefly mentioned the history of sencha, he included an illustration of Baisaō by the Nagoya painter Chō Gesshō (1772–1832), who had studied under Goshun in Kyoto. Ransui also referred to Akinari's *Miscellaneous Comments on the Way of Pure Elegance.* Yet the body of Ransui's text and accompanying copious illustrations focused on the utensils and their usage. One of his many illustrations of utensils depicted a selection carefully organized in a storage cabinet, identified by names familiar to those who practiced chanoyu (fig. 21).

In his discussion of utensils, Ransui included the name of another Kyoto potter, Takahashi Dōhachi I (1740–1804), whom he said manufactured sencha wares. His vessels were very different from those by Rokubei. A versatile master who worked sometimes in porcelain, Dōhachi apparently got into the business of sencha utensil making as a result of his being engaged to fabricate imitation Chinese porcelain teacups and teapots for Kimura Kenkadō and his friends.[31]

Edo writers about sencha continued to emphasize its relationship with chanoyu, but they also strove to define more clearly the setting for sencha gatherings. Perhaps the earliest book on sencha published in Edo was the 1779 *Record of Tea Investigation (Kōcha roku)*, with an interior title page appellation of *Quick Guide to Sencha (Sencha hayashi nan)*, authored by Toto Utaguchi. He advocated drinking sencha with matcha utensils and declared its appropriateness for tea competitions featuring sencha as first described by Ōeda Ryūhō (Shufunotomosha 1981, 417, 489).

More reflective of the growing awareness of sencha in Edo was the somewhat later *Woodblock Book on Boiled Tea (Hōcha shōsho)* of 1803, written by the botanist Sō Senshun (died 1834), who dispensed a detailed account of sencha and its various utensils. The kanshi poet Ōkubo Shibutsu (1767–1837), a frequent traveler who, like his friend Kikuchi Gozan, was befriended by the major literati figures of the Kansai area, contributed a long section at the end, *Notes on a Tea Gathering*

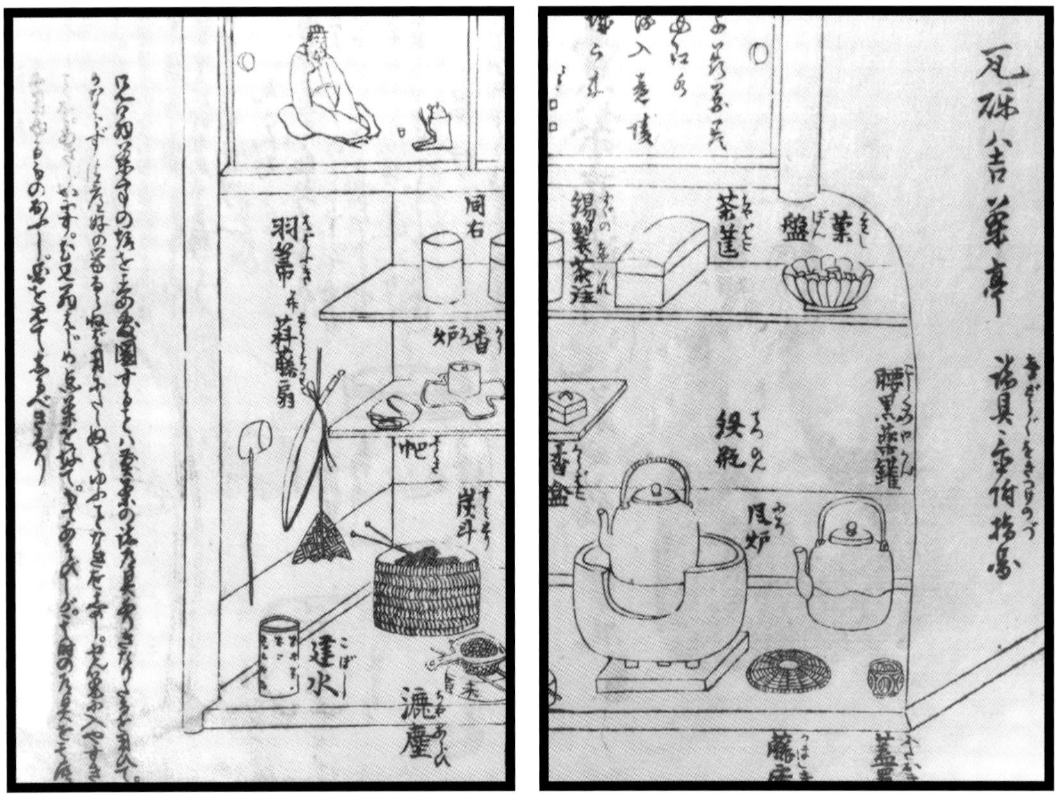

21. SENCHA UTENSILS IN A STORAGE CABINET—1802
Ryūkatei Ransui (dates unknown), from *Quick Guide to Sencha (Sencha hayashi nan)*. Woodblock-printed book; ink on paper. 26 x 36 cm. National Japanese Sencha Association Library, Manpukuji, Uji. Photo: P. Graham.

(Charyō zusan). There he listed all the utensils used at the gathering and their owners, named the eighteen participants, then illustrated and described each utensil individually.

Although many of these were familiar types of sencha utensils, some, such as a carved lacquer teacup stand and a gourd water dipper, appear to have been lifted directly from one of the few Chinese tea treatises that had actually included illustrations.[32] It remains unclear whether Shibutsu and his friends had truly acquired utensils similar to those illustrated in the Chinese text in their zeal to recreate a Chinese ambiance, or had added the pictures of the Chinese utensils to make their gathering seem more impressive to readers. This kind of sencha text, a record of a tea ceremony and a complete description of utensils, must have been inspired by similar writings about formal chanoyu ceremonies. The intended audience was probably the elite samurai residents of Edo who would have already been familiar with such things.

Another Edo publication, a short volume titled *Sencha Techniques (Sencha shiki)* of 1804, surpassed all previous sencha texts in its standardization of procedures and indebtedness to chanoyu. It was authored by Masuyama Sessai (1755–1820), daimyo of the Nagashima fief in Ise who had been born and reared in Edo, moved to Ise from 1776 to 1801, and again resided in Edo from 1801 until his death. Sessai was a devoted scholar and artist himself, and patron of many important artists and Confucian scholars of his day, including Totoki Baigai, who taught at his official academy from 1784 to 1790. This book was particularly influential in Edo scholarly circles, where it helped spread information about the Kansai emphasis on the literati associations of sencha to Sessai's many acquaintances. As Sessai was a high-ranking samurai, he would have been well versed in chanoyu procedures. Consequently, sencha etiquette was, for him, heavily laced with rules of conduct for chanoyu, but modified to accord with literati aesthetics and the requirements of preparing steeped rather than powdered tea.

Instead of providing historical and philosophical background for the subject, Sessai identified and illustrated the essential tools for preparing sencha. Most were virtually the same as those described in Ransui's *Quick Guide to Sencha*, but he also added and identified two of Baisaō's utensils that Kenkadō had owned (a metal brazier and a pottery kettle). Although Sessai insisted that brewing fine-tasting tea remained of paramount importance, the main part of his book consisted of a step-by-step description of a ceremonial presentation of sencha for the edification of prospective hosts. According to the author, the event began with the lighting of incense and a reverential bowing, then progressed to setting out the fire-making equipment, removing the tea-making implements from the portable carrying case (*teiran*), serving sweets, boiling the water, and brewing the tea. Then, as is still customary today, the host would take the first taste of the tea before pouring cups for his guests, and if requested, would prepare a new pot of water for a second round of tea for all. Finally, prior to departure, the guests would be served a dried plum sweet to wash away any unpleasant aftertaste from the tea.

Sessai also clearly defined the fūryū atmosphere in which to serve the beverage. The Sinophile literati atmosphere of the sencha gathering has here been given a formal and prescriptive structure. In no previous sencha text had the chronology of a sencha gathering been so clearly defined. Sessai decreed that five persons were the optimum number appropriate for sencha gatherings: three guests, a host, and an attendant. As the utensils could all be stored in a teiran, he advised that these gatherings could take place out-of-doors at waterfalls, in the mountains, amid bamboo forests, or while floating down a river on a boat. Accompanying activities for such occasions should be the Chinese literati pastimes of composing poetry (*shi*), painting or calligraphy, or playing erudite music. In addition to all the usual utensils for preparing the tea itself, tearooms should have a clean table equipped with brush, paper, inkstone, and ink; musical instruments; a painting on the wall; flowers in a vase; and an image (small statue?) of an important figure associated with sencha such as Lu Yu or Baisaō.

The increasing preoccupation with the particularization of utensils and procedures for serving sencha in these later books is a sharp departure from the writings of Baisaō. They seem more like elaborations of the texts by Ryūhō and Akinari, which were intended as guidebooks on literati lifestyles. They illustrate that by the beginning of the Bunka era (1804–1818), the literati lifestyle was becoming canonized, and that by participating in sencha gatherings, one could adopt the mantle of a bunjin. By this time the standardization of sencha utensils was already nearly complete, so much so that for modern-day sencha practitioners, the names and forms used would be largely recognizable. The utensils described in these books and the many sencha texts to follow in the first half of the nineteenth century were generally of Chinese manufacture, close copies by Japanese makers, or adaptations of well-known chanoyu utensil types. Their diversity of type and style reveals much expansion of the canon of Chinese utensils established by Baisaō, a course that would continue throughout the nineteenth century.

Under the spell of the charismatic eccentric Baisaō, the art of sencha, as the central component of an eccentric and Sinophile lifestyle, first came into fruition. Ironically, although initially disdainful of the liturgies and emphases on material possessions that concerned the followers of chanoyu, sencha adherents soon developed similar fixations with newly devised conventions of their own. They replaced what were to them outmoded sets of values with new ones more harmonious with their own beliefs and aesthetic preferences, but were also willing to adopt elements from the rival and initially scorned tradition of chanoyu. By transforming the Chinese literati custom of drinking sencha into a Japanese ritual, these Japanese intellectuals went beyond the creation of an alternative Way of tea. They assisted in the naturalization of Chinese culture. At the same time, sencha helped create an acceptable niche in Japanese society for those individuals desirous of a lifestyle outside the prescribed social structure of which chanoyu was an integral part. How sencha continued to play a significant role in the lives of the literati as their culture blossomed in the first half of the nineteenth century is the subject of the following chapter.

CHAPTER FIVE

Bunjincha, Sencha of the Literati

By the beginning of the nineteenth century, intellectuals came from all levels of society, and entry into their ranks was granted by virtue of their education, intellect, and, to a certain extent, livelihood (as teacher, physician, artist, writer, etc.). They tended to band together in cliques that were determined by shared interests, bypassing bakufu-imposed divisions of citizens into distinct social classes. They were a diverse group whose ideologies encompassed values both admiring and disdainful of China, the West, and even Japan itself. Some sought to protect the hierarchical class divisions promulgated by the government, while others renounced them.

Among these intellectuals were the bunjin, impassioned admirers of the ideals of the Chinese literati, whose reclusionist tendencies during times of political unrest or as a form of silent protest against unjust rulers served as models of behavior for their own lives. Some of these bunjin who hailed from the samurai class resigned their official posts in protest, thereby denying their descendants samurai status. Others chose to speak out, facing the wrath of the censors and even martyrdom for causes in which they strongly believed. Still others remained apolitical, immersing themselves in intellectual or artistic pursuits, seemingly oblivious to the unsettled conditions that prevailed during much of the late Tokugawa period.

The Japanese bunjin excelled at the scholarly arts of painting, calligraphy, and poetry composition in Chinese—skills marketable among a public fascinated with Chinese culture. These talents enabled them to earn livings as professional writers or artists. Many frequently traveled throughout the country, enjoying the hospitality of provincial hosts who shared similar interests and for whom association with these famous individuals offered increased prestige in their communities. The bunjin, in turn, treated their benefactors and friends to spontaneous exhibitions of their talents by producing paintings, calligraphies, music, or poems in lieu of payment for food and lodging in a tradition called *bunjin bokkyaku* (literati ink guests). Because of their wanderlust, the paths of many bunjin crossed, resulting in the forging of friendships and exchanging of ideas.

Most of these bunjin embraced sencha as a concomitant to their Chinese literati activities. As they attempted to replicate its Sinophile forms, they gave their manner of enjoying the beverage a name, *bunjincha* (literati tea), to distinguish it from other styles of sencha ceremonies that flourished contemporaneously among other groups in society. The increased availability of both Chinese tea texts and material goods, essential to reenacting the Chinese manner of preparing sencha, greatly facilitated their endeavors.

Sencha in the Bunjin Culture of Rai San'yō and His Circle

A central figure to the emergence of bunjincha was the distinguished Confucian scholar, talented calligrapher, and literati painter Rai San'yō (1780–1832). Born in Osaka, the son of a famous scholar of Confucian studies, San'yō was raised in Hiroshima, where his father taught at the fief academy. In 1797 he spent a year studying at the Shōheikō shogunal academy in Edo. Evidently disillusioned, while there he began to lead a dissipated life. He soon abandoned his familial responsibilities and fled to Kyoto. Eventually captured and returned to his family in Hiroshima, he was disinherited and placed under house arrest for six years. During this period he worked steadily on his magnum opus, the *Unofficial History of Japan (Nihon gaishi)*. In 1811 he was freed and settled permanently in Kyoto. From then until the end of his life, San'yō derived his livelihood from teaching Confucianism at a school he founded, supplemented with income derived from sales of paintings and calligraphies, brushed by himself and his Kyoto friends, to provincial patrons during visits to distant provinces, most located west of Kyoto along the Inland Sea.[1] Throughout his life, San'yō continued his studies of Chinese literati arts. A three-month stay in Nagasaki in 1818, for example, allowed him direct contacts with Chinese residents there, including Chinese painters whom San'yō met at the Kagetsu restaurant (fig. 4) (Yamamoto 1983, 379; Nagasaki 1923, 15).

In Kyoto, San'yō organized informal gatherings for friends to study Chinese paintings and literature. Among those closest to him were Koishi Genzui (1784–1849), a physician specializing in Dutch medicine; Shinozaki Shōchiku (1781–1851), a prominent Confucian scholar from Osaka; and several literati painters: Tanomura Chikuden (1777–1835), a samurai from Takeda in northern Kyushu; Uragami Shunkin (1779–1845); Okada Hankō (1782–1846);[2] the cleric Geppō; Nakabayashi Chikutō (1776–1853), a native of Nagoya; and Aoki Mokubei, who was also a potter (Woodson 1983, 123–124). The convivial and intimate atmosphere that characterized meetings of this group must have included the drinking of sencha, as the beverage was by then a requisite component to pursuit of a bunjin life. San'yō's coterie met regularly in the study of his home in central Kyoto, nestled along the banks of the Kamo River. He named his study/studio there, constructed in 1828, the Sanshi Suimeisho (abode of purple mountains and clear water).

A forerunner of later sencha tearooms, with thatched roof, compact proportions, and a small tokonoma alcove, the Sanshi Suimeisho bears general resemblance to traditional chanoyu teahouses, yet lacks the obligatory *nijiriguchi* (a small door for guests to crawl through). Like Ishikawa Jōzan's Shisendō, which may generally be considered its spiritual and stylistic ancestor, San'yō's study reflected his personal taste. The main four-and-one-half mat room, for example, featured an unusually tall, peaked ceiling. San'yō must also have drawn on descriptions of scholars' retreats in Chinese books such as the *Casual Expressions of Idle Feelings*, which provided detailed descriptions of such buildings (Yokoyama 1987, 257–259). Like the structures described in the Chinese texts, San'yō's study contained a small room with a writing desk to the side of a main chamber.

San'yō's abode was not a reproduction of a Chinese scholars' studio, however. Instead, it integrated Chinese design features into a Japanese setting through such details as the fretwork patterns of the railings, the tablet inscribed with the title of the room mounted above the doorway (as found outside buildings at Manpukuji), wicker wainscoting, a reed-covered ceiling, and above a window to the right of the alcove, a shelf meant for display of bunbōgu (scholars' objects and decorative objects for the scholar's study). He also modified the appearance of the tokonama, substituting a flat board for the more common raised, tatami-matted platform (fig. 22). This design was close in appearance to the early form of the tokonoma, suggestive of the Chinese table that was its precursor.

The building also featured a truly exotic element, glass windows set between the wicker wainscoting and shoji of the sliding door panels that opened onto the veranda and encircled the main room (fig. 23). Glazed windows were a rarity in Japan at the time this study was constructed. In fact, in Europe where the technology had been invented, the first factory to produce plate glass windows had opened in the

22. RAI SAN'YŌ'S STUDY
The tokonoma and shelf for scholars' accouterments at the Sanshi Suimeisho (abode of purple mountains and clear water), constructed in 1828. Kyoto. Photo: P. Graham.

Netherlands only in 1773 (Screech 1996, 134). The Japanese knew of glass soon after, for Western residences in Nagasaki incorporated it. Shiba Kokan had included an illustration of a Westerner's room with glass windows in his 1794 *Journey to the West* (Screech 1996, fig. 17), and San'yō must have seen examples during his tour of Nagasaki in 1818. When Japanese first began employing this technology in their own residences is not clear, but San'yō's was undoubtedly one of the first. As the technology was new and expensive, only small glass panels, as here, were used at first.

Although San'yō did not author any books on sencha himself, one of his students, Abe Kenshū (Ryōzandō; fl. first half of the nineteenth century), compiled a sencha text that accurately reflected the preferences of San'yō and his associates. Kenshū was a Confucian scholar, seal carver, kanshi poet, and painter of ink bamboo in the literati manner. Originally from Sanuki province in Shikoku, he moved to Osaka, joining the circles of prominent bunjin there.

Kenshū's book *Ryōzandō's Chats on Tea (Ryōzandō chawa)*, published in 1828 with a preface by the author datable to 1824, used the

23. RAI SAN'YŌ'S STUDY
The glass windows and veranda at the Sanshi Suimeisho (abode of purple mountains and clear water), constructed in 1828. Kyoto. Photo: P. Graham.

term "bunjincha" for the first time to define sencha as practiced by the literati. The text was organized very differently from previous sencha manuals, as it did not provide an overview of how to conduct a sencha gathering, but instead included anecdotes that illuminated the spirit of bunjincha. Commentary was limited to seemingly random observations about tea gatherings and sencha utensils. We learn, for example, that the older word "kibishō" (for teapot) had by then been replaced in common usage by "kyūsu." Also, we discover that reverence for Baisaō had been formalized to the extent that on the twenty-fifth day of each month a memorial service was held in his honor. As the text held Baisaō's utensils in especially high regard and referred particularly to those that had been passed down to Kenkadō, Kenshū and his friends must have been familiar with the 1823 printed version of Kenkadō's sketchbook, the *Pictorial Record of Baisaō's Tea Utensils*.

Kenshū did not dwell on the utensils as much as other writers. The bulk of his text consisted of remarks about the proper ambiance in which to drink sencha and the sorts of pastimes in which to engage on such occasions. It was sprinkled liberally with names of illustrious participants, such as the Edo poet Kikuchi Gozan and the literati painter Okada Hankō. These comments revealed the true purpose of the book, to elucidate the pastimes of the bunjin. Sencha was described as integral to these activities, which included drinking wine, composing poems, brushing paintings and calligraphies, playing musical instruments, and displaying Chinese paintings and antiquities. Clarifying the source of these activities, Kenshū paraphrased Sugai Baikan's descriptions of bunjin asobi among emigrant Chinese painters of Nagasaki and their Japanese pupils. Such descriptions accord with the images of such activities in Araki Kunsen's farewell painting for Baikan (fig. 5).

Straying from literati topics, but perhaps included as a guide to the wide-ranging subjects appropriate for discussion at these gatherings, Shinozaki Shōchiku was quoted on the topic of the first two camels to have entered Japan (in 1821), accompanied by a picture of the famous duo by the Osaka painter Mori Shunkei (fl. 1800–1824). The second part of the text opened with a reference to the Chinese Lanting Gathering, no doubt intended to reiterate the link between Chinese and Japanese scholars, for it was followed by short biographies of assorted Osaka practitioners of sencha whom he identified as sencha *chajin* (sencha tea masters). Significantly, this is the earliest source to designate a separate group of tea masters devoted to sencha.

Another member of San'yō's circle who was devoted to bunjincha was Tanomura Chikuden.[3] A native of the town of Takeda in northern Kyushu, Chikuden served for a time as a Confucian teacher at his clan's school and studied literati painting by correspondence with the flamboyant and celebrated literati painter of Edo, Tani Bunchō (1763–1840). During several extended sojourns east between 1799 and 1811, Chikuden became acquainted with the many famous bunjin of Kyoto and Osaka and joined San'yō's coterie. Around 1811, in a show of support for protesting local farmers, Chikuden submitted a petition to authorities that was subsequently ignored. In protest, Chikuden resigned from official duties and retired to his family's estate in Takeda, where he immersed himself in Chinese literati pursuits.

Chikuden considerably remodeled and expanded the buildings on the estate and modified existing rooms for his own purposes (Aoyama 1986, 391–392). He added an expansive painting studio to the main house and used an existing two-mat chanoyu tearoom as a place to appreciate poetry and painting, activities more closely associated with Chinese literati pastimes and sencha. Yet Chikuden was known to enjoy chanoyu and also used this room for its original purpose (Murai 1980, 237). However, this fondness for chanoyu may be considered an aberration rather than the norm among bunjincha devotees. Chikuden also constructed a large painting studio for instructing pupils (completed in 1826) and a retreat for chatting with friends about art, composing poetry, and drinking sencha and sake. Initially completed in 1806, he remodeled it in 1818 in honor of a visit from Kyoto by Rai San'yō. While the present appearance of the buildings on the estate, now open to the public, is charming, extensive remodeling makes comment on the original appearance of the structures and their interior design features difficult.

After his retirement, Chikuden pursued his studies of Chinese literati arts through frequent and often prolonged periods of travel. During an extended residence in Nagasaki from 1826 to 1827, he studied with visiting Chinese scholar-painters. The numerous Chinese paintings he viewed during this trip profoundly influenced his attitudes toward painting. During this visit he learned much about

Chinese tea-drinking practices, as he was able to participate in its rituals, handle imported utensils, and peruse numerous imported tea treatises (Berry 1985, 101). Chikuden brushed one of his most beautiful paintings with a sencha theme, *Hermit Preparing Tea under a Banana Tree*, during his Nagasaki sojourn (fig. 24). Its contrasting application of ink and light colors, and rough and delicate brushwork, deftly capture the spirit of the subject, an idealized view of two lofty Chinese scholars partaking of sencha amid the scenic beauty of the mountains (Berry 1985, 104).

Soon after his return from Nagasaki, Chikuden published three books about sencha that were highly influential in both his own day and thereafter. One was a Chinese book he edited and adapted for a Japanese audience, the *Pictorial Album of Tea Utensils (Chagu zufu)*, first published in 1829. In his lengthy afterword, Chikuden wrote that the book had been authored by Fu Shiran (J: Fu Shizen), a Fuzhou merchant living in Nagasaki. Chikuden indicated that Fu's book was actually two volumes and was based on a longer, five-part work, by someone referred to as Old Man Sangzhu (J: Sōchoō). Chikuden's text was a one-volume abridgment that a mutual friend, Xian Yinshan (J: Sen Inzen), another visiting Chinese merchant who had accompanied Fu to Japan, had made and presented to Chikuden during his stay in Nagasaki. The main part of the book was an extensive illustrated guide to Chinese tea utensils with identifying captions. Many of the pieces illustrated, mostly ewers and teapots, were clearly the burnished red-, brown-, and buff-colored wares of Yixing, although the ware was not identified by name. This book served as an important source for enriching the Japanese public's understanding of Chinese tea vessels.

Chikuden's afterword illuminated his personal perspective on

24. HERMIT PREPARING TEA UNDER A BANANA TREE—1827
Tanomura Chikuden (1777–1835). Hanging scroll; ink and light colors on paper. 134.5 x 28 cm. Idemitsu Museum of Arts, Tokyo.

sencha. He began with a brief history of the tradition in Japan, stating that Ingen was the first to prepare sencha in a teapot set atop a brazier. Next in line came Baisaō, who he wrote had learned the art by observing Chinese residents of Nagasaki during a visit in 1707. With regard to production of Japanese ceramics for sencha, Chikuden corroborated Rakusui's statement that the first to make braziers and side-handled teapots was Kiyomizu Rokubei, whose excellent products were made to the specifications of Akinari and Kōtei. He then added that foremost among contemporary potters to make fine reproductions of Chinese wares for sencha were the competing Kyoto potters Aoki Mokubei and Nin'ami Dōhachi.

Chikuden also related his attempts to understand Chinese teamaking procedures and uses of utensils. He recorded that he had studied a Chinese tea treatise, *A Commentary on Tea (Cha shu)*, of circa 1607, which had also been cited as a source by earlier sencha writers, beginning with Ōeda Ryūhō. However, recognizing the pitfalls of basing his understanding of the subject on the written word alone, he verified the information through talks with a Chinese acquaintance in Nagasaki, the visiting merchant-artist Jiang Yungge (J: Kō Unkaku; active 1815–1832), younger brother to the more famous visiting Chinese artist, Jiang Jiapu (J: Kō Kaho; 1744–after 1839) (Wylie 1991, 455–456). Additionally, he converted Chinese weights and measurements for amounts of tea and water to those used commonly in Japan.

Chikuden's other two books contained basically identical information on sencha growing and processing in two different literary forms, with different but conceptually similar illustrations of utensils. *Chats on Boiling Tea (Hōcha ketsu)* was first published in 1829. Composed in kanbun, it was presumably aimed at scholars. *Discussion on Tea by Chikuden (Chikudensō chasetsu)*, published in 1831, was written in the more easily understood idiom of vernacular Japanese. By publishing this more accessible version of his scholarly treatise on tea, Chikuden was making a conscious effort to popularize bunjincha beyond the limited audience of Japanese readers of Chinese. Chikuden stressed that water was the kami (a divine spirit in Japan's native Shinto religion) of tea, and that for preparing tea five types of utensils were essential: a brazier, a fresh water ewer, a hot water kettle (which he said could double as a teapot), a leaf tea container, and a teacup. Chikuden, who strove to uphold the humanistic values and practices of the Chinese literati, epitomized the goals of the bunjin of his day. His contemporaries and later admirers, in fact, considered him the embodiment of the elegant (fūryū) bunjin. With mounting political tensions and increased importation of Chinese books and material goods during the late Tokugawa period, Chikuden's lifestyle became an increasingly attractive and accessible alternative.

Yamamoto Baiitsu and Other Advocates of Bunjincha in Kyoto, Nagoya, and Edo

Chikuden's and San'yō's wide circle of friends kept the spirit of bunjincha alive after their deaths and helped to spread its ideals from Kansai to Edo. One of the most influential of the promoters in Kyoto was Yamamoto Baiitsu (1783–1856), who made that city his home for much of his adult life, although he had been born in Nagoya. Baiitsu's best friend from childhood was Nakabayashi Chikutō, who was probably responsible for introducing him to Rai San'yō and bunjincha. The custom was embraced in Edo by the literati artists and Confucian scholars associated with the distinguished samurai-scholar and literati painter Watanabe Kazan (1793–1841) and his foremost disciple, Tsubaki Chinzan (1801–1854).

This era of bunjincha fluorescence coincided in date with the horrific Tenpō-era (1830–1844) famine and pestilence, a national disaster that lasted for most of the 1830s and instigated an economic and agricultural crisis. During this difficult era, the government banned tea ceremonies and tea itself became scarce. Baiitsu wrote a letter from Kyoto to his friend and patron Aoki Jikan in Nagoya detailing this situation, a revealing commentary on the depths of the privations among sheltered, wealthy citizens of the capital:

> *Sencha has recently become quite popular. However, because an official announcement from Edo concerning this season's frugalities has been circulated, there will be no tea ceremonies allowed. The tea from the mountaintops of Uji [and elsewhere] has become increasingly scarce… Beyond this, I have no other news. It is said that there is no money anywhere, and this terrible condition prevails all over. As this is not the sort of thing I wish to continue writing about, and since bad news is not limited to this situation only, I will just end my letter here* (Kanematsu 1910 , 216–217).

Like many disillusioned and frustrated intellectuals of his day, Baiitsu sought solace in his art. Although he was foremost a painter of idealistic Chinese literati themes, he also composed a number of poems in both Chinese and Japanese verse forms. Many, including the two kanshi translated below, reiterated themes from his paintings, voicing his fondness for the literati ideal of eremiticism and appreciation of sencha.

> *I choose a stone and place upon it the burnished teapot.*
> *Drawing water from the falls, I wipe the tea utensils.*
> *In the forest we linger long,*
> *laughing at the white clouds hurrying about in the sky.*
>
> *The sound and smell of brewing tea linger in the dead of night.*
> *In my small study, alone, I roll up my scrolls.*
> *Through the gauze window, the moon's pale shadow starts to rise;*
> *It's the time that this hermit loves best.*
> (Kanematsu 1910, 212–213)

Baiitsu was evidently fond of the small study he described in the second poem, for he brushed a number of small sketches of it, which suggest it consisted of an inner and outer chamber (fig. 25). The room with tiled flooring was probably the anteroom, which, in emulation of Chinese interiors such as that visible in the print of *A Chinese Scholar's Study* (fig. 3), was furnished with a Chinese table, chair, and stools. The interior room had tatami and a tokonoma and seems to have functioned, like Chikuden's and San'yō's studies, as a retreat for drinking sencha and composing painting and poetry. It contained a low Chinese-style table upon which to place tea utensils or scholars' accouterments, a gnarled wooden stand for displaying selected objects or plants, and a portable basket for storing sencha utensils. The utensils depicted in Baiitsu's sketch were undoubtedly Baiitsu's own, as he was renowned for his collection of Chinese paintings, antiquities, and tea utensils.[4]

Baiitsu's more polished paintings included idealized depictions of Chinese scholars enjoying tea in landscape settings and imaginary portraits of both Lu Yu and Baisaō. The proliferation of portraits of

25. TWO SKETCHES OF YAMAMOTO BAIITSU'S STUDY
Yamamoto Baiitsu (1783–1856). Mounted on a folding screen; ink on paper. Top: 13.7 x 17.7 cm; bottom: 12.8 x 17.8 cm. Nagoya City Museum.

these two tea saints by Baiitsu and others of his day corresponded with the popularity of commemorative tea gatherings in their honor. One of Baiitsu's particularly distinctive portraits of Lu Yu is dated to 1836 and brushed in the consciously archaistic manner of late Ming figure painters (fig. 26).

Baiitsu also produced sencha paintings of a very different sort, *uta-e* (poem-pictures), which combined the arts of painting and *waka* poetry, an art form not usually associated with Sinophile artists.[5] Despite his adoration of Chinese culture, Baiitsu seems to have had a strong interest in waka poetry, and a number of his poems in this form are extant (Graham 1983, 133–145). Still, it seems incongruous to find uta-e on the theme of sencha in a small painting of a Nanban-style sencha teapot by Baiitsu (fig. 27). Baiitsu's delight with the subject is evident, for two versions of the painting with the same poem are extant:[6]

chihaya hito	*The vigorous*
uji no konome	*tea leaves of Uji,*
niru nabe ni	*in the boiling water,*
izayō nami no	*make a sound*
otosae zo suru	*like waves.*

This seemingly simple poem-picture is actually a complex integration of Chinese and Japanese visual and verbal imagery. The reference to the sound of boiling water in the poem is based on a passage from Lu Yu's treatise, the tea described comes from Uji, while the poetry style is wholly Japanese.

As an avid sencha enthusiast, Baiitsu hosted and attended numerous tea gatherings of various sizes that were held at assorted locales.

26. PORTRAIT
OF LU YU—1836
Yamamoto Baiitsu (1783–1856).
Hanging scroll; ink and light colors
on silk. 151 x 62.1 cm. Shiga Prefecture
Lake Biwa Cultural Hall, Ōtsu.

He served as one of several hosts at a large, formal gathering in 1835 held at the Maruyama Shōami villa in Kyoto, an elegant sukiya shoin structure with assorted banquet halls and tearooms like the Sumiya and surrounded by an ornate and formal landscape garden. Typical of the parties that took place there is one depicted in the 1799 *Illustrated Guide to Celebrated Gardens of the Capital (Miyako rinsen meisho zue)*, where a calligrapher wields a broom-sized brush over an enormous piece of paper before a crowd of spectators (fig. 28).

Following customs borrowed from chanoyu, the hosts at Baiitsu's ceremony presided over their own *seki* (environments or rooms decorated for service of sencha). Baiitsu described the utensils he used in a letter written to a pupil in Nagoya (Kanematsu 1910, 218–220; Graham 1983, 92). In accordance with his fondness for Chinese literati culture, they seem to have been mainly Chinese vessels, such as Yixing wares,

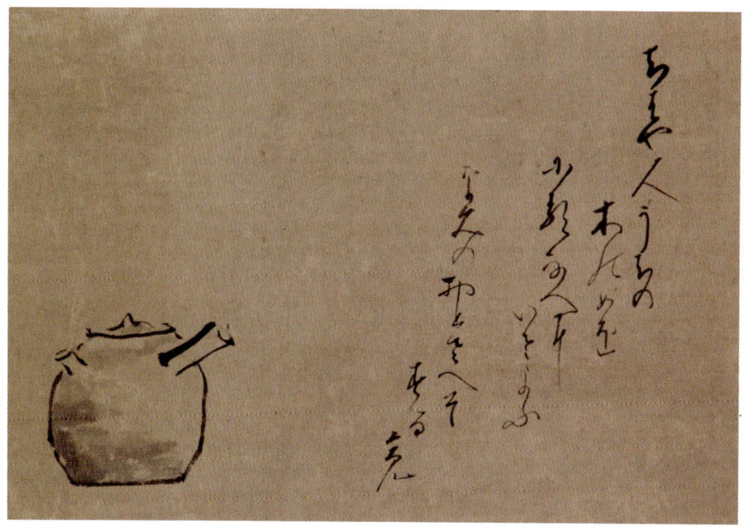

27. NANBAN TEAPOT
AND WAKA POEM
Yamamoto Baiitsu (1783–1856).
Hanging scroll; ink on paper.
20.3 x 35.6 cm. Private collection,
United States. Photo: P. Graham.

in orthodox literati taste. He also included in this record the recipe for a tea sweet concocted especially for the event, another formality borrowed from chanoyu. Its lifelike silverberry nut shape and multiple layering of different colors were said to have enthralled his guests. Many years later, in 1852, another celebrated sencha gathering was held in honor of Baiitsu's seventieth birthday. One hundred and fifty guests were said to have convened in four separate seki in the vicinity of Kyoto's Yasaka shrine (Kumakura 1980, 145).

No doubt because of their expense and the ire they drew from authorities for their disregard of prohibitions, these large gatherings seem only to have been occasional occurrences. Baiitsu regularly attended smaller gatherings that more closely adhered to the ideals of bunjincha. In a letter datable to 1840, Baiitsu described the fūryū atmosphere of one of these to his friend Aoki Jikan in Nagoya:

28. MARUYAMA SHŌAMI VILLA—1799
From volume 2 of *Illustrated Guide to Celebrated Gardens of the Capital (Miyako rinsen meisho zue)*. Woodblock-printed book; ink on paper. 25.5 x 32 cm. Kansai University Library, Osaka. Photo: P. Graham.

> *Last month on the eighteenth day, we held a tea gathering at Mr. Shimomura's villa in Komatsu valley… There were five people attending and we all sat scattered about the garden and in the house. All the spots were quiet and delightful. Mr. Uragami's was tranquil and secluded… His seki and mine were probably the best of the lot… Please tell Mr. Hodo about this event, but please tell no one else. People without interest in this sort of thing would only call us fools and laugh* (Kanematsu 1910, 215).

As Baiitsu indicated in the last sentence of his letter, he did not wish news of this gathering to be spread about. He may have been afraid of reprisals from authorities who had banned tea ceremonies, in addition to his allusion to fear of derision by outsiders who had no appreciation for bunjincha. The Mr. Uragami mentioned in this letter was Baiitsu's and San'yō's mutual friend, the literati painter Uragami Shunkin, who sometimes hosted his own sencha gatherings. One, held in 1833 at Kyoto's famed temple Kiyomizudera, was devoted to tea competitions. An unpublished handwritten record of this event indicates that two of his five guests were Baiitsu and Nukina Kaioku (1778–1863), a noted Kyoto Confucian scholar, calligrapher, and literati painter.[7]

A convivial atmosphere permeated bunjincha gatherings, and those hosted by Baiitsu were no exception. An often repeated anecdote about Baiitsu and sencha recounts that on one particular occasion, in Nagoya in 1854, the guests were so impressed with the flavor of the tea Baiitsu served that they inquired as to its name. Baiitsu responded that the tea was named *Hagoromo* (feather robe). As the guests pondered on this strange name, Baiitsu opened the teapot to reveal that the tea leaves had been tied together with miniature yellow threads in imitation of the appearance of a feather robe.[8]

Although evidence exists for drinking sencha in Edo as early as the mid-seventeenth century, associations between sencha and Chinese intellectual life remained largely unknown until Sinophile intellectuals and artists there, including Tani Bunchō, Kikuchi Gozan, and Ōkubo Shibutsu, began associating with bunjincha aficionados in Kansai in the early nineteenth century. Like bunjincha in the Kansai, Edo gatherings were casual and relaxed. Guests would share their favorite newly acquired sencha utensils and engage in other literati pursuits, including tea competitions. Yet Edo practitioners helped further the formalization of bunjincha through the creation of some of the earliest pictorial records of their gatherings. Unlike the records left by Baiitsu and others in Kyoto, which with few exceptions were handwritten notes to friends or small sketches of utensils, these were printed, that is to say, published documents. Their editions were probably limited, like *surimono* woodblock prints, made for the benefit of friends unable to attend or as elegant mementos for invited guests.

By preserving the appearance of the assemblage of the utensils (*kazari*) during the tea service, these prints encouraged imitation of the kazari. Illustrations of sencha kazari were concurrently being made for the first time by those seeking to establish sencha tea schools (to be discussed in chapter 6). In this case, however, the pictures seem to have functioned as connoisseurship records of the utensils and not, as was the case for tea school records, models for etiquette. One outstanding surviving pictorial record of Edo bunjincha is an accordion-folded surimono-style printed album illustrated by Tsubaki Chinzan and dated to 1838.

This small, sumptuous album features illustrations of seven sencha utensil arrangements, with the meticulously defined utensils rendered in silver and thick, colored pigments (fig. 29). These appear to be Chinese wares or their close Japanese copies. Unusual among the kazari is one page that appears to have been lifted directly from Chikuden's book of Chinese utensils, the *Pictorial Album of Tea Utensils.* As none of the pictures contain captions, it is unclear why this page was included. Perhaps the participants assembled utensils duplicating the Chinese arrangement illustrated in Chikuden's book. The album also includes a portrait of Baisaō signed by Chinzan with a caption by Tachi Ryūwan

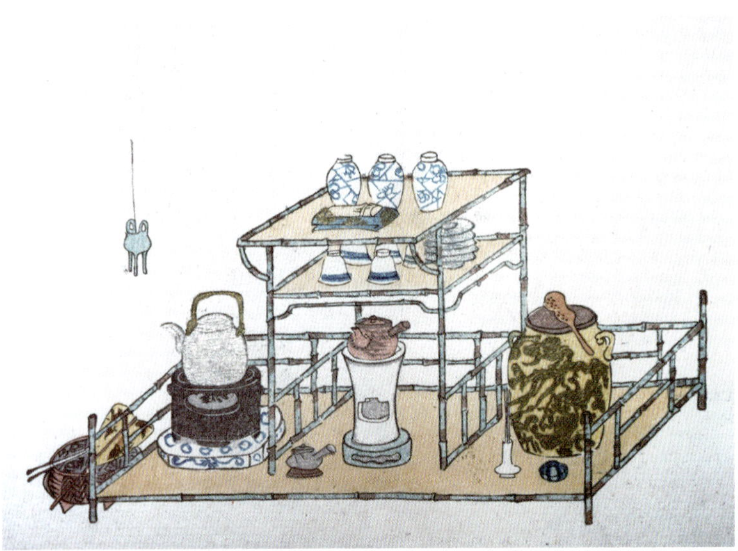

29. ALBUM OF SENCHA UTENSIL ARRANGEMENTS—1838
Tsubaki Chinzan (1801–1854). Section of an accordion-folded surimono-style woodblock-printed book; ink, gold, silver, and colors on paper. 26 x 32 cm (sight). Private collection, Japan. Photo: P. Graham.

(1762–1844), a Confucian scholar and shogunal retainer from Niigata who was a disciple of scholar-painter Kameda Bōsai (1752–1826).

Most surviving illustrations of this period focused on the utensils; only a few contained images of the participants. One of these was a woodblock-printed album, also datable to 1838, *A Small Sencha Gathering (Sencha shōshū)*, which commemorated another gathering of Chinzan and his friends (fig. 30). The group convened at an inn in the Kanda district of Edo on the occasion of the sixty-first birthday of a mutual friend, Iiyama Gihō (1778-?), a merchant from nearby Saitama. Chinzan again brushed the illustrations; the title calligraphy was contributed by Tachi Ryūwan; the preface was composed by Kameda Ryōrai (1778–1853), Kameda Bōsai's son; and Gihō himself penned the epilogue.[9] Chinzan identified all participants by name alongside their caricature-like portraits.

The year 1838 was evidently an active one for Edo fans of bunjincha. In addition to the gatherings already mentioned, that same year Iiyama Gihō published a new edition of the influential Chinese tea treatise *Secrets of Steeped Tea*. The following year he contributed an epilogue to another important volume about sencha, the *Written Record of Poems on Tea (Eicha shiroku).* Tachi Ryūwan edited the volume, a collection of Chinese poems about tea from the Tang through the Ming dynasties, and Kameda Ryōrai penned the preface.

This era of bunjincha efflorescence was short lived, for by the late 1840s formalized schools of sencha had eclipsed it in popularity. Fukada Seiichi (1802–1855), a Nagoya Confucian scholar who was a close friend of Baiitsu, detailed this turn of events in his 1849 *Secrets of Steeped Tea by Bokusekikyo (Bokusekikyo* sencha *ketsu)*, a text generally considered the last in the line of bunjincha tea treatises. His book

30. A SMALL SENCHA GATHERING (SENCHA SHŌSHŪ)—1838
Tsubaki Chinzan (1801–1854). Section of a woodblock-printed album; ink and light colors on paper. H: 12.4 cm. Private collection, Japan. Photo: P. Graham.

outlined the history of bunjincha, beginning with Baisaō and including in its subsequent lineage Ueda Akinari, Murase Kōtei, and the recently deceased Uragami Shunkin. Seiichi lamented that his friend Baiitsu was one of the few alive who preserved the spirit of bunjincha.

Commenting on sencha in his own time, Seiichi acknowledged the existence of two styles of sencha ceremonies. One he identified as bunjincha, which he described as being permeated by an atmosphere of modesty and naturalness. The other he called *zokujincha* (vulgar person's tea), whose practitioners, he wrote, did not understand purity and simplicity. They turned sencha into an institution like chanoyu, devising rules for tea preparation according to levels of formality, with terms borrowed from chanoyu: *shin* (formal), *gyō* (semiformal), and *sō* (informal). He noted that the schools also awarded diplomas to those who demonstrated proficiency in these procedures.

Seiichi also decried the feigned and ostentatious attempts at frugality in chanoyu and warned that sencha, which should aspire to fūga (loftiness), was in danger of becoming debased by chanoyu influences. He stated that although chanoyu practitioners laughingly regarded sencha as a children's game, in actuality the reverse was the case, for it was only sencha that truly revered cleanliness and simplicity. According to Seiichi, the main difference between sencha and chanoyu was that chanoyu masters adhered to native Japanese ritual forms while sencha followers emulated the free spirit of the Chinese literati. Finally, he dismissed the utensils for chanoyu as being too diverse and not altogether appropriate for tea, while he considered those for sencha exceptionally well designed for their function. Seiichi concluded with numerous illustrations of the essential utensils for sencha, accompanied by identifying captions in both Chinese (kanbun) and Japanese (*kana*).

Shogakai (Painting and Calligraphy Gatherings) and the Bunjin

In addition to both grand and intimate gatherings convened for the express purpose of partaking in sencha, the bunjin often attended large and boisterous formal banquets, generally referred to as *shogakai*. These gatherings promoted appreciation of painting, calligraphy, and poetry, sometimes featuring bravura performances by celebrated artists and poets for an admiring audience. They emulated the celebrated gatherings of the ancient Chinese literati, such as the Lanting Gathering or the Elegant Gathering in the Western Garden (*Seigen gashū*),[10] popular themes in both Chinese and Japanese painting. Like sencha ceremonies, these would take place at teahouses and restaurants, such as the Maruyama Shōami in Kyoto, or at private residences. Although these were not sencha tea ceremonies, sencha was invariably served along with food and sake. As they grew in popularity and as participation reached broader segments of the population, shogakai played a critical role in fostering wider appreciation of sencha in Japan.

Shogakai originated in the Kansai area in the late eighteenth century. Kimura Kenkadō is credited as their founder; his first attempts at these endeavors were sales exhibitions for famous painters of the day. The first of these took place in 1770 at Osaka's Ryūsenji. Kenkadō also held large parties that brought together artists, collectors, and writers of prose and poetry. The word "shogakai" seems to have been coined in reference to one of these parties that Kenkadō hosted in the spring of 1783 (Abiko 1982, 102).

One special type of shogakai featured displays of Chinese paintings and calligraphies exclusively.[11] Some were held as tributes to literati figures who were noted connoisseurs, on their important birthdays or as memorials on anniversaries of their birth or death. Both Chikuden and Baiitsu were so honored.[12]

The peripatetic Edo poet Ōkubo Shibutsu was a frequent participant in shogakai, and his descriptions of them are sprinkled throughout two travel diaries that he published, *Journal of Poems Composed during an Excursion to the West (Saiyū shisō)*, 1818, and *Journal of Poems Written during a Second Excursion, to the North (Saibokuyū shisō)*, 1824. One shogakai described in his earlier volume was a banquet that preceded his departure from Kyoto, hosted by the priest-painter Geppō at his home, Chokian (fig. 13). Among the many participants was Yamamoto Baiitsu, who sometimes accompanied Shibutsu, whom he considered a mentor, on his travels.

During his second excursion Shibutsu visited Nagoya, where shogakai were also fashionable. Accompanied by Baiitsu, he stopped for a visit at the Suisetsurō (drunken snow pavilion), an elegant restaurant located on the outskirts of the city. During his stay Shibutsu composed a kanshi that he subsequently included in his 1824 travel diary. This capricious and contrived poem was later published together with an illustration of the Suisetsurō in the woodblock book *Famous Sites of Owari Province (Owari meisho zue)* of 1844 (Graham 1984, 47):

Outside the city at a banquet hall named Suisetsurō
People gathered in former times when the highway was blocked by snow.
At Echizen I was stranded for a day by the snow,
What picture can capture the beauty of today's snow?
The snow is falling intermittently, like spring snow.
The distant view is smoky while nearby it is all snow.
Brewing tea [sencha] in a stone kettle, the fragrance mixes with the snow.[13]
The silver platter full of meat resembles piles of snow.
At this gathering, all we chant is the [Chinese] 'Song of the White Snow'.
The guests are all melancholy like hot water easily melting snow.
At the old age of sixty, I have hair the color of snow.
At Suisetsurō, our heads are drunken with the snow.

Shibutsu also published at the end of his 1824 travel diary a poem Baiitsu composed on this occasion (Graham 1983, 51–52).

Another more private setting for shogakai in the Nagoya region is one of the few buildings of this type from the Tokugawa period to survive. It is a waterside pavilion (fig. 31) constructed in the Ansei era (1854–1860) in Handa City, on the estate of Nakano Matazaemon, a wealthy vinegar merchant. Matazaemon patronized literati painters of Kyoto and Nagoya, including Nukina Kaioku, who was said to have brushed a hanging scroll of a waterfall specifically for the building's tokonoma (Kodansha 1982, 60–61), and who amassed an outstanding collection of Chinese paintings and sencha paraphernalia.[14] Matazaemon's waterside pavilion was located on the property not far from the main house he also had constructed, an expansive sukiya shoin-style residence that incorporated aspects of Chinese design, including a Chinese-style courtyard garden. The fourth-, fifth-, and sixth-generation heads of the family carried Matazaemon's interest in Chinese arts through the Taishō period (1912–1926) and added tearooms for sencha to the main house (Itō and Yokoyama 1983–1985, 2: 32–45).

Reminiscent of similar pavilions that populated Chinese paintings, the waterside pavilion sat beside a pond where small pleasure boats filled with partygoers plied the waters in an idyllic setting for sencha gatherings and shogakai. Exterior Chinese-style features included a deep, overhanging curved tile roof, a veranda cantilevered over the water, and a stone foundation. Inside the L-shaped space of two interconnected rooms were typical Japanese elements, including tatami, shoji, and a tokonoma (fig. 32). The tokonoma, however, encompassed an entire wall to accommodate the large scale of many Chinese and Japanese literati paintings and calligraphies. Other Chinese touches included a cloud-shaped window and intricate Chinese-style patterns for the latticework of the railings and sliding doors. Like Rai San'yō's study, this villa also incorporated glazed windows in the shoji panels, though here the wealthy merchant owner could afford larger and more numerous panes of glass.

Shogakai were also prevalent in Edo, where their form quickly became conventionalized. Tani Bunchō, a forthright self-promoter, hosted one of the earliest, in 1792.[15] At their height in the Tenpō era, Edo shogakai reached unprecedented levels of pomposity, despite the

31. WATERSIDE PAVILION AT THE NAKANO FAMILY ESTATE
Constructed in the Tokugawa period, Ansei era (1854–1860). Honda City, Aichi prefecture. Photo: Matsumura Yasuhiro.

economic distress of the times. Andrew Markus has eloquently described these gatherings as

> *a cultivated symposium, a convivial banquet at which the host and his invited associates produced spontaneous examples of their art or ingenuity. In the course of its development, however, the shogakai embodied less exalted motives: a desire to publish one's name, or inflate a mediocre reputation; the ambition to outdo one's rivals in sheer numbers and ostentation; and most importantly, a craving to transmute the intangibles of talent and reputation into hard currency. Always a self-conscious spectacle, the institution provoked horror, amusement, or some measure of both among the literary figures who, increasingly, figured among its attractions* (Markus 1993, 135).

Unlike the exclusivity of the Kansai-area shogakai held for a close circle of friends, Edo shogakai encouraged commoners to mingle with respected intellectual and artistic figures. Participation was, of

32. WATERSIDE PAVILION AT THE NAKANO FAMILY ESTATE
Constructed in the Tokugawa period, Ansei era (1854–1860). Honda City, Aichi prefecture. Photo: P. Graham.

course, limited to those who could pay. Still, Edo shogakai contributed to expanding the audience for bunjin culture to the middle-class population of the city. By charging admission fees to guests, they also provided the intellectuals and artists an added, and much needed, source of income.

Almost all the artists and intellectuals of Edo participated in these affairs. Among the most respected was Watanabe Kazan, who considered the informal discussions about art that took place at shogakai integral to the sharpening of his connoisseurship and critical thinking abilities. His specific requirements for shogakai included the following recommendations:

> *The tea we drink, sencha, should be used twice, matcha is a bother… tea bowls [cups] must be washed each time with water—to wash with tea is undesirable; it is pleasant to have incense fill the air… those serving tea should be young, attractive women, but if they are not available, members should serve in turn* (Abiko 1982, 100–101).

One well-documented Edo shogakai was hosted by Kazan's disciples and admirers. It took place on the thirteenth day of the first month of 1840, the very day that Kazan left Edo for his hometown of Tawara to begin his final period of seclusion under house arrest for political insubordination. The gathering seems to have been held to raise money for Kazan, who was to receive profits from admission fees (Itabashi 1996, 40, 135). Tsubaki Chinzan immortalized this event in a large, detailed sketch presumably brushed to send to Kazan, who could not attend (fig. 33). The painting has been mounted together with a long letter to Kazan by Chinzan, which enumerates the procurement of various sencha utensils and describes the works the artists painted and sold at the fête. As in his printed book of 1838, Chinzan inscribed the names of these artists alongside their informally brushed portraits.[16] His sketch shows them drinking sencha and sake, eating, reading books, painting literati-style pictures, and admiring artwork strewn about the room and pinned to the walls. Presiding over the congregation is Lu Yu, whose formal portrait hangs in the central tokonoma. This type of portrait is regularly displayed at gatherings such as shogakai where sencha would be served. One example of the sort of meticulously painted portrait of Lu Yu that appears in Chinzan's sketch was brushed by Haruki Nanmei (1795–1878) in 1841 (fig. 34). Typical of such paintings, Nanmei's portrait contains excerpts from Lu Yu's treatise inscribed above the figure.

33. THE PAINTING AND CALLIGRAPHY GATHERING IN HONOR OF WATANABE KAZAN—1840

Tsubaki Chinzan (1801–1854). Mounted as a hanging scroll together with a letter from Chinzan to Kazan; ink and light colors on paper. 30.5 x 54.5 cm. Tabara Municipal Museum.

34. PORTRAIT OF LU YU—1841
Haruki Nanmei (1795–1878). Hanging scroll; ink and light colors on silk. 93.3 x 35.1 cm.
Private collection, Japan. Photo: courtesy Mie Prefectural Museum of Art.

Although many shogakai were held in restaurants of the Yanagibashi district of Edo, another favorite setting was the Yaozentei (pavilion of eight hundred perfections) in the Yoshiwara district, a restaurant that had been established as early as the 1770s (Nishiyama 1984, 271). Because it specialized in Chinese cuisine, the restaurant was a popular haunt of a Sinophile scholar crowd, including Tani Bunchō, Kameda Bōsai, and Ōkubo Shibutsu. The Yaozentei was so famous that its proprietor published a book about its cuisine, the *Handbook of Fashionable Cooking for the Epicures of Edo (Edo ryūkō ryōri tsū daizen)*, with illustrations by the famous Ukiyo-e artist Katsushika Hokusai (1760–1849) and others. Its four volumes were published in serial form between 1822 and 1834.

In the introduction to the book, the owner indicated that his inspiration for opening his establishment was a visit to the Maruyama district of Nagasaki, where he initially learned the art of Chinese cooking. He wrote that he mastered Chinese cuisine from trips to the Kansai where it was also extremely popular (Mitchell 1972, 453–454). Like the Nagasaki Chinese restaurants, banquets at the Yaozentei took place in private dining rooms where guests would sit around a single Chinese-style table. One of the book's illustrations portrays a host welcoming guests to a banquet at a table heaped with food served shippoku ryōri style. The caption identifies the meal as fucha ryōri (fig. 35). Another page illustrates the various utensils, primarily ceramics, that were necessary for the preparation and serving of sencha (fig. 36). As we shall see, the styles and forms for these utensils accorded with the tastes of the bunjin.

35. SCHOLARS GATHERING FOR A PARTY–1834
From volume 4 of *Handbook of Fashionable Cooking for the Epicures of Edo (Edo ryūkō ryōri tsū daizen)*. Woodblock-printed book; ink and light colors on paper. 15.2 x 21.4 cm. Seikadō Bunko Library Foundation, Tokyo.

36. SENCHA UTENSILS—1834
Katsushika Hokusai (1760–1849), from volume 4 of *Handbook of Fashionable Cooking for the Epicures of Edo (Edo ryūkō ryōri tsū daizen)*. Woodblock-printed book; ink and light colors on paper. 15.2 x 10.7 cm. Seikadō Bunko Library Foundation, Tokyo.

Bunjin Influences on the Design of Japanese Ceramics for Sencha

Literati who participated in bunjincha provided the initial catalyst for production of Japanese ceramics for sencha in the late eighteenth century. Although they generally preferred to use authentic Chinese vessels, such as Nanban teapots, unglazed stoneware braziers, underglaze blue porcelain teacups, and Yixing teapots, demand exceeded availability. They also admired Chinese wares with celadon, Swatow, kinrande, and kōchi glazes, which had been imported originally for use by elite society's chanoyu enthusiasts, but were appreciated by all who admired China. In China, however, these wares had not been designed for use as steeped tea utensils, so the bunjin requested Japanese potters to apply these Chinese glazes to vessels appropriate for preparing and serving sencha. With this action, they created an aesthetic for sencha that encompassed, but was not limited to, the aesthetic preferences of chanoyu tea masters.

Some bunjin functioned as designers or managers of commercial workshops, as did Aoki Mokubei. Some, like Ueda Akinari, also became amateur practitioners who created pieces for their own enjoyment. Others, like Murase Kōtei together with Akinari, commissioned wares from established Kyoto kilns. Yet others, mainly literati painters, served as decorators of wares for commercial kilns, whose customers appreciated literati arts. The first Japanese sencha wares were produced by Kyoto pottery workshops where artisans benefited from their associations with the Kansai region bunjin who were leaders in the sencha movement. The most easily manufactured ceramics for sencha were copies of Nanban teapots and kettles from provincial Chinese kilns such as those made by Kiyomizu Rokubei I. Manufacturing porcelain tea utensils in the vast array of popular Chinese styles initially proved to be a greater challenge. Unlike the large pottery towns in Arita and elsewhere in western Japan, where porcelain had been produced since the early seventeenth century, Kyoto had no established porcelain industry of its own.

From the time of Ogata Kenzan, however, Kyoto potters had been making stonewares with overglaze enamels in the Chinese taste. By the third quarter of the eighteenth century, the growing vogue for Chinese-style porcelains required that Kyoto potters find a way to produce the ware in order to remain competitive. Porcelain potters from Kyushu recognized the advantage of their monopoly on porcelain manufacturing in Japan and strove to keep their technical knowledge secret. It therefore required ingenuity and research on the part of potters elsewhere to duplicate their techniques, and Kyoto potters were among the first to succeed.

Experiments with adapting Arita ware porcelain glazes—primarily overglaze enamels, underglaze blue, and celadon—to Kyoto clays had begun with seventeenth-century potters such as Nonomura Ninsei (active ca. 1647–1660), but it was Ninsei's follower Kenzan who first experimented, with only limited success, with porcelain clay (Kawahara 1985, 18–22; Wilson 1991, 102–103). Following in Kenzan's footsteps, other Kyoto potters embarked on the same quest, but did not succeed in production of true porcelain until around 1781. Credited with this feat is Okuda Eisen (1753–1811), a descendant of naturalized Chinese immigrants who had fled China at the time of the Qing conquest. Eisen's ceramics came to be much admired in sencha circles; he and his pupils are also credited with initiating styles for sencha wares that have become standardized and perpetuated up to the present.

When young, Eisen was adopted by the wealthy Okuda family, proprietors of a successful pawnshop. They encouraged his studies and allowed him to live at the Zen temple of Kenninji. This temple, an important repository of Chinese artifacts, was also a center for the study of Chinese culture and philosophy, in part due to its patronage by families of immigrant Chinese, including that of Hayashi Razan (Kawahara 1985, 22). Eisen eventually inherited his family's business, but he left its operation to a manager and from about the age of thirty-five immersed himself in ceramics. Although he is considered an amateur studio potter who never sold his wares, Eisen was a serious student of the craft.

It is generally assumed that Eisen's affluence provided him with the free time and financial resources needed to undertake experiments for perfecting the production of porcelain. He may have acquired some of his techniques during visits to Seto, where porcelain manufacturing was also just beginning (Pollard 1989, 31; Nakanodo 1981, 112). In Kyoto, he mastered the basics of his craft from the little-known potter Ebiya Kiyobei (fl. first half of the eighteenth century), who had also taught Kiyomizu Rokubei I.

Unlike Rokubei's sencha wares, which emulated unglazed Chinese stonewares, Eisen's few remaining vessels reveal indebtedness to very different sources: brightly glazed provincial Chinese export wares. Dating from the 1780s and after, they were made for a variety of purposes, including use in chanoyu. The styles for these ceramics were the same as those preferred by Kenzan: kōchi, underglaze blue, and Swatow.[17] Although these were in styles that appealed to connoisseurs of chanoyu, their rough-textured surfaces, forms in the shape of archaic bronze vessels, and casually brushed designs of birds, flowers, and scholarly figures are more reflective of bunjin taste, and indeed the Sinophile literati of Kyoto were Eisen's most ardent admirers. His Swatow-style ewer with a design of phoenix and flowers was, like many of his pieces, appropriate for either chanoyu or sencha (fig. 37).

Even though he was not a professionally trained artisan, Eisen attracted many pupils who significantly influenced the subsequent course of Japanese ceramics in Kyoto. These figures include Nin'ami Dōhachi (1783–1855), Kinkodō Kamesuke (1765–1837), and Aoki Mokubei (1767–1833), who is widely acknowledged as Eisen's most important follower. Although Mokubei is most famous for ceramics, his literati paintings are also much admired. Unlike his ceramics, which were commercial products, his paintings were created for his own enjoyment and date mainly from the last decade of his life.

The son of a wealthy teahouse owner who was a former retainer to the daimyo of Owari, Mokubei studied various Chinese arts in his youth, including literati painting and connoisseurship of Chinese antiquities. His fondness for the latter resulted in one of his sobriquets, Kokikan (connoisseur of old vessels), the name by which he often signed his wares. His elder mentors included Daiten Kenjō, Kimura Kenkadō, and Kō Fuyō, whose collection of Chinese antiquities—jades,

37. SWATOW-STYLE EWER
Okuda Eisen (1753–1811), ewer with decoration of flowers and phoenix. Porcelain with overglaze enamels. H: 28.3 cm. Tekisui Museum of Art, Kobe.

bronzes, and old coins—Mokubei studied and tried his hand at copying. Friends included members of the circles of San'yō and Chikuden, and Tanaka Kakuō, founder of the Kagetsuan school of sencha. Kakuō, who came to know Mokubei around 1824, proved to be one of his most important patrons. Numerous surviving letters and other documents attest to their intimate relationship and the influence Kakuō wielded on the design of sencha utensils Mokubei made for him.[18] Chikuden, who chronicled his friends and associates in his *Records of Chikuden's Painting Teachers and Friends (Chikudensō shiyū garoku)*, a memoir written in his last years, indicated that Eisen was Mokubei's teacher.[19]

Mokubei's lifework as a potter came about seemingly by chance after he began visiting Kimura Kenkadō in 1796. There he found inspiration in one of Kenkadō's many Chinese books, a handbook on porcelain production at Jingdezhen, the *Discussions on Ceramics* (C: *Tao shuo*; J: *Tosetsu*) of 1774 by Zhu Yen (also known as Zhu Liting). This book was included in a Chinese compendium owned by Kenkadō, the *Secret Book of the Majestic Dragon* (C: *Longwei mishu*; J: *Ryūi hisho*), first published in 1794.[20] It was more than a mere "how-to" guide for aspiring potters, however. Its author, a scholar-bureaucrat, produced a comprehensive history of ceramics in China from earliest times through the eighteenth century that encompassed both technical information on pottery manufacturing and the functions of different types of vessels.

Mokubei translated the *Discussions on Ceramics* into Japanese soon after reading it and arranged to have it published immediately. During proofing he discovered a number of mistakes, but put off finalizing his corrections as he was too busy with pottery commissions. Meanwhile, another translation was published in Edo in 1807, by the Confucian scholar Kasai Inze (died 1823). Mokubei's translation was finally published posthumously by his son, Shūkichi, in 1835, with a preface dated to 1827 by Rai San'yō and Mokubei's original afterword of 1804. Ultimately this book played a significant role in the dissemination of information necessary for widespread production of porcelain in Japan during the first half of the nineteenth century (Kawahara 1985, 39–41).

Mokubei's diverse oeuvre reflects his study of a vast array of ceramic types. Designs of European (Delft), Chinese (largely shonzui), and Korean celadons of the Koryo period (918–1392) fill his sketchbook, the *Album of Connoisseurship of Old Vessels (Kokikan zujō)*, of circa 1808.[21] Mokubei, a devoted fan of sencha, is most highly praised for the creativity of the sencha wares that form the largest part of his oeuvre, but he also made tea bowls for chanoyu as well as dishes and trays for serving food and sake and small pieces for other functions. Some of his styles for sencha wares were inheritances from his teacher Eisen, but his range was far broader. His unglazed sencha teapots and braziers were inspired by those favored by Baisaō, but he also produced sencha teapots and cups in classic Chinese styles appreciated in chanoyu circles, including kōchi, shonzui, kinrande, celadon, Jingdezhen red ground overglaze enamels, Ding, and Dehua wares.

Mokubei functioned as a master designer who relied on assistants to mass-produce his wares. A consummate professional, he streamlined his production process by using a basic mold for the body of many of his smaller vessels, distinguishing pieces by different glazes, painted designs, and individualized spouts, lids, and handles. Such is the case with a celadon-glazed fresh water ewer with a mold-impressed design and a distinctive pierced handle (fig. 38). Characteristic of Mokubei's eclecticism, he has here successfully adopted the celadon glaze, a favorite among fans of chanoyu, to a ware for sencha.

38. FRESH WATER EWER
Aoki Mokubei (1767–1833). Porcelain with celadon glaze. H: 20 cm. Private collection, Japan. Photo: P. Graham.

39. SIDE-HANDLED TEAPOT WITH DESIGNS OF PLANTS AND FLYING BIRDS
Aoki Mokubei (1767–1833). Kinrande-style porcelain with clear glaze, overglaze red ground, gold leaf, and metal rim on lid. H: 9 cm. Private collection, Japan. Photo: courtesy Yanagi Takashi.

Mokubei's wares influenced by chanoyu taste also included kinrande-style vessels. Arita potters of the seventeenth century were the first in Japan to produce kinrande-style wares, but they did not attempt to emulate the standard technique employed by Chinese potters for applying the gold in thin foil sheets. Instead, they painted their gold designs with a brush. Later, only Mokubei and his great rival Eiraku Hozen tried their hand at the gold-foil technique, based on their study of imported Chinese pottery manuals. However, their many followers who made wares in this style utilized an easier method of applying the gold in powdered form. Mokubei's distinctive sense of design for kinrande is evident in a teapot in which the delightfully awkward, intentionally casual delineation of the golden birds and plants complements the sumptuous quality of the gold and red surface (fig. 39).

Mokubei's antiquarian interests also influenced the appearance of his wares. Among his oeuvre are a number of white wares with shapes or surface patterns inspired by the restrained elegance of white-glazed porcelains from various Chinese kilns: Ding wares of the Song dynasty, Ming Jingdezhen wares, and the more popular seventeenth-century Dehua ware from Fujian.[22] Mokubei's wares in this mode appealed to the many bunjin sencha enthusiasts who collected and admired old Chinese bronzes and ceramics, particularly those who had been trained as Confucian scholars. These sencha participants would have been familiar with Chinese bronzes from their use as altar vessels during Confucian rites. They incorporated such objects into sencha gatherings as part of bunbōgu displays of Chinese antiquities or used them as flower containers. Among Mokubei's most successful creative adaptations of archaic Chinese motifs and pottery styles on white ware is a small fresh water ewer with an elegantly curved overhead handle in the manner of

40. FRESH WATER EWER WITH OVERHEAD HANDLE AND MOLDED DESIGN OF SACRED FUNGUS
Aoki Mokubei (1767–1833). White-glazed porcelain. H: 14.8 cm. Idemitsu Museum of Arts, Tokyo.

41. SET OF TWELVE SENCHA UTENSILS
Formerly owned by Kyūkyodō, Kyoto, with all but the mat, Chinese pottery kettle, and wooden teacup saucers by Aoki Mokubei (1767–1833). Porcelain and stoneware with assorted glazes. Tokyo National Museum.

Jingdezhen wares and a delicate molded relief pattern of the Chinese Daoists' sacred fungus (fig. 40).

Encompassing much of Mokubei's range is a group of twelve sencha utensils assembled several decades after his death by the Kyoto merchant and bunjin patron Kumagai Naotaka (1846–1875), proprietor of the Kyūkyodō stationery and incense shop (fig. 41). They form a nearly complete set of sencha serving utensils, requiring only a large cloth mat upon which to arrange them, a Chinese Nanban-style kettle, and wooden teacup saucers. Mokubei's vessels from this set include some of his most famous pieces in a variety of his representative styles. Among these is a large green-glazed metal-handled fresh water pot in the kōchi style, a manner for which he was much renowned, and its accompanying unglazed stand incised with poems and bamboo. Also extraordinary is an unglazed white stoneware cylindrical brazier with a bold design of a blossoming plum tree and moon in copper red openwork relief that sits atop a green-glazed, kōchi-style stand. Several other pieces reveal Mokubei's propensity to elevate the craft of pottery to the realm of fine art in literati taste with designs comprised of calligraphic inscriptions, Chinese poems from the Six Dynasties through the Northern Song era: a pair of rectangular underglaze blue leaf tea containers, a set of five teacups with calligraphy in overglaze red enamel, and a tea scoop made from a calligraphic specimen written in ink on silk and attached to a folded mounting. Completing the group are wares reflective of other sources: a small cylindrical tube for storing the teacup cleaning cloth decorated with an abbreviated underglaze blue design of a Chinese landscape in the Kangxi style, a plum blossom-shaped underglaze blue kosometsuke-style incense holder, a Nanban-style teapot, and a Korean-style tea sweet bowl.

Throughout the Bunka and Bunsei eras (1804–1830), ceramics suitable for sencha in Nanban styles were being imported to Japan in ever larger quantities, as inscriptions on their accompanying boxes attest. However, even in Mokubei's day, these wares were sometimes confused with the finer, somewhat similar products of the Yixing kilns as Japanese collectors had not seen enough actual examples of Yixing to distinguish between the two. Mokubei's knowledge of these wares came from connoisseurship training with Kō Fuyō, the person responsible for describing Baisaō's Gikōkan kettle (fig. 15) as Yixing. Mokubei perpetuated this misinformation in a copy he made of this very kettle (fig. 42). He even impressed a seal for the famous Yixing potter Li Zhongfang (active 1573–1619) underneath the handle, as if it had been copied from the original.[23]

Mokubei had some direct knowledge of Yixing wares, however. He was asked to authenticate, for example, a burnished red Yixing ware teapot, the size of which (12.5 cm high) made it usable for either tea or wine; it had apparently been owned by Baisaō. Mokubei, considered an authority on Chinese ceramics by his peers, attributed it to one of the most famous Yixing potters, Shi Dabin (ca. 1567–after 1661), whose name he must have learned from books.[24] Among his surviving pieces are examples of his attempts to emulate Yixing wares, both their shapes and unglazed brown surfaces, although duplicating their burnished finishes was beyond his technical capability.[25]

Mokubei's involvement in sencha escalated in his later years, as did the frenetic pace of his production of wares for its service. In what was fated to be his final major commission, he decided to host a large sencha gathering for one hundred guests at Kyoto's Kitano shrine in the early spring of 1833, at the time of the blossoming of the shrine's

42. HOT WATER KETTLE
Aoki Mokubei (1767–1833). Hot water kettle erroneously known as Gikō utsushi (copy of Yixing ware pot). Unglazed, cream-colored stoneware. H: 10 cm. Kyoto National Museum.

famous plum trees. The setting was a favorite locale for sencha parties in honor of Baisaō, who had frequently set up his tea stall there. Mokubei intended to distribute sencha tea sets, consisting of six cups and one teapot, to each invited guest.

Unfortunately, Mokubei had only some neighbors to help with this enormous project because his chief assistant had died in the previous year. As his wares were very thin and fragile, the highest technical expertise was required of his workers. Without experienced help, problems during the firing of the kiln resulted in damage to many of the pieces and he was forced to postpone the gathering. On a second try, he successfully fired the six hundred cups and some of the teapots (records are unclear about the exact number). The effort so exhausted Mokubei that he died soon after. From these and other vessels still remaining in her father's studio, Mokubei's daughter assembled tea sets for distribution to guests who attended her father's funeral (Mitsuoka 1990, 102–103).[26]

43. SIDE-HANDLED TEAPOT—1833
Aoki Mokubei (1767–1833). Side-handled teapot inscribed with the phrase "*Minun shiseki*" (sleeping among clouds, crawling in the rocks). Unglazed, cream-colored stoneware. H: 10.5 cm. Private collection, Japan. Photo: P. Graham.

44. SET OF FIVE SENCHA TEACUPS—1833
Aoki Mokubei (1767–1833). Porcelain with gohonde glaze. H: 5 cm. Iruma City Museum.

The unglazed moldmade cream-colored stoneware teapots Mokubei designed for this Kitano gathering are among the most elegant of his plain Nanban-style teapots, featuring an inscription in clerical script of a four-character phrase in raised relief. The phrase "*Minun shiseki*" (sleeping among clouds, crawling in the rocks) obliquely idealized the Chinese literati, who sought refuge from the difficulties of the world by dwelling in seclusion in mist drenched mountains (fig. 43). The teacups, on the other hand, were designed in a style known as *gohonde*, a pinkish white ash glaze, of a type originally employed on Korean chanoyu tea bowls and copied by Japanese potters at the order of prominent chanoyu tea masters (fig. 44). These two styles form a curious aesthetically contrasting set.

Although Mokubei often made vessels in porcelain with underglaze blue decoration, other kilns and potters were more famous for this style. Underglaze blue, the least technically challenging decorated porcelain to produce, was the first type of embellishment on porcelain in Japan. Its appeal persisted owing to the skill of its decorators, whose fine and varied painterly designs invoked association with the Chinese literati.

By the early nineteenth century, two Japanese kilns, Hirado in Kyushu and Seto near Nagoya, had become famous for their distinctive styles of underglaze blue decoration on porcelain. Seto was best known for its heavily patterned shonzui style, which Mokubei sometimes employed. One of the Seto potters, Kato Tamikichi (died 1824), initiated mass production of shonzui-style wares there about 1807.[27] The underglaze blue designs on Hirado wares were very different in character. During the late eighteenth and early nineteenth centuries, Hirado ware was made for the exclusive use of the Hirado fief daimyo in styles suitable for the elegant Chinese ambiance of daimyo-style chanoyu. It featured sensitively brushed pastoral scenes of China, Chinese scholars, children, or animals brushed onto vessels composed of the finest white porcelain clay available in Japan (Cardeiro 1989; Lawrence 1997; Singer and Goodall 1997).

Less well known than Seto and Hirado were the underglaze blue products of another Kyushu kiln, Kameyama in Nagasaki, which designed products more closely attuned to the taste of sencha fans. Established on the precincts of a local Shinto shrine, the Wakajima Jinja, it was founded in 1804 as a private commercial enterprise but eventually was sanctioned by Nagasaki's shogunal administrator. From 1814, Kameyama produced sencha and sake utensils and other small functional vessels for daily use from the pure white porcelain stone of Amakusa, the same material as the Hirado potters, which they decorated exclusively in underglaze blue. Although most famous for blue-and-white wares, the kiln also manufactured copies of Swatow and overglaze enamels. They made Swatow-style ceramics beginning in 1839, in response to the Sinophile mania sweeping the nation, with imported clay from Suzhou. As Suzhou was a center of literati culture and not of ceramic production in China, its coarse, gray clay was not comparable to the fine quality of porcelain from other regions. The resulting Japanese wares resembled Swatow vessels in texture and appearance. Plagued by natural calamities that interfered with production, the kiln was restructured under the direction of Nagasaki administrators in 1859 and thereafter made more commercially viable products for export and wider domestic consumption. It continued to decline and finally closed in 1865.[28] During its heyday, though, local literati painters, including Kinoshita Itsuun (1799–1866), and their visiting friends, such as Tanomura Chikuden, frequently collaborated with potters in decorating Kameyama wares for sencha with casually brushed underglaze blue designs of landscapes, flowers, or fruits and vegetables.[29] Typical of their work is a set of teacups with lively, light-hearted depictions of *daikon* (Japanese radish) and shrimp by Itsuun (fig. 45).

Although literati painters occasionally dabbled in forming and decorating ceramics for their own amusement, by the middle of the nineteenth century utensils and accouterments in a Sinophile taste associated with sencha were routinely being created as collaborative efforts of potters and literati scholars and artists.[30] By the very end of the Tokugawa period, this collaboration became transformed into a routine commercial undertaking. One literati artist to participate in this endeavor was Hine Taizan (1813–1869), whose fan-shaped porcelain plaque for adorning the wall of a sencha tearoom is a particularly fine example (fig. 46). The plaque is treated as a painted fan and decorated with an austere landscape in one of the artist's favorite styles, that of the reclusive Chinese Yuan dynasty literati painter Ni Zan (1301–1374). The box that accompanies the piece indicates that it was fabricated at the Shohei kiln (a popular name for Kinbeizan ware), which was located near Iwakuni in Yamaguchi prefecture. The kiln was founded in 1868 and Taizan died in 1869, so the date for this work can be closely approximated.[31]

The bunjin contributed to the general public's fascination with their lifestyles through their prolific writings, impressive artworks, and forceful personalities. They helped spread appreciation of sencha through participation in shogakai, authorship of tea treatises written in vernacular Japanese, and production of paintings with sencha themes. They

45. FOUR SENCHA TEACUPS
With designs of daikon (large radish) and shrimp. Kameyama ware, Nagasaki; porcelain with underglaze blue decoration by Kinoshita Itsuun (1799–1866). H: 5.5 cm. Nagasaki City Museum. Photo: courtesy Itahashi Ward Museum of Folklore, Tokyo.

46. LANDSCAPE IN THE STYLE OF NI ZAN—CA. 1868
Kinbeizan ware, Yamaguchi prefecture; fan-shapes plaque, porcelain with underglaze blue decoration by Hine Taizan (1813–1869). 17.8 x 38.1 cm. Private collection, United States. Photo: P. Graham.

were also instrumental in establishing aesthetic standards for sencha utensils through patronage of potters and other artisans who devised sencha tea utensils.

Yet they alone were not responsible for adapting the essential elements of bunjincha to a broader constituency. This task was further accomplished by other promoters of sencha who sought to integrate it more fully with the aesthetics and etiquette of chanoyu. Those who contributed to the final assimilation of sencha as a formal ritual in Sinified Japanese taste and the concurrent proliferation of sencha arts and architecture that followed are the subject of the following chapter.

CHAPTER SIX

The Assimilation of Sencha into Japanese Society

Concurrent with the flourishing of bunjincha among the Japanese literati, sencha also gained favor among samurai, courtiers, and commoners, all of whom, for a variety of reasons, considered it an elegant beverage to serve guests. This growth in popularity occurred in response to two main factors. One was practical: the tea tasted better as a result of adoption of new processing techniques. The other was social: many of these sencha drinkers possessed an intense desire to be perceived as cultivated, and participating in Chinese literati avocations such as sencha attested to their sophisticated taste. In this latter context, sencha utensils became reflections of their owners' sense of style and discrimination, further encouraging production of finer quality sencha accouterments. Yet learning the correct means of preparing and serving the tea required teachers and materials that instructed users on proper etiquette. This was the final step in the process toward widespread adoption of sencha in Japan.

Gyokuro (Jade Dew), Steeped Tea for Connoisseurs

Although leaf tea had been processed in Japan from the mid-seventeenth century, its popularity only increased substantially after 1738 when Nagatani Sōen perfected his processing technique for sencha. His tea was comparable to superior imported Chinese varieties, but it was more widely available. It fulfilled the need for a tea product for those who neither had interest in the elaborate etiquette of chanoyu nor could afford its expensive utensils. Nagatani Sōen's descendants continued to produce sencha of such high quality that they extracted an annual fee from the family business of their Edo distributors, the Yamamotoyama teashop of Nihonbashi, up to 1874 (Kumakura 1980, 126).

As markets for sencha increased, competition among merchants and growers intensified. The sixth-generation head of the Yamamotoyama teashop, Yamamoto Tokujun (Kahei) undertook an exhaustive study of the history of tea cultivation and preparation in Japan in order to develop a better, more desirable product. He published the results of his research in the 1834 *Small Book about Sencha (Sencha shōjutsu)*, which he composed in vernacular Japanese. He included listings of where sencha was cultivated and descriptions on how to use its utensils.

Tokujun used his research to develop a new and improved leaf tea product, which he began selling to the public in 1835. After observing matcha tea cultivation techniques, Tokujun instructed sencha growers of Uji to adopt the use of an arbor to shade the delicate tea plants and to protect them from damage by unseasonably late frost. This covering also reduced the tannin and increased the caffeine content. Concurrently, Tokujun employed a new method for quick-drying the steamed tea leaves. These innovations preserved the attractive bright green color of the leaves and increased the sweetness of their flavor. So famous was Tokujun's shaded tea arbor for sencha plants that it appeared in another book he wrote about sencha, the 1848 *Concise Guide to Sencha* (*Sencha tebiki no tane*), illustrated by Katsushika Ōi (fl. second quarter of the nineteenth century), Hokusai's daughter (fig. 47).

This new tea was named gyokuro (jade dew) after the appearance of the byproduct created when the steamed tea leaves were rolled (Shufunotomosha 1981, 447–448; Tanihata 1984, 20; Kumakura 1980, 126–131). Gyokuro, whose taste turns bitter if it is steeped in water that is too hot, was, and still is, prepared by the encha method in which water is heated in a kettle on a brazier and another vessel, a teapot, is employed to steep the tea.

47. THE YAMAMOTO TEA PLANTATION IN UJI—1848
Katsushika Ōi (fl. second quarter of the nineteenth century). From *Concise Guide to Sencha (Sencha tebiki no tane)*. Woodblock-printed book; ink on paper. 8 x 32 cm. National Japanese Sencha Association Library, Manpukuji, Uji. Photo: P. Graham.

After the invention of gyokuro, the popularity of leaf tea soared and, for the first time ever, surpassed chanoyu, although this situation lasted only through the first decades of the Meiji period (Kumakura 1980, 138). The complexities of the manufacturing process for gyokuro accounted for its high cost and marked it as a product that only connoisseurs could afford. Consequently, leaf tea of various lower qualities continued in production in quantities that far exceeded gyokuro. From this time forward, gyokuro was classified separately from sencha and bancha as the highest grade of green leaf tea in Japan. Gyokuro became the standard tea for sencha gatherings, though for some special occasions, such as services of tea in honor of Baisaō, sencha would be used and brewed by the older preparation method of throwing the leaves into freshly boiled water.

Sencha Utensils for a Wider Market

Regardless of the setting for enjoying sencha, from bunjincha and shogakai gatherings to informal service at restaurants and teahouses or as the focus of a formal tea ceremony, the same types of sencha utensils could always be used. Thus objects for steeped tea that appear in the backgrounds of many Ukiyo-e prints, such as a pictorial calendar for the year 1811 designed by Totoya Hokkei (1780–1850) (fig. 48), are vessel types associated with the bunjin. For the calendar, the artist depicted a plain, unglazed pottery brazier and kettle resembling the wares of Kiyomizu Rokubei I.

Sencha utensils were different, however, from vessels used in the preparation of common tea or bancha. Bancha teacups were larger, as the milder flavored, less costly tea could be consumed in greater quantities. Water for bancha was heated in heavy iron kettles (*tetsubin*) (Arts 1988). These were used in only the most informal services of sencha. More frequently, when metal kettles were employed to heat water for

48. COURTESAN, CLIENT, AND COMIC ENTERTAINER
Totoya Hokkei (1780–1850), pictorial calendar for the year 1811. Surimono-style woodblock print; ink, colors, silver, and gold on paper. 13.8 x 18.7 cm. Spencer Museum of Art, University of Kansas, Lawrence; William Bridges Thayer Memorial.

sencha they were of lighter weight and made from finer materials: copper, silver, or gold. Generally known as *ginbin*, these sat upon large hibachi-shaped braziers (*binkake*) such as pictured in a page from Chinzan's 1838 surimono-style woodblock album (fig. 29).

The popularity of gyokuro had profound impact on the Japanese ceramics industry. Increased tea drinking resulted in greater demand for utensils. Both established and newly opened pottery workshops began producing more and varied utensils tailored to the encha brewing method for gyokuro. As utensil makers increased, they began to personalize and sign their wares, making subtle modifications in styles to accord with their clients' means and tastes. They nevertheless followed standards set by Kyoto potters, especially Mokubei, who specialized in sencha utensils to a greater extent than did any other potter of his day. Many of these newly devised sencha wares were created in styles virtually indistinguishable from products for chanoyu (Tanihata 1984).

Mokubei and other Kyoto potters assisted in founding a number of pottery workshops where sencha wares were made. Sometimes they traveled to these kilns to oversee operations directly, but they also provided technical assistance in the form of publications, such as the *Pottery Manual (Tōki shinan)* of 1830 by Kinkodō Kamesuke. So closely were ceramics for sencha associated with Kyoto potters (whose wares were generally known as *Kiyomizu*, after the district of the city where their workshops proliferated) that they were among the most famous of Kyoto's local products. Utagawa Hiroshige (1797–1858) indicates this in his 1839 Ukiyo-e print *Kiyomizu Ceramics and Blossoms from the "Landowner's" Cherry Tree in Kyoto (Keishi kiyomizuyaki jinushi no sakura)*, from the series *Famous Products of the Provinces (Shokoku meisan)* (fig. 49). The lion-handled teapot illustrated was a popular style from the 1830s.

Creative Kyoto potters drew inspiration from many sources, including the earlier Kyoto master potters Ninsei and Kenzan; Chinese kōchi, shonzui, kinrande, and celadons; and European Delft ware, the exotic appearance of which was especially popular at midcentury when interest in Western culture intensified. One style in high demand, initially popularized by Mokubei, featured overglaze enameled designs of Chinese figural subjects. Brush paintings in miniature form, these designs became a vehicle for the personal artistic expression of the potter-decorators who made them.

49. KIYOMIZU CERAMICS AND BLOSSOMS FROM THE "LANDOWNER'S" CHERRY TREE IN KYOTO-1839
Utagawa Hiroshige (1797–1858). (Keishi kiyomizuyaki jinushi no sakura), from the series *Famous Products of the Provinces (Shokoku meisan)*. Woodlblock print; ink and colors on paper. 113 x 168 cm. Chazen Museum of Art, University of Wisconsin-Madison, Bequest of John H. Van Vleck.

Among those who excelled at this style of decoration was Nin'ami Dōhachi. Wrapping around the surface of one of his fresh water ewers like a handscroll are images of scholars lounging about in a garden setting (fig. 50). Dōhachi brushed above the figures the central section of Lu Tong's famous "Tea Song" poem in Mokubei-style aka-e (overglaze red). His animated, sketchlike figures and simplified landscape combined with the brightly colored glazes—purple, green, yellow, red, and pink—to create a charming and spirited interpretation of the theme. Dōhachi's talented younger brother, Ogata Shuhei (1783–1839), also produced sencha wares, such as a fine example of a brazier decorated

50. FRESH WATER EWER WITH THE TEXT AND IMAGES OF LU TONG'S "TEA SONG"
Nin'ami Dōhachi (1783–1855). Porcelain with underglaze blue and overglaze enamels. H: 14.5 cm. Private collection, Japan. Photo: P. Graham.

with a sophisticated landscape in underglaze blue with a long inscription in Chinese dated to 1837 (fig. 51). This piece is one of many sencha utensils collected for use by Kyoto's famed Sumiya restaurant.[1]

Another important Kyoto potter who produced sencha wares was Eiraku Hozen (1795–1854). At a young age Hozen was adopted by the Kyoto potter Eiraku Ryōzen (1770–1841), who specialized in chanoyu pottery braziers for daimyo patrons. Hozen developed his own specialties, however, one of which was kinrande. His meticulous and precise designs in this style result from the careful application of cut gold leaf to the overglaze enameled surface (fig. 52). Although this is the same technique used by Mokubei (fig. 39), the surface design has a very different character. Indeed, though they lived and worked in the same city, Hozen and Mokubei are thought to have never associated (Pollard 1989, 43; Nakanodō 1981, 117).

Although Mokubei's styles for sencha utensils inspired the professional studio potters of Kyoto, another local potter, the nun Ōtagaki

51. BRAZIER WITH LANDSCAPE SCENERY–1837
Ogata Shūhei (1783–1839). Porcelain with design in underglaze blue. H: 16 cm; diam: 12.7 cm. Sumiya, Kyoto.

52. SET OF FIVE SENCHA TEACUPS—MID-19TH CENTURY
Eiraku Hozen (1795–1854). Kinrande-style porcelain with overglaze red enamel, underglaze blue, and gold leaf. H: 3.8 cm. Saint Louis Art Museum, Museum Shop Fund.

Rengetsu (1791–1875), created her own distinctive style of sencha vessels that also became extremely popular.[2] Rengetsu, a celebrated waka poet and a calligrapher of Japanese kana syllabary, studied poetry with Ueda Akinari between 1805 and 1809. After the tragic early deaths of both her husband and child, she began supporting herself by making

53. SET OF FIVE TEACUPS FOR SENCHA—MID-1800s
Ōtagaki Rengetsu (1791-1875). Glazed earthenware. Each approx. 3.5 x 5.1 cm diam. Denver Art Museum: Gift of Drs. John Fong and Colin Johnstone. Photography © Denver Art Museum.

ceramics: sake bottles, food dishes, flower containers, incense burners, teacups and pots for sencha, and tea bowls and water containers for chanoyu. She had professional potters fire them for her in local workshops (Maeda 1979; Kyoto Prefectural Library 1984; Feltens 2023). Like all her ceramics, she embellished and personalized her sencha wares with her waka poems composed in delicate script, sometimes incised into wet clay, other times brushed on the surface with iron oxide pigment. Rengetsu must have learned something about sencha and its ceramics from Akinari, for her misshapen, handmade teapots and teacups resemble his in spirit (fig. 53). However, her favorite thick, cream-colored glaze more closely resembled the gohonde glaze that Mokubei used on his last set of teacups (fig. 44).

As the drinking of sencha spread nationwide from the mid-1830s, many potters at older, well-established kilns, such as Seto, Bizen, Tamba, and Shigaraki, began adding sencha utensils to their repertoire of chanoyu vessels for everyday use. Rengetsu's manner of joining poetry with pottery exerted direct influence on potters from Shigaraki, whom she came to know personally (Cort 1979, 243–245). The mass-produced sencha products of provincial kilns such as Shigaraki, however, remained destined for use among those who could not afford the higher-priced sencha wares of Kyoto's elite studio potters.

Adopting the Iemoto System, Creating Schools for a Sencha Tea Ceremony

For nearly one hundred years after Baisaō began promoting sencha as an alternative to chanoyu in the 1730s, devotees eschewed the formalism and factionalism that had developed among chanoyu followers in the wake of Sen no Rikyū's death in 1591. In that earlier era, a host of charismatic leaders and their disciples and descendants began propagating their own interpretations of an orthodox chanoyu tea ceremony. In many ways the evolution of sencha schools mirrored these developments, and it is useful to review the emergence of structured schools of chanoyu as a precursor to sencha's formalization.

By 1757 chanoyu lineages were being perpetuated through adoption of the "headmaster system" (iemoto *Seidō*) (Varley 1989, 173). This system was applied to diverse Japanese traditions, including most performing and martial arts, flower arranging, and even some types of literature (Gardner Museum 1993). It facilitated the transmission of knowledge and skills within a household (*ie*) from one generation to the next. Some aspects of the iemoto system appeared as early as the eighth century, though its apogee is generally considered to have occurred during the Tokugawa period, when it functioned as a means of differentiating distinct schools (*ryū* or *ha*).

Although it was adopted in various ways by practitioners of the different arts, as applied to the Tokugawa period five main features of the iemoto system have been distinguished: hereditary succession; secret transmission of the teachings (*hiden*); adoption of a permit system to clearly define teachers and pupils; a hierarchical, authoritative organizational scheme; and maintenance of the lineage through cultivation of loyalty among both teachers and students (O'Neill 1984, 635–637). The iemoto system could flourish during this time because large numbers of avid amateur participants pursued various means of self-cultivation. In this context the boundaries between professionals and amateurs became increasingly blurred as amateurs became adept at their arts and rose in rank as paid teachers.

In some arts the number of iemoto remained fairly stable, while for others their quantity increased as high-ranking teachers decided to found their own lineages. Thus the iemoto system could in different circumstances either legitimize innovation or perpetuate established methodologies. Although the largest, most influential chanoyu lineages adhered to the latter model, one, the Sekishu school, did not. This school was founded by a daimyo, Katagiri Sekishu (1605–1673). His students were also daimyo, many of whom opted to follow their own paths after mastering the art rather than submit to domination by a school structure (Varley 1989,174). A similar situation would prevail in the development of schools for sencha, due to its indebtedness to the ideals of the Japanese bunjin, who followed the Chinese literati in respecting self-expression and individuality.

Nevertheless, hierarchies and competing lineages did develop within the world of sencha. The 1828 *Ryōzandō's Chats on Tea* provides the first hint of such a fragmentation in its description of bunjincha as a specific type of sencha gathering associated with a particular group of people. Yet bunjincha cannot rightfully be considered as a lineage itself, but rather it was a source of philosophical and aesthetic concerns for the later sencha schools.

Bunjin followers of sencha prevailed in Kyoto under the influence of Baisaō and several generations of his admirers. But owing to the influence of the most important early proponents of sencha, such as Ōeda Ryūhō, Kimura Kenkadō, and Ueda Akinari, sencha as an alternative tea tradition initially made more and varied converts among the residents of Osaka than elsewhere in Japan.

Ōsato Kōan, a native of Edo, compiled information on twenty-two of these individuals in an unpublished, illustrated handwritten manuscript, the *Collection of Great Sencha Tea Masters of Naniwa [Osaka] (Naniwa* sencha *taijin shū)*, of 1835. The author indicated in his afterword that he had created the album to inform the people of his home city about sencha's heritage. He wrote that as it was a popular beverage consumed at all times of the day, its traditions needed to be better understood. He wrote about Baisaō as the father of sencha in Japan and provided information on contemporary sencha practices and leaders in Osaka, each of whom he illustrated.[3]

The manuscript contains short biographies of those figures, including one woman, Shinozaki Sachiko (fig. 54), the wife of the Confucian scholar Shinozaki Shōchiku. In organizational structure and style, it mimicked pictorial handscrolls that depicted famous ancient Japanese poets. These had become extremely popular during the Tokugawa period and featured imaginary portraits of the poets seated alongside a short biography and selection of their writing. Among the sencha masters pictured, some were celebrated literati painters and Confucian scholars, while others were obscure figures who shared a common

54. PORTRAIT OF SHINOZAKI SACHIKO–1835
From *Collection of Great Sencha Tea Masters of Naniwa [Osaka] (Naniwa sencha taijin shū)*. Hand-painted album; ink and light colors on paper. 29.2 x 21.6 cm. Osaka Prefectural Nakanoshima Library. Photo: P. Graham.

interest in literary arts, collecting antiquities, or pursuing an eremitic existence. Some were samurai, while others were merchants, physicians, or Zen priests.[4] Twelve of those included here were also listed in a section on sencha tea masters in one of the popular "who's who" compendia of the region, the 1837 edition of the *Continuing Record of Old Friends of Osaka (Zoku Naniwa kyōyūroku)*. While some of these compendia were arranged in iroha order (the equivalent of an alphabetical listing), others, including this one, were divided into sections according to the person's occupation or avocation, with sections on painters, calligraphers, poets, Confucian scholars, physicians, tea masters, and the like. If a person excelled at more than one art, his or her name would be included in each relevant section. This text appears to have been the first to contain a separate section for sencha tea masters. Heading this category was Tanaka Kakuō, known by his studio name of Kagetsuan.

Tanaka Kakuō and the Kagetsuan School

Tanaka Kakuō (1782–1848) was born into a family of sake brewers whose famous Ebisudai sake was shipped as far away as Edo.[5] At age sixteen he inherited the family business and proceeded to expand it, while continually seeking to improve its product. During the course of his research, he realized that fine quality water was an essential element and discovered an excellent source on his own premises, the "chrysanthemum" well. Water from this well came from the famed Kiyomizu (pure water) spring, which gave its name to the district of Osaka in which Kakuō lived (Kiyomizu-chō). By 1823 Kakuō was a well-known sencha tea master whose early concern for water was widely held as contributing to his later successes in brewing fine-tasting sencha.[6]

Kakuō studied chanoyu during his youth, when he also began drinking sencha. His complete devotion to sencha resulted from the influence of his Ōbaku Zen teacher Monchū during the Bunsei era (1818–1830). Kakuō's rapid rise to prominence in the realm of sencha is chronicled in various contemporaneous publications. The most extensive mention of him appears in the 1859 (latter) edition of the garden manual *Notes on Constructing Artificial Hills and Gardens (Tsukiyama niwa tsukuriden)*, by Akizato Ritō (whose preface dates to 1828). Included is an illustration of Kakuō's small thatched tea hut, the Kagetsuan (hermitage of flowers and moonlight), and its surrounding garden, evocatively titled *The Jade Stream Garden of Kagetsuan, the Secret Haunt of Master Tanaka at Rōkashima* (Rōkashima was the district of Osaka in which his property was located) (fig. 55). Ritō augmented the illustration with the following text:

> *The Kagetsuan towers above the west bank of the Higashi [east] Yokobori River just where it connects with the Yodo River. At the highest point of the promontory is its veranda, which affords a view of the port. The Ikutama forest floats in the mist and to the south is the Kaoku Bridge. In the garden, branches of willows from China's West Lake and bush clover from the imperial palace compound mingle together. There is a "spirit hiding rock" and a "spirit calling rock. "It is a garden that possesses every element of Jade Stream Garden [Lu Tong's garden]. The hut contains portraits of Lu Yu and Lu Tong, and a stone statue of Baisaō is also enshrined. On the sixteenth day of each month a memorial service for Baisaō is held. Friends from all over gather then to engage in elegant pursuits and without fail, on this day every month the master brews tea all day long. Additionally, on the sixth day of the third month, a special memorial service for Lu Yu*

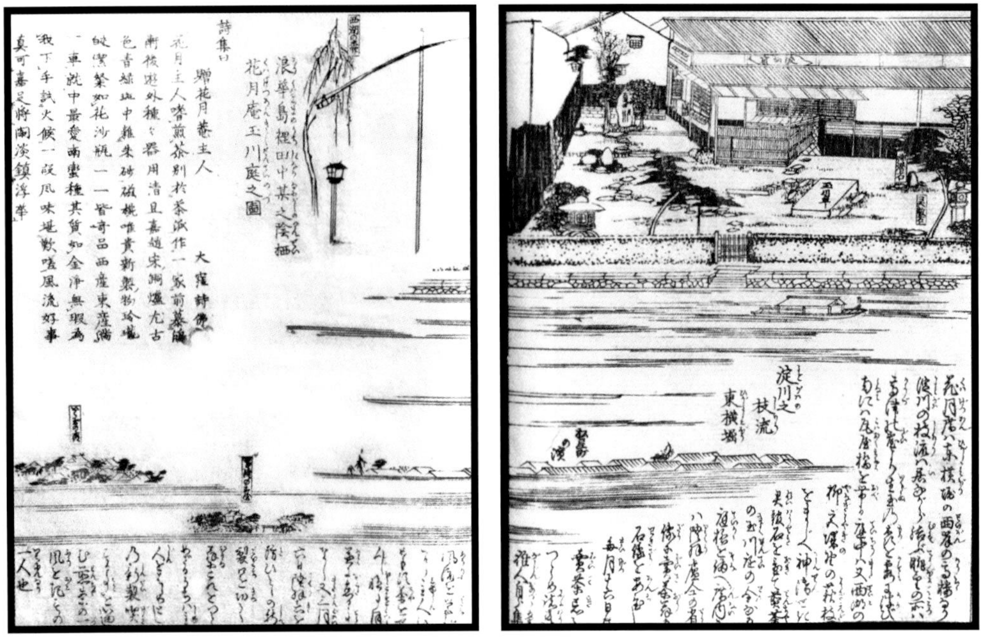

55. THE JADE STREAM GARDEN OF KAGETSUAN, THE SECRET HAUNT OF MASTER TANAKA AT RŌKASHIMA (RŌKASHIMA NO UCHI TANAKA SOREGASHI NO INSEI, KAGETSUAN GYOKUSEN TEI NO ZU)
From volume 2 of the latter edition of *Notes on Constructing Artifical Hills and Gardens (Tsukiyama niwa tsukuriden)*, preface dated 1828, published in 1859. Woodblock-printed book; ink on paper. 26 x 32 cm. Kyoto University Library. Photo: P. Graham.

is held. After offering some tea to Lu Yu's spirit, the first harvest of the new year is consumed. This is one of sencha's traditions.

A description of Kakuō was also included in the form of a long kanshi, "On Meeting the Master of the Hermitage of Flowers and Moonlight, "composed in 1827 by Ōkubo Shibutsu, who wrote there that he had learned how to brew sencha and had come to appreciate its spiritual significance under Kakuō's tutelage:

The master of the Hermitage of Flowers and Moonlight enjoys sencha, for which he created his own lineage.
Fond of the great Kō Yūgai of the past, he employs various utensils, reserving special esteem for Chinese-made ones.
His Song dynasty bronze brazier has a fine patina, the green and blue spots meld with the red sand.
Each of the pottery vessels is strange and wondrous, products of the West and the East fill up an entire carriage.
He prefers above all his Nanban objects, fine, like gold, they are pure and flawless.
For a novice like me, attempting to light the coals, I struggle at even the first step, but finally succeed in improving the flavor of my brew.

Enjoying things that are simple but elegant, I have a natural affinity for this activity.
From this time forward, I derive contentment from simply listening to the silence of the floating flowers.[7]

Kakuō was not merely celebrated for his ability to brew fine-tasting tea, but for rituals he created to enhance its appreciation. These rituals came to be identified as his means of pursuing the ideals of fūryū in the book *Records of the Elegant Pleasures of Life in Osaka (Naniwa fūryū hanjoki)*, published sometime during the Tenpō era. This volume described in both words and pictures what fūryū meant to assorted notables of Osaka. Kakuō's friend Yasui Bokuzan (fl. early nineteenth century) provided a sketch for the volume showing the tea master in his hermitage along with two friends (fig. 56). The caption reads: "In the clear moonlight, sketching a picture by the light of the full moon, he boils tea to capture the lofty spirit of Lu Yu."

As this description indicates, Kakuō was adept not just at brewing sencha, he was also well versed in various literati arts and indeed was famous for those avocations. Another of the era's "who's who" compendia, *The New Edition of Records of Residents of Naniwa [Osaka] (Shinkoku Naniwa jinbutsushi)*, of 1824, records his name in its category of participants in elegant literati activities (*bunga*), a category that encompassed painters and poets. Kakuō had studied waka poetry with a famous poet of Kyoto, Kagawa Kageki (1768–1843), also a friend of Ōkubo Shibutsu, and mingled, as a patron in the tradition of bunjin bokkyaku, with numerous literati in Osaka and elsewhere during various sojourns. Among these friends was the Confucian scholar Fujisawa Hakuen (also known as Tōgai; 1794–1864), who ran an influential

56. TANAKA KAKUŌ AT THE KAGETSUAN
Yasui Bokuzan (fl. early nineteenth century), from volume 2 of *Records of the Elegant Pleasures of Life in Osaka (Naniwa fūryū hanjōki)*, Tokugawa period, Tenpō era (1830–1844). Woodblock-printed book; ink and light colors on paper. 24 x 16 cm. Kansai University Library, Osaka. Photo: P. Graham.

57. PORTRAIT OF TANAKA KAKUŌ
Yamamoto Baiitsu (1783–1856), inscribed by the twenty-ninth abbot of Manpukuji, Hakugan Enyō (1767–1836). Hanging scroll; ink and light color on paper. 78 x 25.4 cm. Private collection, Japan. Photo: P. Graham.

private Confucian academy in Osaka, the Hakuen Shōin (est. 1825). His descendants have remained loyal supporters of Kagetsuan up to the present.

Kakuō's literati associates also included Ōkubo Shibutsu, Aoki Mokubei, Tanomura Chikuden (Sakai 1987), and Yamamoto Baiitsu, who painted his portrait (fig. 57). Kakuō appears here dressed in his formal sencha master attire, a crane robe, like that worn by Baisaō, topped by a crane-shaped cap (*fuyōkin*). Holding a *nyoi* scepter (C: *rui*; named for its shape inspired by the legendary Chinese Daoist fungus of immortality), Kakuō is solemn and dignified as he sits surrounded by the tools of his trade, a basket containing assorted sencha paraphernalia and a small three-level stand that houses his most important utensils, a tea scoop on the upper shelf, a teapot in the middle level, and a brazier with kettle below. Hakugan Enyō (1767–1836), the twenty-ninth abbot of Manpukuji, inscribed a kanshi about Kakuō on the scroll above his seated figure.

During the 1830s Kakuō traveled extensively, and his fame as a master of sencha grew. He hosted numerous sencha gatherings. One that took place in Edo in 1832 was attended by about ten people, including Tani Bunchō, Ōkubo Shibutsu, and the Kokugaku scholar Hirata Atsutane (1776–1843). While in the capitol, he was also invited to prepare sencha for the eleventh shogun, Tokugawa Ienari (1773–1841). When he returned to Osaka, Kakuō was befriended by the Kyoto courtier Ichijō Tadaka as well as daimyo from the Owari and Kii domains.

Kakuō was famous for eccentric exploits, such as the following episode, which demonstrates his extraordinary devotion to sencha. Yearning for his tea to be as authentically Chinese as possible, Kakuō sought to prepare tea with water from China's West Lake. Because he could not travel to China himself, he requisitioned water from China via authorities in Nagasaki. A year after submitting his request, three bottles, containing eighteen liters of water each, finally arrived on a Chinese trading vessel and were forwarded to the offices of Osaka's administrators, who notified the surprised Kakuō of their arrival. Delighted, Kakuō gathered together ten of his closest friends to share his bounty. However, they all agreed that to deny others the opportunity to taste authentic Chinese water was selfish, so they devised a plan to share it with the entire population of their city. They decided to place the water into a large, small-mouthed ceramic pot and bury it in the upper reaches of the Yodo River. This way, the precious Chinese water would seep out slowly into the river, the city's drinking water source, where it would be consumed in minuscule doses by all. Mokubei was commissioned to fabricate the pot in imitation of an antique Chinese leaf tea storage jar in Kakuō's collection. After much discussion with government bureaucrats who had gotten wind of the plan, and who initially opposed it out of fear that the Chinese water would poison the drinking supply, the task was eventually carried out on the fifteenth day of the eighth month of 1833.

Another of Kakuō's well-documented sencha events was a formal ceremony he hosted as part of a memorial service for his teacher Monchū in 1835, on the seventh anniversary of his death.[8] Many of the same people who appeared in the 1835 *Collection of Great Sencha Tea Masters of Naniwa* were listed as attendees. Artworks on display included calligraphies by Zen monks associated with the sencha lineage: Monchū, Baisaō, Daiten, and Kōsen (1633–1695), Manpukuji's fifth abbot. In contrast to Baiitsu's famous sencha gathering at Maruyama Shōami in the same year, the utensils Kakuō used represented a more diverse range of Chinese and Japanese ceramics, and many were closer in style to vessels appreciated in chanoyu circles. They included Chinese Nanban wares, kōchi, and kosometsuke underglaze blue wares, but also Japanese copies of these and other wares, including Swatow, celadons, and white Korean porcelains.

By 1838 Kakuō had adopted the mantle of iemoto of Kagetsuan and wore, as the formal attire of his position, a crested kimono and *haori* (short formal jacket), which the Kii daimyo, Tokugawa Kerutomi, presented to him that year. Thereafter he held sencha ceremonies at many locations, such as by the gates of famous Kyoto temples, at the founder's hall of Nara's Hōryūji, and even in the Sento Goshō (the retired emperor's villa) in Kyoto.

Kakuō's positive reception from citizens of diverse social backgrounds may in part be due to his adaptation of rules of etiquette
(*temae*) for tea preparation from chanoyu, with which the general public was undoubtedly familiar. These have been recorded in a long document, *A Detailed Explanation of the Elegant Commodity of Boiled Tea (Seifūryū hōcha shoshiki shōkai)*, which he apparently composed some time during the Tenpō era. Three slightly dissimilar manuscript editions of this text are extant, copied out by his disciples or by professional scribes in the Meiji period. As the manuscript has never been reproduced in printed form, it must be considered a secret text (*hidensho*) that was used to convey his teachings to select initiates. This accorded with methods for transmission of chanoyu rules of etiquette and reveals Kakuō's indebtedness to the chanoyu structure.

Within its seven volumes, fine line drawings illustrate the appropriate arrangement of the utensils for preparing sencha in a variety of settings, social situations, and according to the two main preparation techniques of sencha and encha. Utensil usage and arrangement differed according to rules that were indicative of levels of propriety. Borrowing the terminology for these rules from chanoyu, procedures were divided into stages extending from informal (sō), to semiformal (gyō), to extremely formal (shin), with various levels of formality within each category. There were also separate methods for tea competitions, again dependent upon whether one was utilizing sencha or encha preparation techniques for the tea.

The illustrations indicate the use of a wide range of vessels. Although Kakuō devised his own assemblages of these, they generally reflected preferences of the bunjin. Most frequently, illustrations showed several braziers of different types used in the same service, sometimes arranged on formal stands. This kind of organization has already been seen in the 1838 accordion-folded printed book illustrated by Chinzan (fig. 29). Utensils could also be placed directly on a mat, as in the illustration reproduced here, for the arrangement of the third informal level of the semiformal style (*Gyōsō sansō kazari no zu*) (fig. 58).

Additional drawings depicted a waiting bench for guests and the interior of a small three-mat sencha tearoom, perhaps the earliest reference to a tearoom designed especially for sencha service (fig. 59). Bunjin had never devised such rooms, as they drank sencha in their studies or in formal parlors (*zashiki*) adorned with Chinese-style decoration. At first glance, this tiny room appears to be indistinguishable from tearooms for chanoyu, with a tokonoma, a wooden board running down the center of the room to separate the host from the guests, and a low shelf by a window for displaying writing implements. However, it possessed some unusual features: a large, round, Chinese-style window of the sort that became ubiquitous in later sencha tearooms, and a wooden board in the tokonoma, like that seen in Rai San'yō's study (fig. 22).

Throughout his life Kakuō actively promoted Chinese literati activities and participated in sencha as an avocation, while deriving his livelihood from his sake business. Although his taste in sencha utensils remained true to the literati spirit, in his formalization of the methods and settings for the drinking of sencha according to rules derived from chanoyu, he departed from the spontaneity and informality that characterized bunjincha gatherings. Through his influence sencha became transformed into a refined ritual so closely resembling chanoyu that by the 1840s Fukada Seiichi was compelled to lament in his *Secrets of Steeped Tea* by Bokusekikyo that it was no longer being distinguished as a separate tea tradition. Similarly, compendia of famous personages of the 1840s no longer distinguished sencha masters from those adept at chanoyu. Kakuō's name, for example, appeared in the section titled simply "chajin" (tea master) of two books of that decade, the *Record of Famous Schools of Naniwa [Osaka] (Naniwa meiryū ki)* and the *Record of Famous People of the Time in Naniwa [Osaka] (Naniwa tōji jinmei roku)*, both published in 1845.

Because he had no son, Kakuō adopted his eldest daughter's husband, Tokuō (1805–1885), who, as his successor, adopted the surname Tanaka. After Kakuō's death, Tokuō carefully preserved all his father-in-law's possessions in a storehouse and taught his children Kakuō's sencha etiquette. His elder son inherited the family business, and when he retired around the time of the Meiji Restoration, his younger son, Tanaka Issō, began to earn his living as a professional teacher of the Kagetsuan school of sencha. Issō was then designated the third-generation iemoto of Kagetsuan.

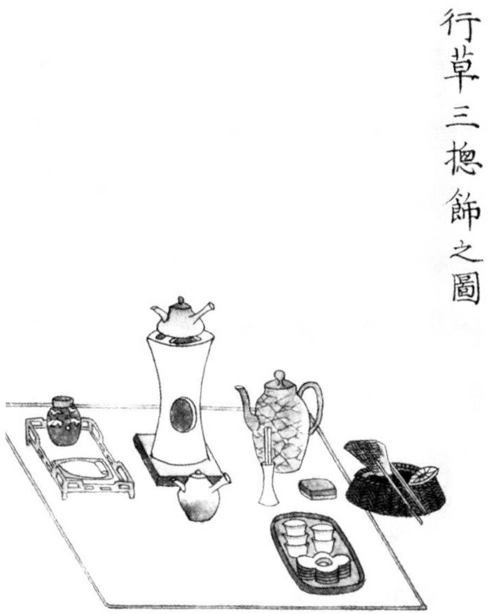

Far left:
58. SENCHA UTENSIL ARRANGEMENT OF THE THIRD INFORMAL LEVEL OF THE SEMIFORMAL STYLE
From volume 1 of the Kagetsuan school manual *A Detailed Explanation of the Elegant Commodity of Boiled Tea (Seifūryū hōcha shoshiki shōkai),* Meiji-period (1868–1912) copy of an original from the Tokugawa period, Tenpō era (1830–1844). Handwritten album; ink on paper. 26 x 16 cm (sight). Private collection, Japan.

Left:
59. A THREE-MAT SENCHA TEAROOM
From volume 6 of the Kagetsuan school manual *A Detailed Explanation of the Elegant Commodity of Boiled Tea (Seifūryū hōcha shoshiki shōkai),* Meiji-period (1868–1912) copy of an original from the Tokugawa period, Tenpō era (1830–1844). Handwritten album; ink on paper. 26 x 16 cm (sight). Private collection, Japan. Photo: P. Graham.

Disseminating a Tea Ceremony for Sencha through Teachers and Texts

Contemporaneous with Tanaka Kakuō's efforts in Osaka, Ogawa Kashin (1786–1855) (fig. 60) began promoting sencha in Kyoto. He regarded sencha as a formal ritual intimately tied to principles associated with the Japanese imperial tradition that could be traced back to Chinese beliefs. The school he ultimately founded is commonly regarded as the second oldest sencha lineage.

Kashin, who came from a samurai family in the service of the Fukui daimyo of Echizen province, was said to have enjoyed sencha from his youth. Later he settled in Kyoto where he became a physician.[9] Kashin's involvement with sencha intensified after his move to Kyoto, and some accounts indicate that he may even have been involved in the research that led to the perfection of gyokuro in 1835 (Kyoto 1973, 540). The next year he abandoned his medical practice to devote himself completely to promoting the benefits of sencha for both body and spirit.

Unlike Tanaka Kakuō, Ogawa Kashin's name does not appear in Tokugawa-period publications enumerating those who frequented the

60. PORTRAIT OF OGAWA KASHIN
Kōsai (active ca. mid-nineteenth century). Hanging scroll; ink and colors on silk. 95 x 36.5 cm. Private collection, Japan. Photo: courtesy Ogawa Kōraku.

fashionable intellectual and artistic circles of his day. Indeed, Kashin's apparent ideological distance from these individuals is reflected in the criticism of his Ogawa school in Fukada Seiichi's bunjincha treatise; Kashin's was the only school cited by name as one of the disparaged lineages of zokujincha. Many of the documents and other materials related to the early history of the Ogawa school were destroyed in fires during the Meiji period, but two that do survive, the *Record of a Boiled Tea Ceremony (Hōcha ki)* of 1851 (which only exists in copies dated 1909) and *Kōrakudō's Talks on Tea Drinking (Kōrakudō kissa ben)* of 1857, indicate that Kashin's closest supporters were not the intellectuals or artists of his day but rather Kyoto's aristocrats.[10]

Like the literati, the courtier class was considered an elite group within Japanese society. Although they comprised the highest class, the aristocrats were in fact controlled by the military regime, who nevertheless accorded them certain privileges and responsibilities. The shogunate provided courtiers with a stipend and kept them occupied with mandated court ceremonies. They also pursued assorted elegant activities befitting their exalted status. During the late Tokugawa period, courtiers had the support of many intellectuals, both Sinophile and Kokugaku scholars alike, who worked to overthrow the weakening and ineffectual shogunate and restore the Imperial House to power. The mutual interest in sencha on the part of these groups became a point of commonality and a mark of their outsider status (Ogawa 1975a, 10–11). Although high-ranking samurai, including the shogun, did indeed participate in sencha, it was not a prescribed form of etiquette as was chanoyu. Sencha's hints at anti-authoritarian idealism as promulgated by celebrated masters such as Baisaō and Akinari were too conspicuous, while it was simultaneously seen as too plebeian as a result of its strong support among the middle classes. Although Tanaka Kakuō introduced sencha to some of the courtiers, Ogawa Kashin formulated the ideology that tied sencha to their loyalist cause. This association may also have contributed to the growing appreciation of sencha among a public dissatisfied with the shogunate, and by extension its rituals, such as chanoyu, in the waning years of the Tokugawa period.

Kashin's *Kōrakudo's Talks on Tea Drinking* is a plainly written manual on sencha preparation techniques, but it also contains a highly theoretical discourse on the relationship of tea to Daoist cosmology. Ogawa Kashin apparently orally transmitted the text from his deathbed, in 1854, to his disciple Tachibana Moromi, and it was published posthumously in 1857 on the occasion of the third memorial service of his death. The courtier Horikawa Yasuchika provided a preface, a short history of tea appreciation in Japan.

The main body of the text covers practical matters first in sections on precepts, boiling methods, preparation of the teapot, varieties of tea, and tea utensils. Three relatively abstract sections follow: fire, water, and wind—subjects derived from ancient Chinese cosmology. Kashin's association of these elements with tea stemmed from his belief that sencha was a living entity for which systematic preparation methods existed in nature. Uncovering these could be accomplished by devising a ritualistic presentation method for sencha that adhered to the principles and respected the elements—yin and yang (*in-yō*), fire, water, and wind—which regulated the natural order of the universe and the calendar.

Although Kashin was the first to apply these concepts to tea, they were well known among Japanese aristocrats, for they had guided court liturgy in Japan since the Heian period. Emperor Saga, an early proponent of tea and literati culture, is credited with codifying much of the liturgy (Miller 1971, 107). During the Heian period, Japan was governed by legal codes adapted from the Chinese imperial tradition. These laws had originally been devised as part of the complex early Han (second century B.C.) cosmological system that decreed the emperor as arbiter of yin and yang, ruler of the four cardinal points, and governor of the four seasons and five elements.

These beliefs grew into the complex liturgies of religious Daoism, whose imperial bureaucratic offices regulated life first in China and then in Japan with the establishment of the bureau of Yin and Yang (*Onmyō-ryō*) in 709. This bureau's authority was expanded and codified during the Heian period, when it promulgated the annual calendar and oversaw the implementation of ceremonies around which life revolved (Miller 1971). By linking sencha to principles that had dominated the imperial court at its height, Kashin's appeal among the courtier class was assured.

Kashin asserted in his treatise that the contents of the teapot contained the essence of heaven and earth. Drinking tea, he said, invigorated the body, but the spirit could only be harmonized with the universe when quietly seated beside a brazier observing the convergence of the natural forces in the tea. As the wind picked up, the fire burned hotter. The fire caused the water to boil, and then, as these essential elements were synchronized, their natural rhythms brought forth the true flavor of the tea (Shufunotomosha 1981, 413).

Like the literati and other promoters of sencha, Kashin placed great importance on brewing the best-tasting tea possible. Like them, he studied processing and preparation techniques, sources for water, and so on. However, he departed from the literati by stressing the underlying importance of attuning sencha preparation to the annual cycle of the four seasons and twelve months (*shiki juni setsu*). By modifying the procedures according to the calendar, he could adjust for variables of humidity and temperature that affected the taste of the tea. This interest in the impact of seasonal fluctuations on tea's physical properties must have been aroused by Kashin's study of the natural sciences during his training as a physician. Kashin may also have adapted some of his brewing techniques from methods of preparing Chinese medicines and gongfu tea (Ogawa 1986a, 34–35). Additional concerns with the hygienic benefits of the beverage led to his devising certain procedures unique to his Ogawa school: a distinct method of wiping the teacups with a clean cloth, offering tea sweets with chopsticks instead of fingers, and drinking a cup of plain hot water between servings of tea (Ogawa 1975a, 7).

Kashin emphasized that preparation techniques and the flavor of the tea took precedence over the appearance of the utensils. He asserted that other sencha masters made sencha into *dōgu cha* (utensil tea), as they were more concerned with using authentic Chinese utensils, implements imitating those that Baisaō had employed, or Japanese copies of such vessels. He claimed not to care whether utensils were Chinese or Japanese, old or new, so long as they functioned well. This attitude also encouraged creativity on the part of Japanese makers of sencha utensils, for it allowed them freedom to experiment with a wider range of styles than had previously been deemed acceptable in sencha circles. Still, Kashin did not disregard veneration of utensils entirely. One page from his *Record of a Boiled Tea Ceremony*, for example, features an elaborate stand for seven tea caddies (apparently for the service of tō-cha)-, like similar containers for precious chanoyu utensils, each caddy was wrapped in its own cloth bag (fig. 61).

61. SENCHA TEAROOM OF THE OGAWA SCHOOL
From *Record of a Boiled Tea Ceremony (Hōcha ki)*, 1909 copy of an 1851 original. Handwritten album; ink on paper. 26.5 x 31 cm. Private collection, Japan. Photo: courtesy Ogawa Kōraku.

Despite his claims to disregard literati preferences, their ideals permeated the ambiance of Kashin's sencha world. In fact, the *Record of a Boiled Tea Ceremony*, which documented a tea ceremony that Kashin hosted at Kodaiji in Kyoto in 1851, included descriptions of many types of Chinese wares and their Japanese copies in styles known to have been appreciated in bunjin circles. Kashin also displayed at this gathering paintings and calligraphies by several Kyoto literati painters who were his contemporaries: Nakabayashi Chikutō, Uragami Shunkin, and Nukina Kaioku. The prominence of these artworks by native literati artists was at odds, however, with the literati practice of bestowing highest status on Chinese works of art and authentic Chinese utensils. With this shift from veneration of China's literati traditions to those of Japan itself, Kashin played an important role in furthering the naturalization of sencha.

Kashin and his followers created a distinctive atmosphere in their tearooms by having utensils designed to their specifications, often imprinted with yin and yang symbols, and by furnishing the rooms with specially designed objects. For example, in accordance with the taste of Kashin's aristocratic patrons, they sometimes displayed curtain stands (*kichō*), which had been used to divide rooms in ancient Heian aristocratic mansions. Their rooms also featured a hearth screen consisting of four panels, with the two in the center angled to form the shape of a mountain; hence its appellation of "mountain screen" (*sanjibyō*). Its design, characterized by the placement of a number of small paintings and calligraphies scattered across its surface in the manner of ancient courtly *shikishi* (decorated papers with poems written upon them), appears in the *Record of a Boiled Tea Ceremony* (fig. 61).

Although the motivations of Kakuō and Kashin in promoting a formalized sencha etiquette differed, their efforts had similar results. Through their followers sencha became accessible to diverse segments of the population. Although these two had the most widespread and lasting influence, they were not sencha's only popularizers.

One of the most important of these other promoters was a Rinzai priest, Yatsuhashi Baisa (1760?–1828). Born into a samurai family in Fukuoka, Baisa joined the Buddhist priesthood when young (a common profession for younger sons of samurai families) and went to study at a temple in Nagasaki. Around 1786 he moved to Kyoto, where he became affiliated with Myōshinji and mingled with literati sencha aficionados. Later he opened a teashop in Edo, but left around 1805 to wander along the Tōkaidō road selling sencha, like Baisaō, from a portable bamboo carrying case. During his roamings he found an abandoned temple, Yatsuhashi Muryōshōji, in Mikawa province (Aichi prefecture), near the location of the fabled eight-plank bridge (*yatsuhashi*) described in the ninth-century *Tales of Ise (Ise monogatari)*. Settling there, he made restoration of the temple his life's work. He continued to proselytize sencha in that region and is today considered the founder of Nagoya's Baisa school of sencha.[11]

Beginning in the late 1840s pocket-sized guides to sencha lore and practice became widely available to supplement personal instruction by teachers. These books made sencha understandable to aspiring devotees and contained short biographies of the most important sencha masters—Lu Yu, Baisaō, and Ueda Akinari—and annotated illustrations of utensils (mostly teapots and braziers) and their proper assemblage. Significantly, they did not include step-by-step procedures to follow in preparing the tea, for that remained the domain of the teachers. The earliest of these texts was the *New Selections of Sencha at a Glance (Shinsen sencha ichiran)*, published in 1847, by Sakura Seidan (Seidanrō shujin). It included some of the same Chinese utensils Chikuden had published in his *Pictorial Album of Tea Utensils* and served as the model for another popular volume, the 1851 *Outline of the Pure Spirit of Sencha (Seifū* sencha *yōran)*, by Toen. Similar in scope and format was Yamamoto Tokujun's *Concise Guide to Sencha* of 1848, which was published simultaneously in Edo, Osaka, and Kyoto.

By far the most ambitious of these popular guides was the *Elegant Sayings about Sencha* (*Sencha kigen*), published in 1857 (volume 1) and

1858 (volume 2), by Tōgyū Baisa (1791–1857), an influential student of Tanaka Kakuō. This Baisa was born in Kyoto and when young became a Sōtō Zen priest. Later he moved to Osaka and owned a teashop, but abandoned it and relocated to Edo. Eventually he returned to Kyoto, where he taught sencha and became acquainted with many local literati and artists, including the potter Kiyomizu Rokubei II (ca. 1797–1860). Several of these friends contributed to the second edition of his book: Uragami Shunkin designed a portrait of Lu Yu for the preface and Nukina Kaioku contributed a poem.

Tōgyū Baisa's book became extremely influential in the late Tokugawa and early Meiji periods, as it provided the most extensive chronology of sencha in Japan up to its time. According to him, the lineage of sencha began with the scholar-recluse of Kyoto, Ishikawa Jōzan, who had before this time been absent from such chronologies. Within Tōgyū Baisa's configuration of the lineage, Baisaō Kō Yūgai was followed by Yatsuhashi Baisa, identified as Baisaō II, then himself as Baisaō III (bypassing his teacher, Kakuō). Enumerated thereafter were an enormous number of latter-day followers of sencha from throughout Japan, including samurai and women (Shufunotomosha 1981, 824–837).

Sencha in the Culture of the Samurai Elite

Though many of the individuals involved with the promotion of sencha came from samurai backgrounds, they were not, with few exceptions, from the highest samurai rank of daimyo. Most of those men continued to prefer chanoyu over sencha, as participation in the former was required for individuals of their status. Still, some adopted sencha as a private pastime in conjunction with their pursuit of the literati arts deemed appropriate civilizing activities by the bakufu. For these men, participation in Chinese customs such as sencha helped to define their status. Sencha apparently was admired as much for the elegant ambiance in which it was consumed as for its flavor.

In fact, it is a sencha tearoom designed for a daimyo, the Sankatei (pavilion of three flowers), that is the oldest tearoom for sencha in existence today (fig. 62). It was designed in the Kaei era (1848–1854) for the Edo residence of the thirteenth daimyo of the Maeda clan of Kaga province (Ishikawa prefecture), Maeda Nariyasu (1811–1884). In 1949 the structure was relocated to its present site, where it was attached to the residence that Nariyasu had constructed for his mother in 1863, the Seisonkaku, located in Kenrokuen Park in Kanazawa. The Sankatei consists of three main interconnected rooms: a five-mat sencha room that adjoins a four-mat room for depositing one's sword (*saya no ma*) and a three-mat study, identified also as a room for serving the fragrant flower or herb tea, kōsen. The complex also includes a storage room (*mizuya*) and a separate three-mat waiting room (Kitao 1957, 10–39; Yokoyama 1987, 261).

With its rich and idiosyncratic details, it may be considered an extravagant distant cousin of the Chinese-influenced interior design of rooms where Japanese bunjin enjoyed sencha. Tsubaki Chinzan, in fact, was commissioned in 1852 to carve a design of bamboo and a rock into a large standing stone for installation in the adjacent garden. Perhaps the most distinctive feature of the interior, walls painted deep blue and purple, has now been covered over. However, the effect can be interpolated from observing a similar color scheme preserved in several second-story rooms of the Seisonkaku (Hashimoto 1981, pls. 169,170).

Another unusual design feature is the presence of a bronze bell suspended from the ceiling adjacent to the tokonoma in the tearoom. The rooms also feature elegantly shaped etched-glass windows. The most exotic element in this suite filled with curiosities may be the giant narwhal's horn that spans the nearly nine-foot-long transom (*ranma*) separating the sencha room from the sword deposit room.

Generally though, the Sankatei abounds with architectural details in Chinese taste, including a wisteria vine ceiling in the study area; unusually shaped windows, such as a large, round paper-covered window on an exterior wall and a cutout opening between rooms shaped like a double gourd; paper-covered shoji with elegant Chinese-style bamboo lattice patterns; elevated shelves for display of scholars' objects; and Chinese hardstone door pulls. A Qing dynasty black lacquer four-panel screen has been used as a sliding door (*fusuma*) to separate the sencha and kōsen rooms. Its surface is covered with literati emblems: the side facing the sencha room features mother-of-pearl inlaid designs of the symbolic plants denoted by Chinese literati as the "four friends," or shikunshi (plum, bamboo, orchid, and chrysanthemum), while the reverse contains calligraphy in *maki-e* (inlaid lacquer with sprinkled gold), a line from Wang Xizhi's famous Lanting Gathering preface. There are also insets of Chinese fabrics, underglaze blue porcelain and lacquer panels, and simulated ink cakes incorporated into the walls and cabinet doors as decorative adornments.

The opulent and exotic atmosphere of the Sankatei owes much to the architectural interiors of the finest restaurants of the entertainment areas, such as Kyoto's Sumiya, and to long-held daimyo preferences for Chinese material culture. However, in its eclectic fusion of Japanese, Chinese, and Western elements, the rooms have redefined traditional Japanese interior space in a new aesthetic specifically identified with sencha.

The Sankatei is a unique example of a sencha tearoom complex designed for a daimyo. Other daimyo, however, incorporated similar aesthetic elements into rooms designed as their private retreats, essentially places where they drank leaf tea (sencha) informally, served chanoyu, and practiced literati (bun) activities. A surviving example of a structure of this type is found at the Ii family residence in Hikone, a rambling estate originally constructed by the fourth-generation family

62. SENCHA TEAROOM IN THE SANKATEI (PAVILION OF THREE FLOWERS) Constructed in the Tokugawa period, Kaei era (1848–1854). Among a suite of rooms at the Seisonkaku Kenrokuen, Kanazawa. Photo: Matsumura Yoshiharu.

daimyo, Ii Naooki (1656–1717). Like the Sankatei, these rooms date from the mid-nineteenth century. The suite is known as the Rakurakutei (pavilion for the enjoyment of various pleasures) in reference to the four scholarly arts of calligraphy, painting, playing go, and music that would be enjoyed there. Although today the spirit of wabi dominates the aesthetic of chanoyu tearooms, in the late Tokugawa period Chinese aesthetics were so fashionable that even enthusiastic proponents of chanoyu, such as the Ii family, whose members included the powerful daimyo Ii Naosuke (1815–1860), an author of various books on the subject, succumbed to this influence.

The Rakurakutei contains a chanoyu tearoom adjoining a raised tatami-matted study (fig. 63), both larger in scale than similar rooms at the Sankatei.[12] In deference to the family's inclinations toward chanoyu, Chinese aesthetic elements are here more subdued and wabi taste is reflected in some prominent interior features such as the unfinished twisted tree limb used as the main pillar of the tokonoma. Chinese design features include the several large, decoratively shaped windows, lattice patterns covering the shoji, and the placement of a plaque with the name of the suite, Rakuraku, inlaid in mother-of-pearl in scholarly clerical script, inset into the transom between the two main rooms.

In addition to participating in sencha themselves, daimyo contributed to its further promulgation through sponsorship of ceramic kilns in their jurisdictions. During the nineteenth century most of their kilns specialized in porcelain and produced scholars' objects and sencha utensils. Some of these kilns had been established earlier in the Tokugawa period, but many were founded in the early nineteenth century following directives from the bakufu to encourage local craft industries as a means of improving a weakened economy. In many instances, potters from Kyoto, who were considered experts in the fashionable new styles in bunjin taste, were called in to oversee the operations. The Zuishi kiln of the Tokugawa daimyo of Kii province (Wakayama prefecture), for example, was established in 1801 by Mokubei, who also helped to revive the Maeda daimyo's ceramics industry in Kanazawa by working at the Kutani ware Kasugayama kiln (in 1806).

Kutani quickly became one of the most important and commercially successful centers of production for porcelain sencha wares and scholars' objects in the late Tokugawa and Meiji periods.[13] Other Kyoto potters who assisted at Kutani included Hozen's son Eiraku Wazen (1823–1896), who initiated the production of kinrande wares there, using the powdered-gold application technique. Kutani became particularly famous

63. THE RAKURAKUTEI (PAVILION FOR THE ENJOYMENT OF VARIOUS PLEASURES)
Constructed in the mid-nineteenth century. Suite of rooms at the former residence of the Ii daimyo family, Hikone. Photo: P. Graham.

64. TEAPOT WITH NARRATIVE AND FLORAL MOTIFS
Kutani Shōza (1816–1883). Kinrande-style Kutani ware porcelain with overglaze enamels and gold. H: 5.5 cm. Private collection, Japan. Photo: P. Graham.

65. SENCHA TEACUP FROM A SET OF FIVE
Meihō (fl. Tokugawa period, mid-nineteenth century). Kinrande-style Kōtō ware, Hikone; porcelain with overglaze red enamel and gold. H: 4.5 cm. Hikone Castle Museum.

for this style in the early Meiji period under the leadership of Kutani Shōza (1816–1883), the most famous and creative Kutani potter of the era. His designs are characterized by the incongruous pairing of scenes of different subjects on a single vessel. His wares are opulently decorated, as in a delicate teapot for sencha (fig. 64). Here he has painted a pastoral narrative of a fisherman on one side and a bird-and-flower motif in a medallion on the other. Prominent among the overglaze colors on this teapot is a rosy pink, used to define the flower petals. One of Shōza's favorite pigments, this color owes its appearance to his adaptation of Western chemical compounds imported during the Meiji period.

Eiraku Hozen also established important kilns for daimyo patrons. In 1827 he accompanied his adopted father to Kii province, where they established a personal kiln, the Kairakuen, for the local daimyo, which produced wares for chanoyu and other formal occasions.[14] Eiraku also taught his methods of applying decoration on kinrande wares to potters at the Kōtō kiln at Hikone, active between 1829 and 1862 under the sponsorship of three successive generations of Ii daimyo: Naoaki, Naosuke, and Naonori. Representative of their kinrande products is a sencha teacup from a set of five decorated with Chinese figures in medallions, signed by the potter Meiho (fig. 65). Kōtō potters also excelled at underglaze blue, celadon, and copies of Kutani and Imari wares.[15] Since this kiln existed for but a short span of time and did not distribute widely, and since many of its wares were later destroyed in fires, it is not well known today.

Other daimyo kilns that produced sencha wares within the sphere of influence generated by Kyoto literati and potters have likewise become obscure, as they also ceased production in the early Meiji period. They include the Sanda and Ochiyama kilns in Hyōgo prefecture (Sasayama 1991, 48–60; Sasayama 1988), famed for their celadons, and the Tozan kiln sponsored by the Sakai daimyo at Himeji (Mitsuoka 1975).

By the end of the Tokugawa period, sencha had become transformed into much more than a casually ingested beverage. As its promoters adopted chanoyu etiquette and aesthetic preferences in karamono, the assimilation of sencha into Japanese culture was complete. No longer was it the private avocation of intellectuals and eccentrics. Its champions had rationalized an appropriateness for samurai, aristocrats, and the middle classes alike. Entire industries, from tea schools to craft workshops, were devoted to its promotion. Sencha's Chinese literati-inspired aesthetic had so completely infiltrated public consciousness that the marginal role of the sencha ceremony in modern Japanese society seems a surprising turn of events. The fate of sencha after the Meiji Restoration is the subject of the final chapter of this book.

CHAPTER SEVEN

Sencha in Modern Japan

The Meiji Restoration of 1868 constituted a radical break with the past in terms of internal politics and international relations, though corresponding changes in values—evident in the Japanese public's preferences for art, literature, daily and ritual customs, ethical teachings, etc.—came about more slowly. The leaders of this new age set in motion a program of modernization under the rubric of *bunmei kaika* (civilization and enlightenment), seeking to refashion Japan in the image of industrialized Western powers. Yet so entrenched were Chinese ideals and their associated arts and customs that they could not easily be dislodged.

By the middle of the nineteenth century, rituals associated with drinking sencha had become widely practiced by people from virtually all walks of life, but still its aesthetics and tenets remained closely affiliated with admiration for classical China. The continued presence of sencha and its material culture in the modern era—from the Meiji period to the present—reflects not only the depth of penetration of its philosophy and aesthetics into Japanese society, but also the tenacity of the Japanese Sinophile literati scholars (*Kangakusha*) during an era in which their high regard for China's cultural legacy was deemed by many to be nostalgic and obsolete. This chapter surveys the variety of individuals in Japan's modern era who continued to embrace sencha and explores the richness of arts devoted to it as one facet of the aesthetic environment of modern Japan.

Sencha's continuing evolution in the modern era can be charted through printed books and other pictorial records. These are divisible into four distinct types of documents: (1) commemorative records of sencha gatherings that illustrate the environments (seki) where sencha was served and the arrangements of the utensils (kazari) within them; (2) studies of the art objects (principally of Chinese manufacture) associated with sencha; (3) reprints of older Chinese and Japanese books on sencha; and (4) guides to the use of standardized types of utensils according to rules (temae) set by sencha schools.

Sencha and Chanoyu in Relation to Japan's Modern Identity

By the 1880s, in reaction to the zealous adoption of Western ways, Japanese political leaders recognized the need to cultivate for Japan a unique cultural identity as a modernized but still distinctly Asian nation. Although numerous aspects of Japan's cultural patrimony encompassed assimilated Chinese values, many questioned and sought to overturn Japan's traditional deferential relationship with China as that country became fragmented by internal power struggles and subjugated by Western forces. These attitudes helped provoke the Sino-Japanese War of 1894–1895. Japan's subsequent military victory over China was so stunning that it strengthened feelings of superiority over other Asian nations as well. Japanese leaders ultimately concluded that it was only in their country that the wisdom of the East, which had originally emanated from China, could now be preserved. Widely promoted in the Meiji period, this concept had its roots in the ideology of Tokugawa-period Confucian scholars.

Sinophile intellectuals, epitomized by Naitō Konan (1866–1934), maintained conflicting sentiments toward China; they continued to praise its past achievements but expressed dismay at its present weakness, which they sought to rectify through the offering of various kinds of assistance. By the late nineteenth century, Kangaku supporters of classical Chinese culture and thought, with whom Naitō sided, and all of whom seem to have participated in sencha, were often coming into conflict with modernist scholars of *Tōyō* (East Asia). These so-called pan-Asianists (*Tōyōgakusha*) deemed Kangakusha old-fashioned idealists and focused instead on contemporary developments in Asia.[1]

These attitudes led to two contradictory developments that further affected both the relationship between China and Japan and the definition of Japan's national identity. On the one hand, there was a sense of urgency to appropriate China's cultural artifacts and intellectual heritage in the guise of preservation of the material culture that represented Eastern values. On the other was a desire to create a less China-oriented cultural identity for Japan. The former led to the collecting and cataloguing of Chinese art, including the first systematic surveys of the great cave temples. The latter stimulated the promotion of Japanese artistic traditions less obviously indebted to those of China. Both these attitudes affected the reception of sencha in modern Japan, as its appreciation continued to be intimately tied to respect for traditional Chinese culture.

In contrast, the rituals and aesthetics of chanoyu, though remotely based on Chinese tea preparation techniques and encompassing an appreciation of karamono, were conceived and practiced solely in Japan. Thus the suitability of sencha as an element of "Japanese" culture both to the world outside and among the Japanese public was questioned by the new pan-Asianists, such as Okakura Kakuzō (Tenshin; 1862–1913), who promoted chanoyu instead (Okakura 1903; Okakura 1906).

Even before Okakura's time, from the very beginning of the Meiji period, impetus for reappraisal of the status of chanoyu emanated from chanoyu tea masters themselves, particularly those associated with the Urasenke school. They intensified efforts to reform and expand their following by allowing the use of chairs for guests (formally adopted in 1872), holding large public tea ceremonies to overcome the image of chanoyu as an elitist occupation of samurai and wealthy merchants (from 1877), and cultivating participation by women as a means of instructing them in proper etiquette (begun in the 1880s but entering the formal curriculum of women's education from 1913). The reputation of sencha was finally surpassed by chanoyu as the powerful new industrialists of the late Meiji period became enthusiastic participants and collected its related arts. Thus chanoyu became a status-enhancing avocation for this new "merchant class" (Guth 1993, 72–75; Varley 1989, 188–191).

In general, sencha did not fare well in the competition with chanoyu for patrons; it did not enjoy the advocacy of those in positions of economic power, nor did it have a single strong institutional base, like Urasenke, from which to rally. Yet its proponents tried to refashion its identity and expand its constituency in ways similar to what was occurring within the chanoyu establishment. As early as the 1870s, sencha, together with other Chinese literati arts, was being promoted as an edifying activity for ladies. Several paintings from this decade by a female literati painter from Osaka, Noguchi Shōhin (1847–1917), including the delicately brushed *Women Practicing Literati Arts in a Garden*, 1872 (fig. 66), depict women enacting bunjin activities, with sencha prominent among them.[2]

By the 1890s, however, motivations for women to participate in sencha had changed. Sencha was, for them, no longer associated with the mastery of Chinese-influenced literati arts. Rather, participants learned the custom as a means of acquiring gracefulness in a task that was, and remains today, an essential skill employed in the entertaining

66. WOMEN PRACTICING LITERATI ARTS IN A GARDEN—1872
Noguchi Shōhin (1847–1917). Hanging scroll; ink and light colors on silk. 111.5 x 37 cm. Private collection, Japan. Photo: courtesy Yamanashi Prefectural Museum of Art.

of guests in Japanese society. Woodblock prints, such as a triptych by Mizuno Toshikata (1866–1908), *Serving Guests Sencha in a Room with a Fine View*, dated 1890 (fig. 67), suggest this shift in the formal poses of the seated guests and the orderly arrangement of the utensils. However, that the air of refinement still clung to Chinese artifacts is evident in the Chinese-style furnishings, such as the rug, hearth screen, tables, flower arrangements, and hanging scroll. As in the sencha rooms of the late Tokugawa period, Chinese elements—the lattice designs of the railing and the cracked ice-patterned windows—are combined with more standard Japanese interior design features, in this case, an elevated, tatami-covered tokonoma.

Sencha and Literati Culture in the Meiji and Taishō Periods

In the early Meiji period, most members of the new political elite continued to uphold Chinese literati values and pursuits as morally correct. These leaders had received their educations prior to the Meiji Restoration, when Chinese Confucian teachings served as the mainstay of the educational curriculum. They acquired a taste for related literati avocations in their formative years and encouraged continued respect for writings in Chinese (kanbun). Donald Keene has observed that writing in kanbun was, by the Meiji period, no longer considered an alien language; it was instead the language of the educated, to be used when composing serious books for a literate audience (Keene 1985). Under the influence of these Chinese-educated leaders, Chinese antiquities remained the art of highest status among collectors. Ex-samurai politicians also admired and collected related Japanese arts and artworks by Japanese literati painters from similar backgrounds.

67. SERVING GUESTS SENCHA IN A ROOM WITH A FINE VIEW—1890
Mizuno Toshikata (1866–1908). Woodblock-print triptych mounted as a section of a long handscroll; ink and colors on paper. 35.5 x 70.5 cm. Iruma City Museum.

Rai San'yō, Watanabe Kazan, and Tanomura Chikuden, for example, were accorded particular esteem, and disciples of these artists were patronized by the new leaders (Addiss 1982; Guth 2006).

Of the many literati painters active from the late Tokugawa period through the Taishō period, Tanomura Chokunyū (1814–1907) and Tomioka Tessai (1836–1924) were the two most admired by the new elite politicians not only for their talent as artists, but also for their pre-Restoration associations with supporters of the loyalist movement. Not surprisingly, they were also the most influential promoters of sencha in literati circles. Friends of very different temperaments and ambitions, their pictorial records and studies on sencha reveal complementary approaches to its preservation and modernization.[3]

Chokunyū, a native of Takeda, Tanomura Chikuden's hometown, was from a family of *ikebana* (flower-arranging) teachers. A child prodigy in painting, he became a student of Chikuden at age eight and was adopted by him soon after. Later he studied Chinese poetry with Shinozaki Shōchiku in Osaka. Settling in Kyoto in 1868, where he met Tessai, Chokunyū became an influential teacher and promoter of literati painting and related culture. He served as the first director of the Kyoto Prefectural Painting School (Kyoto-fu Gagakkō) when it opened in

1879 and later, together with Tessai, was instrumental in founding the Japanese Literati Painting Society (Nihon Nanga Kyōkai). He was also an Ōbaku monk.

The records of sencha gatherings in which Chokunyū participated reveal that he strove tirelessly to promote sencha as an educational activity. In 1863 he published the earliest and most famous example of this effort in a three-volume illustrated book, *Pictorial Record of the Azure Sea Tea Gathering (Seiwan chakai zuroku)*, an account of two related sencha gatherings that took place in Osaka in 1862 and 1863 (Kramer 1985, 150–157). Volumes one and two were devoted to the first gathering, volume three to the second. The first gathering convened to commemorate the one-hundredth anniversary of the death of Baisaō. Its main event was the erection of a stone tablet on the bank of

the Yodo River at the supposed site of Ōbaku Ingen's pronouncement that the scenery resembled that of China's West Lake, a place famed in Chinese literati lore. The agenda of the second gathering seems to have been less specific. To finance these gatherings and the erection of the memorial stele, Chokunyū painted one hundred portraits of Baisaō, which he sold to his friends.

Both gatherings featured seki devised by various sencha coteries, or sencha masters and their disciples. These rooms were all illustrated in the book, accompanied by thematically related poems in Chinese and detailed descriptions of the important sencha utensils they contained (of Chinese, Japanese, Korean, Ryukyuan, and European manufacture). Among the treasures displayed in one of the seki (fig. 68) were the famous utensils made by Akinari, his crab-shaped brazier and kettle (fig. 20). Still, despite the eclectic nature of the accouterments, the appearance of the settings remained overwhelmingly Chinese, with rooms furnished with an abundance of Chinese wooden and bamboo tables, trays, stools, ancient bronzes, and ceramics.

The book's format, an exhaustive, illustrated record of the objects connected with a sencha gathering, came to serve as the model for the seemingly mandatory publications commemorating such events in the succeeding Meiji and early Taishō periods. As many earlier participants in bunjincha had also been respected authorities on Chinese antiquities, the shift in emphasis in this text, from descriptions of the sencha tea ceremony itself to a detailed account of the utensils, was a natural extension of bunjin interests. It foreshadowed the new climate in which art collecting was to become an avocation of the culturally enlightened in the modern age.

The most distinguished defender of the values outlined in the *Pictorial Record of the Azure Sea Tea Gathering* during the Meiji and Taishō periods was the literati painter and scholar Tomioka Tessai. Born into a Kyoto merchant family, Tessai had a scholarly temperament from his youth, when he studied poetry with the nun Ōtagaki Rengetsu. After an extended stay in Nagasaki in 1861–1862 to elude shogunal authorities seeking to punish imperial loyalists such as himself, and a brief return to Kyoto where he opened a private academy, Tessai embarked on a long period of wandering, taking up permanent residence in Kyoto in 1881. There he moved into a house that had once belonged to Ogawa Kashin, founder of the Ogawa school, though he had no particular affinity for sencha as practiced by that master (Tessai 1991). Introspective and modest by nature, Tessai considered himself foremost a scholar and eschewed public fame as a painter despite his prodigious output. Still he received many honors for his paintings and is widely acknowledged as the greatest creative genius among Japanese literati

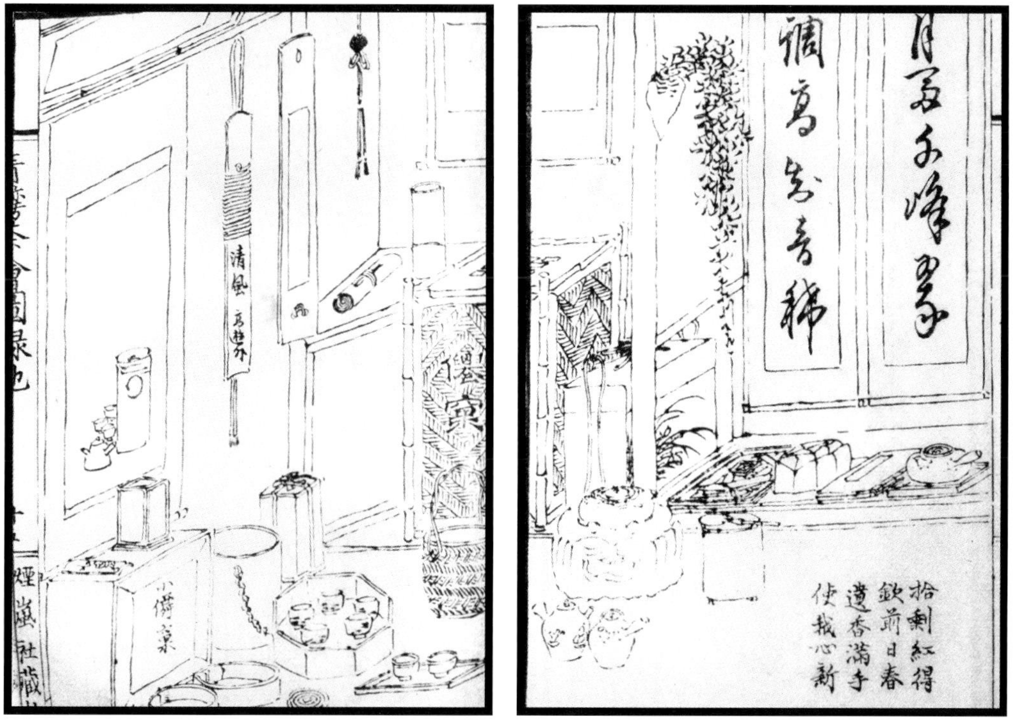

68. ARRANGEMENT OF SENCHA UTENSILS IN A ROOM—1863
Tanomura Chokunyū (1814–1907), from volume 2 of *Pictorial Record of the Azure Sea Tea Gathering (Seiwan chakai zuroku).* Woodblock-printed book; ink on paper. 19.5 x 23 cm. Osaka Municipal Museum of Art. Photo: P. Graham.

painters of the modern period. His many other learned avocations revolved around his devotion to sencha and other literati arts, including book collecting, seal carving, connoisseurship of old paintings, and collaboration with Kyoto artisans in the production of sencha utensils (Conant 1995,166–167; Tessai 1991; Kyoto Municipal Museum 1985, cat. nos. 431–477).

Tessai contributed to the continued fascination with Chinese literati and sencha through numerous paintings that idealized the bunjin lifestyle. His works showed scholars brewing sencha in solitary reverie or attending boisterous literati gatherings. Part of the charm in his paintings of sencha themes lay in his self-deprecating humor, such as exhibited in his casually brushed *Blind Men Critiquing Beauty* (fig. 69), in which a group of sightless old men grope at a painting and assorted sencha utensils—several braziers, a basket carrying case for utensils, tea caddies, an inkstone, and an ancient Chinese bronze vessel.

Tessai also significantly elevated the level of scholarship on the material culture associated with sencha in his two-volume *Tessai's Tea Records (Tetsusō chafu)*, published in 1867. The first volume, *Record of*

69. BLIND MEN CRITIQUING BEAUTY
Tomioka Tessai (1836–1924). Hanging scroll; ink and light colors on paper. 22.9 x 29.2 cm. Nelson-Atkins Museum of Art, Kansas City (Gift of I. Groupp and Julieann White Groupp).

Clay Pots of Yixing (Gikō jihu fu), is a connoisseurship study, the first of its kind, of assorted Chinese Yixing ware teapots illustrated alongside the names of their makers. In his volume he translated into Japanese the earliest-known treatise on Yixing wares in China, *An Account of the Teapots of Yangxian* (C: *Yangxian minghu xi*; J: *Yōsen meiko kei*), by Zhou Gaoqi, written during the Wanli era of the Ming dynasty (1573–1620). Although Yixing wares had been appreciated and used by earlier sencha masters, and the names of famous Yixing potters were known, they had not been well understood due to lack of reliable information. Tessai's publication changed that by increasing access to original Chinese sources. The second volume of Tessai's book, *Sketches of Pure Scholar's Accouterments (Bunbō seiyaku zu)*, defined in pictures and explanations the appropriate Sinified atmosphere in which to enjoy sencha, with some of the illustrations borrowed from those published in Chikuden's books, and others closely resembling the seki found in Chokunyū's tea-gathering record of 1863.

Among the influential new Meiji leaders with whom Tessai and Chokunyū associated was Kido Takayoshi (1833–1877), also a serious collector of the paintings of San'yō and Chikuden and patron to talented literati artists.[4] Kido's circle also included the Osaka art dealer Yamanaka Kichirōbei (Shunkōdō; 1847-1917), whose family firm was soon to become a leading supplier of East Asian art in the Western market, and the merchant Kumagai Naotaka, proprietor of the Kyūkyodō. Together with these friends, Kido participated in sencha gatherings that, soon after the Meiji Restoration, became occasions for public exhibitions of Chinese antiquities, paintings, and calligraphies. Kido and other Meiji leaders promoted these exhibitions, modeled after shogakai, as a means of spreading the literati values that they considered an essential component of education for the general public. One of the earliest of these exhibitions of antiquities took place at an unnamed Kyoto teahouse in 1869 and was hosted by seven literati of Kyoto, who also served their guests sencha (Kido 1983–1986, 1: 213).

Two years later, in 1871, a larger and more formally organized exposition, precursor to the many that were held throughout Japan into the first decade of the twentieth century, opened in Kyoto. Conceived by Kyoto's governor Makimura Masanao (1834–1896), with assistance from Kyoto's intellectual and artistic elite, it contained numerous Chinese Ming and Qing paintings of the sort that would have been appreciated in sencha circles. The main intent of the exhibition, however, was to promote Kyoto's arts and crafts industries, which Makimura championed in the slogan "enrich the country through the arts" (*bijutsu fukoku*) (Conant 1995, 19).

In the mid-1870s exhibitions of sencha accouterments and Chinese paintings and antiquities took place in various cities around Japan. Tanomura Chokunyū served as one of the foremost promoters and chroniclers of these ventures. Chokunyū documented several in painted handscrolls and another in an illustrated woodblock book. One of the handscrolls records a gathering that took place over a five-day period in 1873. One hundred and thirty guests convened to celebrate the sixty-first birthday of an administrator from Harima (Hyōgo prefecture), Kameda Tamekazu (1811–1883), and bid him farewell prior to his departure for Tokyo on official business (Ogawa 1975b).

In January of the following year, Chokunyū organized another sencha arts extravaganza, this one for the general public. He recorded its appearance in a set of three long handscrolls. In the epilogue to the scrolls he wrote that the exhibition took place in his home district of Toyokuni (northern Kyushu), over a period of three days and nights. Friends had asked him to arrange it as a means of helping to impart understanding of the values of "civilization and enlightenment" (he used the term "bunmei kaika") to the area's commoners. As its goals were educational, it received the blessing of the provincial governor. Some twenty to thirty regional officials and eight hundred local men, women, and children came to view the displays. Chokunyū wrote that he considered himself useless and aged, but he agreed to formulate this exhibition to aid in the transformation of the social trends of the nation in the aftermath of the Restoration.[5]

The large, detailed, colored paintings create a far more impressive effect than the small, woodblock-printed illustrated books that were the standard records of sencha gatherings. The handscrolls were organized like the books, with an illustration of each room followed by careful

70. BONSAI DISPLAY—1874

Tanomura Chokunyū (1814–1907), from *Pictorial Record of a Sencha Tea Ceremony*. Section from a set of three handscrolls; ink and colors on paper. 26.7 x 963.9 cm (overall). Saint Louis Art Museum, purchase: funds given by the Mr. and Mrs. Oliver M. Langenberg Endowment Fund, Mr. and Mrs. David Mesker, Mrs. Winifred Garber, Viola Story in memory of Eugene "Buddy" Story, Florence Morris Forbes, Mrs. James Lee Johnson, Jr., and Mr. and Mrs. Charles Lowenhaupt, and funds given by the John R. Goodall Trust, Mr. and Mrs. Lawrence B. Langsam, Mrs. Charles W. Lorenz, Mr. Jack Ansehl, Miss Helen M. Longmire, Mr. and Mrs. David W. Mesker, the Gateway Apparel Charitable Trust, Mr. and Mrs. James Lee Johnson, Jr., Mr. Thomas F. Schlafly, Mrs. Charles A. Thomas, and other donors through the 1992 Annual Appeal, and Museum Purchase.

descriptions of the Chinese and Japanese objects displayed and the names of their owners.

The fête encompassed eight different seki, which guests passed through in succession, beginning with a gallery of some thirty-nine paintings and calligraphies, mostly Chinese, all carefully reproduced. Artists represented include some venerable names in literati circles: Chinese artists Wu Zhen, Shen Zhou, Yi Fujiu, and a joint work by Japanese literati painters Rai San'yō and Tanomura Chikuden. Next came a small room or hallway containing flowers in pots (binka) and an oversized gourd, followed by the first of three seki devoted to environments decorated in sencha taste with all the accessories necessary for serving the beverage. The fourth seki was devoted to potted plants and dwarf trees (bonsai), which Chokunyū sketched with great sensitivity (fig. 70).

This inclusion of flowers and plants must have been inspired by similar practices in chanoyu, but here the plants selected possessed allusions to Chinese rather than Japanese culture: bamboo, prunus, peonies, and pines. Their containers and stands were similarly Chinese in style. Chokunyū must have become acquainted with Chinese-style flower arrangements through his teacher, Chikuden, who had authored a *Treatise on Flower Arranging (Binkaron)*, which incorporated ideas

71. SERVING SENCHA WHILE SEATED IN CHAIRS—1874
Tanomura Chokunyū (1814–1907), from *Pictorial Record of a Sencha Tea Ceremony*. Section from a set of three handscrolls; ink and colors on paper. 26.7 x 963.9 cm (overall). Saint Louis Art Museum, purchase: funds given by the Mr. and Mrs. Oliver M. Langenberg Endowment Fund, Mr. and Mrs. David Mesker, Mrs. Winifred Garber, Viola Story in memory of Eugene "Buddy" Story, Florence Morris Forbes, Mrs. James Lee Johnson, Jr., and Mr. and Mrs. Charles Lowenhaupt, and funds given by the John R. Goodall Trust, Mr. and Mrs. Lawrence B. Langsam, Mrs. Charles W. Lorenz, Mr. Jack Anselil, Miss Helen M. Longmire, Mr. and Mrs. David W. Mesker, the Gateway Apparel Charitable Trust, Mr. and Mrs. James Lee Johnson, Jr., Mr. Thomas F. Schlafly, Mrs. Charles A. Thomas, and other donors through the 1992 Annual Appeal, and Museum Purchase

from Chinese Ming texts.[6] The arrangements of the plants featured in Chokunyū's scrolls and books were regular features of sencha gatherings and form a general category of ikebana known as sencha hana (sencha-style flowers) or bunjin bana (literati-style flowers) (Ogawa 1986b).

Continuing on through the rooms, the fifth seki featured an unusual setting for sencha, incorporating Chinese, Western, and Japanese design features including a Chinese rattan chair for the host; wooden slipcovered chairs for the guests placed around a six-sided, black-and-red lacquer table (fig. 71); and a tokonoma containing artworks by Rai San'yō and Uragami Gyokudō alongside a flower arrangement that featured the surprising addition of a crab (not visible in the photo). The next room was devoted to a display of scholars' accouterments (bunbō seki). Writing utensils were set upon a low Chinese table covered by a Chinese rug, while a tiger skin was spread below the table on the floor. The last sencha seki was more conventional in appearance, with utensils arranged on a mat. The handscrolls concluded with a table set for a shippoku ryōri-style Chinese banquet.

Later in the same year, 1874, Chokunyū was involved in another, even larger sencha celebration for the general public in Osaka sponsored by the Azure Sea Tea Association. The art dealer Yamanaka

72. A ROOM FOR SERVING SENCHA—1875
Tanomura Chokunyū (1814–1907), from volume 4 of *Pictorial Record of Famous Utsensils Used at the Azure Sea Tea Gathering (Seiwan meien zushi)*. Woodblock-printed book; ink on paper. 17 x 20 cm. Private collection, United States. Photo: P. Graham.

Kichirōbei (Shunkōdō) wrote a small four-volume woodblock book recording this event, *Pictorial Record of Famous Utensils Used at the Azure Sea Tea Gathering (Seiwan meien zushi)*, published in 1875, which Chokunyū illustrated. As many wealthy merchant-collectors of Chinese art lived in the Osaka area, the treasures displayed were impressive.

The gathering featured extensive displays of Chinese paintings and calligraphies (listed but not illustrated), bonsai and cut flowers arranged in antique Chinese vessels, and thirteen separate sencha seki with portions of each devoted to bunbōgu (fig. 72). The rooms contained ubiquitous Chinese furnishings: tables, stools, bronze vessels, plants, musical instruments, writing implements, and assorted decorative objects and baskets. Short descriptions followed the illustrations, while separate pages featured drawings and discussions of noteworthy Chinese utensils and antiquities—Yixing wares, ancient bronzes, musical instruments, jades in archaic shapes, flower baskets, and the like. This book, distinguished as the first to exclusively focus on Chinese antiquities appropriate for sencha, was soon followed by other specialized studies of Chinese arts related to sencha.

The earliest of these connoisseurship studies was the 1876 *Pictorial Record of Famous Teapots (Meiko zuroku)*, in which the author, Oku Randen (Saburobei; 1837–1897), a wealthy Tokyo merchant who served in the Lower House of the Diet, illustrated and described thirty-two teapots, mostly Yixing wares, owned by himself and his friends (Lo 1986, 252). Unlike Tessai's book, which had highlighted the teapots of illustrious potters, those in this text were identified first by color and shape. To this day, the classification and connoisseurship of Yixing wares in Japan is dependent upon this approach.

In the late Tokugawa period, appreciation of Yixing wares had been closely associated with the bunjin followers of sencha, such as Mokubei, Chikuden, and Baiitsu. With the publication of Tessai's volume and this book, however, the ware gained greater exposure and grew fashionable among a wider group of sencha aficionados who adopted the use of Yixing teapots exclusively for serving gyokuro. Representative of the Yixing wares available to collectors in Japan around the time of the book's publication in the 1870s is a large collection owned by the Kozone family of Nagasaki (fig. 73). These wares were probably acquired directly from Chinese traders in Nagasaki by this family of wealthy and politically well-connected merchants who, judging from the variety and quality of these examples, must have had first pick of newly imported vessels.

The intellectuals and merchants in Japan's major urban centers succeeded in spreading their passion for Chinese arts in literati taste throughout Japan, for throughout the Meiji and well into the prewar Shōwa period, collectors of literati arts (both Chinese and Japanese) abounded. The collectors included scholars who taught at local academies, the wealthy farmers and merchants who were their pupils, and free-spirited artists and writers. Many of these individuals amassed substantial collections of Chinese antiquities and Japanese arts in Chinese taste, which they displayed in Chinese-style suites of rooms designed to complement their enjoyment of sencha. The design of most of the sencha tearooms from the late Meiji through the early Shōwa periods closely resembled tearooms for chanoyu, though a sense that the room was appropriate for sencha was manifested in the details: designs of door pulls, shapes of windows, patterns of railings, and the like.[7] In some of the surviving examples, Chinese-style interior ornamentation dominated a single wing or room of a house that was otherwise designed in a more typical Japanese residential style. In others, Chinese elements were integrated throughout the entire dwelling.

73. GROUP OF YIXING WARE TEA UTENSILS
Chinese, eighteenth-mid-nineteenth centuries. Burnished, unglazed, buff and brown stoneware. H: 6.5 to 12 cm. Kozone Kichirō collection, Nagasaki. Photo: courtesy Itabashi Ward Museum of Folklore, Tokyo.

74. THE ANTEROOM OF THE SHINAKAN (CHINESE-STYLE PAVILION)
Constructed in 1907, Tsukamoto Yasushi (1869–1937), architect, at the Shibata family residence. Nagahama City, Shiga prefecture. Photo: Misawa Hiroaki.

Perhaps the most impressive example of the former is the Shinakan (Chinese-style pavilion), a wing of a sprawling townhouse in Nagahama on the eastern shore of Lake Biwa. Owned by the Shibata family, affluent wholesalers of crepe (*chirimen*), the house was originally constructed in 1694. It was enlarged in 1907 by the tenth-generation family head, Genshichi. The architect he commissioned for the project, Tsukamoto Yasushi (1869–1937), was an 1893 graduate of, and later professor at, the Tokyo Imperial University's School of Architecture. Sent abroad to study Western architecture soon after he graduated, Tsukamoto is best known for his devotion to the French Art Nouveau style (Finn 1995, 214). Yet, judging from this example, he had great appreciation for Chinese domestic architecture, which he must have learned about during a trip to China in 1906.

Genshichi's interest in Chinese culture led to his friendship with prominent Kyoto scholars and artists of similar persuasion, who would visit his home and partake in lively discussions in the salonlike setting there. Among those friends were Naitō Konan and the master potter, calligrapher, and seal carver Kitaōji Rosanjin (1883–1959), who contributed the design for a large etched-glass window in the anteroom (fig. 74). Replete with elegant Chinese designs for patterned latticework, molding, and fancifully shaped windows, the ambiance was enhanced by tiled flooring; Chinese tables, stools, and chairs; curtains; light fixtures; and a coffered wooden ceiling. The tearoom proper was a standard Japanese size, six mats, but the floor was covered entirely by tiles, which extended into the oversized tokonoma (Itō and Yokoyama 1983–1985, 6: 33–43).

Equally impressive for its recreation of a Chinese environment, but quite different in character, is the Chōkōen (garden of fishing and

75. ROOM IN THE CHŌKŌEN (GARDEN OF FISHING AND CULTIVATION)
Estate of Tokutomi Sohō, constructed ca. 1920–1930. Kumamoto City. Photo: courtesy Issa-an, Osaka.

cultivation) in Kumamoto, constructed for the eminent scholar-journalist Tokutomi Sohō (1863–1957), an influential promoter of Japan's modernization. It dates to the late Taishō or early Shōwa period (ca. 1920–1930), presumably inspired by architecture Sohō viewed during his first sojourn to China in 1906. During this trip, Sohō visited many famous cultural sites, including Tiger Hill in Suzhou and the West Lake of Hangzhou (Fogel 1996, 212–213).

Sohō's education had begun with the Chinese Confucian classics, the passion of his father, and he later studied Christianity, Western learning, and English, which he combined into a single curriculum at his private academy in Kumamoto. He nevertheless reserved highest respect for Rai San'yō, about whom he authored several scholarly studies (Pierson 1980, 32). Like San'yō's Sanshi Suimeisho, Sohō had his estate reconstructed as a private retreat, with its adjacent main rooms designed as a study and sencha tearoom.

The building integrates numerous Chinese-influenced features: a cut stone veranda, elegantly shaped windows, patterned railings, interior doorways covered with curtains or painted sudare (bamboo blinds), rugs, and Chinese furnishings (fig. 75). Yet it is the building's setting, in a landscaped garden amid picturesque mountains, for which it is most distinguished. In 1688 the land had been granted to Sohō's family patriarch, a village headman, by the local daimyo, Hosokawa Amitoshi, as reward for meritorious service. The estate's name was taken from a four-character phrase Amitoshi composed in Chinese, "*Kōun chōgetsu*" (cultivating the clouds and fishing for the moon). Sohō had the estate encircled by a Chinese-style stone wall inset with pierced green-glazed tiles mass-produced for export in China. After entering the central gate (fig. 76)—a set of red-painted double doors in an arched stone gateway—one passes through a dense bamboo grove along the route to the main building, situated beside a shallow pond surrounded by banana and pine trees (Aoyama 1986, 393–394; Kateigaho 1982, 93–96).

The spirit of sencha as practiced by these antiquarians and scholars of eccentric proclivities was evocatively and sympathetically evoked by the novelist Natsume Sōseki (1867–1916) in his book *The Three-Cornered World* (J: *Kusa makura*), published in 1906. Sōseki's artist-protagonist sought refuge in the countryside, where he was invited to attend a tea ceremony at the home of a retired gentleman. He described his apprehension at attending the gathering:

76. MAIN GATE TO THE CHŌKŌEN (GARDEN OF FISHING AND CULTIVATION)
Estate of Tokutomu Sohō, constructed ca. 1920–1930. Photo: courtesy Issa-an, Osaka.

> *When I heard the word "tea," my enthusiasm waned a little. There is nobody as ostentatious , or as persuaded of his own refinement of taste as the man who performs the tea-ceremony… Those who partake in the tea ceremony are really only tradesmen, merchants and the like who have not the first idea of what the words "artistic taste" mean* (Natsume 1968, 68).

However, the tea ceremony turned out to be sencha, which the scholar's daughter described as "tea without any ceremony," certainly a reference to bunjincha, as it was described as an opportunity for the old man to "show off his nick-nacks" (Natsume 1968, 69, 115–119). Sōseki used his commentary on the sencha tea ceremony to compare the merits of Chinese, Japanese, and Western aesthetics for his readers, noting that

> *instead of a cushion, there was a beautiful rug spread there, which was obviously Chinese… [Its] charm lay in its lack of frivolous detail… This lack is not only noticeable in Chinese carpets, but in all their furniture and ornaments. Looking at them, you cannot fail to realise that they were created by a stolid, patient people. What makes these objects so superlative is their ability to absorb one's interest utterly and completely. Japan produces her works of art with the attitude of a pickpocket, while in the West everything must be on a grand scale, and inseparable from the material world* (Natsume 1968, 110–111).

Sōseki also described in detail the tiny teapots and cups by Mokubei that the host used for the occasion, and eloquently praised the exquisite taste of gyokuro tea:

> *The average person talks of "drinking" tea, but this is a mistake. Once you have felt a little of the pure liquid spread slowly over your tongue, there is scarcely any need to swallow it. It is merely a question of letting the fragrance penetrate from your throat right down to your stomach. On no account should it be swilled round the mouth and over the teeth, for this is extremely coarse.*

> *"Gyokuro" tea escapes the insipidness of pure water and yet is not so thick as to require any tiring jaw action. It is a wonderful beverage. Some complain that if they drink tea they cannot sleep, but to them I would say that it is better to go without sleep than without tea* (Natsume 1968, 113).

Sōseki has here invoked a world that at the time of his writing was rapidly disappearing. Although Tessai continued to promote sencha until his death in 1924, and a few other prominent men of letters (for example, Tokutomi Sohō and Asakura Fumio) constructed sencha rooms in the early Shōwa period, this erudite lifestyle was becoming more of an aberration than a standard. By the early twentieth century, interest in scholarship on classical Chinese arts, including the study of kanbun and the appreciation of Japanese literati painting, had declined owing to the displacement of Chinese aesthetics and scholarship by ideas from the West, with which they were largely incompatible (Keene 1985, 85; Guth 2006).

Concurrent with these cultural transformations, sencha practitioners were beginning to place greater emphasis on the history of the custom in their own country than on its indebtedness to China. Apart from the continued reverence of Baisaō, increased respect for Kimura Kenkadō became particularly strong. Leadership of this new direction came not from the bunjin, but from the professional sencha schools, particularly Kagetsuan of Osaka, which possessed many sencha utensils that both Baisaō and Kenkadō had owned.

In 1901, on the one-hundredth anniversary of Kenkadō's death, Kagetsuan-school tea masters and other admirers in Osaka held a commemorative gathering featuring displays of his writings, paintings, books, and other personal possessions. A record of this event was published, the *Illustrated Catalogue of Old Man Kenka's Posthumous Works (Kenka iboku tenran zuroku)*. Its text was one of the earliest sencha publications to be typeset, but the book also included woodblock-printed illustrations. On the one-hundred fifteenth anniversary of Kenkadō's death in 1916, the group held another memorial exhibition, also accompanied by an exhibition catalogue, *Illustrated Catalogue of the Exhibition of Posthumous Works by Kenkadō (Kenkadō ibokuhinten shuppin zuroku)*. This was a public event at the most up-to-date of venues for art exhibitions, Osaka's preeminent department store, Takashimaya, which was the first in the country to contain a gallery for displaying art (it had opened in 1911). These two publications marked the beginning of a new era for sencha, dominated by the institutions that carried its traditions into the twentieth century.

The Modern Institutionalization of Sencha

Throughout the Meiji and early Shōwa periods, Kagetsuan, with a familial succession that remained unbroken from the time of its founder, continued in its leadership role among sencha devotees. Issō (1845–1922), the long-lived third-generation iemoto, was largely responsible for the school's transition into a modern institution. He helped secure its status by involvement with public sencha gatherings, like those to commemorate Kenkadō, which illuminated its links to venerable sencha masters of the past. As iemoto from around 1867 to his death, Issō completely devoted himself to the propagation of sencha. Upon his death, Issō's eldest son, Tanaka Futani (1874–1939), became the fourth iemoto of Kagetsuan. He has been followed by his son Tanaka Seiha

(1904–1979) and grandson Tanaka Akihito (born 1957), the present and sixth-generation head of the school.

The Kagetsuan school's influence remained strong for many reasons, including the exalted lineage of its iemoto, whose family possessed a historically important sencha utensil and painting collection, and the deep respect accorded the Tanaka family for their knowledge of sencha etiquette. In 1877 the school's prestige was validated and enhanced when Isso and his father, Tokuo, were invited to serve sencha to the Meiji emperor. This took place during festivities at the Osaka Prefectural Government office to mark the opening of railroad service between Kyoto and Osaka. For this occasion Isso donned formal Western attire, a swallow-tailed coat (Tanaka 1973, 322–323).

Under Isso, a well-devised training system for students was established at Kagetsuan. They were taught in specially designed sencha tearooms that Isso had constructed at his family home in Uemachi, Osaka. Datable to the late Meiji period (late nineteenth to early twentieth centuries), this two-story tearoom complex remains today among the best examples of Japanese sukiya shoin-style tearooms designed with interior features in sencha taste.

The first floor comprises a four-mat entryway (*genkan*), two tearooms, one six and the other four and one-half mats, and a utensil storage and preparation room (mizuya). The second floor consists of two adjacent rooms of six and eight mats that can be opened to create a large open space in the manner of an elegant literati salon. Though the rooms appear at first glance quite similar to chanoyu tearooms, with tatami mats and plain wood surfaces, they include many of the features closely identified with a sencha aesthetic: tokonoma alcoves with boards flush with the tatami flooring and a conspicuous absence of a crawl door for the entrance of guests, obligatory in chanoyu tearooms. The smaller of the two tearooms also has more the appearance of a scholar's study than a tearoom, with its built-in writing desk suitable for display of bunbōgu and books (fig. 77). The room also contains subtle Chinese design features, a small, round shoji-covered window embellished with Chinese-style bamboo latticework and a hanging Chinese bamboo shelf for display of scholars' objects, whose original function was as a backpack frame for itinerant Chinese peddlers and priests.[8]

Kagetsuan-school sencha was also promoted through influential books, which can be considered among the earliest examples of modern sencha manuals. These manuals were easily distinguished from earlier Meiji-period records of sencha gatherings and exhibitions of sencha-related antiquities as they discussed the functions of utensils in specific temae, rather than focusing on their intrinsic aesthetic or historical qualities. The first such modern guide to Kagetsuan-school sencha was the 1917 *Illustrated Book of Rules for the Pure Enjoyment of Sencha According to Methods of the Kagetsuan School (Kagetsuanryu hōshiki zufu sencha seiganki)*, published in the traditional bag-binding (*fukuro toji*) format. Authored by Sakata Keizō (Shūken), who ultimately left Kagetsuan to found his own school (Kagetsuan Shūkenryū), it was produced and distributed by an art dealer, Mizutani Seisaburō. It featured paintings from Kagetsuan's collection (portraits of Lu Yu, Baisaō, Ōbaku Monchū, and Tanaka Kakuō) with detailed biographies of the individuals pictured. It also contained information on Kagetsu-an-school philosophy and methods, a glossary of names for tea utensils, and photographs of utensils arranged in kazari according to temae taught at the school.

77. SENCHA TEAROOM AT THE KAGETSUAN TEA SCHOOL
Constructed late nineteenth-early twentieth centuries, Osaka. Photo: Okamoto Shigeo.

In 1927 Sakata authored a more detailed how-to guide for Kagetsuan-school temae, the *Popular Methods of Preparation for Sencha (Tsūzoku sencha hōshiki)*. This was one of the most important publications on sencha etiquette of the early Shōwa period, as it provided detailed instructions on every step of the preparation and serving process for aspiring students. The educational level of its target audience was evidently rather low, for nearly all Chinese characters (*kanji*) were accompanied by phonetic pronunciation guides (*furigana*). With this publication, the transmission of sencha protocol moved from the realm of secret teachings handed down from master to disciple, to rules of conduct accessible to a general public.

Meanwhile the Ogawa school continued to flourish in Kyoto. Like Kagetsuan, the Ogawa lineage became formalized with professionalization of an iemoto under Kashin's son, the second-generation family head, Ogawa Tamemi (Kiraku; 1820–1892). The lineage continued with the third-generation head, Ogawa Hisataka (Kairaku; 1854–1894), son of Tamemi. After Hisataka's untimely death, his younger brother, Ogawa Jijirō (Katei Kōraku; 1864–1937), became iemoto. During Jijirō's early years as iemoto, sencha had gone out of fashion among the courtiers who had been the Ogawa school's primary patrons, and he was obliged to pursue outside employment. He took a job in Nagasaki as a bureaucrat in the Ministry of International Trade and Industry.

While Jijirō was away from Kyoto during the 1920s and 1930s, Reizei Tamenori, descendant of a courtier family who had long supported the Ogawa school, served as substitute iemoto. He assisted in popularizing Ogawa-school sencha among a broader audience by redefining its values and rituals in terms relevant to the lives of ordinary people (Ogawa 1982, 28). The effort apparently succeeded, for when Ogawa Jijirō finally returned to Kyoto, local newspapers gave him a banner headline.[9] Jijirō's successor as iemoto was his daughter, Ogawa Shioko (1899–1972), whose formal title was Ogawa Kōraku V.

Even outside Japan's major urban centers, where the Kagetsuan and Ogawa schools were most active, by the early twentieth century sencha had become a familiar custom in most cities and towns. Many of the practitioners in provincial communities devised their own methods for sencha's preparation, which they shared with friends and disciples in small coteries. Out of these groups grew autonomous ryū (schools), which bore only perfunctory relationships to the well-established sencha schools of Kyoto, Osaka, and Tokyo. About fifty distinct sencha schools may have already existed by the beginning of the Shōwa period, and some of their leaders began publishing manuals on sencha preparation from the first decade of the twentieth century.[10]

By the late 1920s new attitudes toward preservation of Japan's cultural achievements encouraged a reassessment of sencha and hastened its emergence as a cultural institution that in ways paralleled similar developments in chanoyu. The person most directly responsible for this transformation was Fukuyama Chōgan (Gyōan; 1873–1946), an abbot of the Manpukuji sub-temple of Hōrinin who was active in temple governance. Fukuyama sought to promote sencha as a unified tradition through emphasis on its early association with Ōbaku monks. Focusing especially on the preeminence of the Ōbaku monk Baisaō, who was responsible for sencha's initial popularization, he conducted the first systematic research on Baisaō, which he subsequently published in 1933 (Fukuyama 1933). This text included reprints of all of Baisaō's major writings and a detailed chronology of Baisaō's life (Baisaō nenpu), which he had first published in 1928. Fukuyama's study, though not without errors, remains an invaluable source of information today.

To link Baisaō more closely with Ōbaku, Fukuyama encouraged Manpukuji to establish the Baisadō (alternately pronounced "Maisadō"), a memorial hall for holding commemorative services to Baisaō, and to construct the Yūseiken (house with a voice), a sencha teahouse, in 1928, open to all sencha devotees. Although the pivotal roles of Ōbaku monks—Ingen, Baisaō, and Monchū—had been acknowledged by premodern writers of sencha texts, the close identification of the Ōbaku religious institution with the formalized sencha tea ceremony must be considered a modern phenomenon. No actual sencha ritual existed in Ingen's time, and it was common knowledge that both Baisaō and Monchū had left the clergy in order to devote themselves to sencha's propagation. Nevertheless, by closely allying Manpukuji with sencha, Fukuyama effectively broadened the patronage of his temple and boosted its status in ways similar to the benefits Rinzai Zen temples derived from associations with schools of chanoyu.

While Fukuyama was promoting this reappraisal of Baisaō, other scholars were evaluating the contribution of the first upholders of his legacy—the late Tokugawa bunjin—to the history of the sencha tradition. Yukawa Gen'yō published his *Biographies of Elegant People of the Early Modern Era (Kinsei gajinden)* in 1930, which contained some one hundred and twenty biographical sketches of Tokugawa bunjin who excelled at painting and calligraphy. Although the works of some of the more prominent of these artists had been appreciated in sencha circles since the early Meiji period, the all-inclusive nature of his book was intended by the author as a guide for selection of artworks that were suitable for display at sencha gatherings. The author focused exclusively on Japanese literati artists, a reversal of the preferences of earlier bunjin themselves.

A much smaller group of Japanese literati artists who had been directly involved with bunjincha was featured in the 1943 book *The Way of Sencha (Senchadō)* by Nakajima Yōsuke.[11] In addition to providing a history of sencha in China and Japan and explaining the main points of Ueda Akinari's *Miscellaneous Comments on the Way of Pure Elegance*, the author included a short chapter on the relationship of sencha and bunjin values, with biographies of prominent bunjincha literati painters, including Chikuden, San'yō, and Baiitsu. He concluded with information on heirs to this tradition in the Meiji period who were responsible for popularizing sencha in his hometown of Fukui, particularly Yamamoto Chikuun (1820–1888), a literati painter and seal carver who was in his day a respected connoisseur of Chinese paintings and sencha utensils.[12]

Nakajima, writing in the midst of World War II, indicated in the preface to his book that he wrote about sencha to arouse nationalistic sentiments in his readers during the difficult wartime era. To him, the elegant simplicity of sencha's moralistic values, derived from the Chinese literati, inspired loyalist convictions in the bunjin sencha devotees whom he admired as nationalist heroes of the past. With this statement, Nakajima both mythologized the bunjin and their beliefs as spiritual progenitors of modern sencha, and put sencha-related values forward as a suitable model for instilling allegiance in Japan's military cause. The irony of enlisting Chinese belief systems in the war against China is typical of Japan's imperialist-period contradictions.

In the immediate postwar era, as revival of interest in traditional Japanese arts emerged, leaders of sencha schools restructured their organizations for greater popular appeal. Still leading the way was Kagetsuan, the practices of which were described in the highly detailed *Rules of Etiquette for Sencha (Sencha temae)* by Saeki Futoshi in 1949. Like Sakata Keizō's 1927 text upon which it was modeled, it placed less emphasis on explanation of the historical tradition of sencha and its early practitioners, and more on providing detailed information about rules of conduct for preparing tea. This actually may have been the first book to utilize the term "temae" in its title, a term more closely associated with etiquette for chanoyu. Furthermore, the book was published as the sole volume devoted to sencha in a general series, *Books on the Tea Ceremony (Chadō bunko)*, on chanoyu. Its inclusion in this series reinforced sencha's legitimate but subservient position within the world of tea in Japan dominated by chanoyu.

Shortly thereafter, in 1951, seven sencha-school iemoto collaborated to host public tea gatherings at famous Kyoto scenic locales: in spring these took place at Nijo Castle, in summer at Gion's Yasaka shrine, and in autumn at the Heian shrine (Shufunotomosha 1981, 415). In 1956 various sencha-school iemoto from throughout Japan convened at Manpukuji. The result of their meeting was the formation of the National Japanese Sencha Association (Zen Nihon Senchadō Renmeikai), the establishment of which stimulated further revival of interest in sencha. Under this group's influence, publications on sencha increased in both number and quality. The earliest, and to this date still the best, modern critical commentary on primary textual materials relating to sencha was published first in 1965 (and reprinted in 1983) by Hasegawa Shōshōkyo (1905–1989), a Kagetsuan-school adept (Hasegawa 1965).

Sencha's status as an officially sanctioned traditional Japanese art was finally achieved in 1970, when sencha tea ceremony demonstrations took place as part of the International Exposition in Osaka that year; perhaps sencha's association with Osaka's historic traditions influenced its inclusion. Japan's resumption of full diplomatic relations with China in 1972 may have contributed to its continued growth during the 1970s. From that decade come numerous volumes devoted to sencha, which both illustrated and explained in detail the temae of assorted individual schools and provided historical accounts of the tradition in general. These books were mostly authored by individuals associated with various sencha schools, and the main audience continued to be an expanding roster of pupils.

In the 1980s the National Japanese Sencha Association intensified its efforts to popularize sencha. Officially incorporated in 1966, it has been situated since its inception at Manpukuji, with the present offices and meeting rooms dating to a 1985 expansion of the association's original home in the Yūseiken. The association continues to serve as an umbrella organization for member sencha schools, though not all of the nearly one hundred in existence belong.[13] The Kagetsuan and Ogawa schools, for example, initially participated but later dropped out, along with several of their independent offshoots.

According to the original bylaws of 1966, there are five categories of membership in the National Japanese Sencha Association. The highest category is the regular member (*seikaiin*), comprised of sencha iemoto. As of 1994 there were forty such members, each of whom paid annual dues of ¥30,000 (in 1994, roughly $300). The second highest level is the councilor member (*sanjikaiin*), nominated by the regular members and comprised of senior teachers of the various schools. In 1994 there were 4,781 such members who paid annual dues of ¥2,000 each. Following this category is the ordinary member (*futsūkaiin*), lower-ranking sencha instructors, again nominated for membership by the regular members. Their individual annual fee in 1994 was a mere ¥500 (about $5). An additional category of membership is the supporting member (*sandōkaiin*), consisting of individuals who endorse the purpose of the organization—crafts makers, tea suppliers, and the like—who, in 1994 paid an annual membership fee of ¥20,000 each. The last category of membership is the honorary member (*meiyōkaiin*), individuals who have performed some meritorious service on behalf of the organization. They are chosen by a resolution of the general assembly.

The association sponsors many activities, including a large sencha gathering that has been held annually each May at Manpukuji since 1955. The event is open to all, who, for a fee, can participate in sencha ceremonies hosted by selected iemoto of member groups (see frontispiece). In this festival-like atmosphere, the approximately four thousand visitors admire antique sencha utensils and related artifacts owned by members; view exhibitions of Ōbaku arts and contemporary sencha crafts; and purchase utensils, tea, and books from vendors. The association also hosts more intimate sencha ceremonies as part of memorial services for Baisaō at the Baisadō on the sixteenth day of each month; invites all visitors to Manpukuji to participate in sencha ceremonies every Sunday; produces a monthly magazine for members; sponsors occasional leisure activities such as cruises; and, since 1988, has participated in demonstrations of sencha at tea organizations in the Peoples' Republic of China. Sencha, as practiced by the schools affiliated with this group, varies widely in form and content.

While the Manpukuji association spearheads many of the efforts to popularize the sencha tea ceremony, the two largest and oldest independent sencha schools, Kagetsuan and Ogawa, remain active as well. Though their headquarters are located in Osaka and Kyoto respectively, they both maintain branches in various cities throughout Japan, where their temae is taught by certified instructors (Ogawa 1982, 142–143). In contrast, most National Japanese Sencha Association member schools are limited only to their home city.

The Ogawa school's sixth-generation iemoto (from 1971 to 2017) was Ogawa Kōraku (Narabayashi Tadao; born 1940), nephew of the previous iemoto, Shioko. He is a prolific writer of scholarly and popular texts about sencha's historical development and aesthetics. Under his direction, for example, the school began publishing a scholarly journal, *Ogawa-ryū* sencha (Ogawa-school sencha) in 1973. Since 2017, the Ogawa school headmaster is now Ogawa Kōraku VII (born 1971), the eldest son of Ogawa Kōraku VI. Respect accorded the Kagetsuan school comes from its lengthy, unbroken lineage and the impeccable provenance of its artistic treasures, which are brought out on special occasions for students' inspection and included in major art exhibitions. Kagetsuan is also the only sencha school to host sencha ceremonies annually as part of Kenninji's Yotsugashira festivities.

Utensils for Sencha in Modern Japan

Makers of fine crafts for serving sencha and furnishing its tearooms continue to flourish, perpetuating lineages and aesthetic standards that date from sencha's apogee in the late Tokugawa and early Meiji periods. From the early twentieth century, however, sencha utensils have been overshadowed in the public eye by products for chanoyu and Western-influenced crafts, both sculptural and functional. Nevertheless, close inspection of sencha crafts reveals a richness and variety that mirror the diversity of the tea's proponents. In characteristic Japanese fashion, the best of the studio artisans producing sencha crafts are highly skilled technicians who imbue their products with a sense of their personal artistic spirit through innovations in technique and creative adaptations of traditional forms and designs.

The most essential sencha utensil is the teapot; its infinite array of forms and styles reveals the genius of Japanese craftspeople for innovative designs within set parameters (Nitta 1990; Morse 1901). During the Meiji period, as steeped leaf tea came to be widely consumed, teapots were fabricated at virtually all Japanese kilns. Among these, potters at the Kyoto, Tokoname, and Banko kilns produced the most technically refined, innovative, and popular styles for teapots of their day.

For many Kyoto potters, sencha waned in importance as opportunities increased for production of tablewares for sale abroad and for participation in international expositions. One notable exception was the potter Miura Chikusen I (1854–1915), who continued to specialize in ceramics for sencha closely modeled after earlier Kyoto potters' works: celadons, kinrande, sometsuke, shonzui, overglaze enamel, and Swatow. He learned these techniques from his teacher, Takahashi Dōhachi III (1811–1887), prior to establishing his own kiln in 1883. Chikusen was also a member of Kyoto's community of Sinophile scholars; he studied painting with Tanomura Chokunyū and consorted with Tomioka Tessai. His patrons came from this group, as well as from sencha practitioners associated with established old sencha schools such as Kagetsuan. A sencha tea set with elegantly painted literati-style underglaze blue designs of bamboo, plum blossoms, rocks, and kanshi poetry (fig. 78) testifies to Chikusen's scholarly inclinations.

Chikusen is distinguished as the founder of two separate lineages of pupils, both of which have successfully preserved the orthodox Kyoto styles for sencha wares into the present age and contributed to new directions in porcelain artistry in Japan. The first includes eldest family sons Miura Chikusen II (1882–1920), Miura Chikusen IV (1911–1976), and Miura Chikusen V (born 1934). The second lineage was established

78. SENCHA TEA SET WITH DESIGN OF BAMBOO, PLUM, ROCKS, AND POEMS
Miura Chikusen I (1854–1915), ten cups, water cooler, and a teapot. Porcelain with decoration in underglaze blue. Cups h: 4.7 cm; teapot h: 7.5 cm; water cooler h: 6.3 cm. Iruma City Museum.

by Miura Chikusen III (1900–1990), third son of Chikusen I. He took the title Chikusen III in 1921, but changed his name to Chikken in 1934, when the first son of Chikusen II became the family head as Chikusen IV. Chikken's expertise in porcelain was recognized by the Japanese government in 1955, when he was designated a Living National Treasure (*Ningen kokuhō*). One of his prominent pupils was Kawase Chikuō (also known as Chikushun I; 1894–1983), who initiated the making of porcelains in Japan with Ming-style *doucai* (competing colors) glazing, overglaze designs outlined with underglaze blue. Chikuō's son, Chikushun II (born 1923), carries on the family's trademark overglaze enamel and underglaze blue styles today. Chikushun II's son, Kawase Shinobu (born 1950), whose fame has eclipsed that of his father, has moved in another direction as a specialist in porcelains with celadon glazes (Baekeland and Moes 1993, 133–134, 139–140; Faulkner 1995, 42).

As the popularity of Chinese Yixing ware escalated in the late Tokugawa and early Meiji periods, regional potters began trying to emulate its appearance in response to requests from local clientele. It remained difficult to reproduce these unglazed teapots, which were dependent upon the quality of unknown clays and unfamiliar Chinese forming techniques. One place with a suitable brown and red iron-rich clay was Tokoname in Aichi prefecture, where the potter Akai Tōzen II (1796–1858) and others began to experiment with Yixing-style wares by the mid-1840s (Yamada 1986).

As the tea brewed in these teapots was deemed to have a better flavor, production at Tokoname thrived. From 1854 Tokoname potters began attempting to reproduce the smooth-burnished surface texture of Chinese Yixing wares. They finally succeeded in 1878 with the assistance of an immigrant Chinese literatus from Anhui, Jin Shiheng (J: Kin Shiko) (Tokoname 1986). He also taught potters the Chinese slab-formed beating method (*panpan sei*), in which a slab-built tube was beaten into desired shapes. Today though this difficult technique has largely been abandoned in favor of hand-built, wheel-thrown, and molded forming production methods. Under Jin's tutelage, specialized decorators started engraving on leather-hard pots the fine-lined calligraphy and pictorial motifs that have remained hallmarks of Tokoname pottery into the present.

The Tokoname potter credited with initiating production of wares with this burnished finish was Sugie Jumon (1828–1897). One of his finest creations is a chrysanthemum-shaped teapot with an intricately fashioned petal-shaped lid that fits precisely into corresponding niches in the lip of the pot (fig. 79). Unlike later Tokoname wares formed on a wheel, Jumon made this teapot utilizing the more arduous Chinese slab-formed technique. By the mid-Meiji period, burnished teapots and matching sets of cups in this style were being mass-produced at numerous Tokoname factories, many of which are still active today. Finer quality limited production wares also continued in production for discerning clients by studio potters descended from Jumon and his most famous disciple, Yamada Jōzan I (1868–1942).[14]

Not far from Tokoname, another distinctive style of teapot for sencha began to be produced by Banko ware potters in the late Tokugawa period. A ware identified as Kō-Banko (old Banko) had first been made in Kuwana, Mie prefecture (Ise province), by a wealthy merchant, Numanami Rōzan (1718–1777), who may have studied with Ogata Kenzan. Rōzan specialized in stoneware chanoyu utensils with overglaze enamels in the styles of Ninsei and Kenzan, utilizing clay and glazing chemicals possibly imported from China (Morse 1901, 96–97).

After Rōzan's death, pupils continued to manufacture Banko in nearby communities. Meanwhile its production languished in Kuwana until 1831, when a local antique dealer, Mori Yūsetsu (1801–1882), somehow obtained Rōzan's old formulas for clay and glazes and revived the ware under sponsorship of the Matsudaira daimyo who ruled the region. Known as Yūsetsu Banko, the kiln mainly produced sencha teapots. Throughout the late Tokugawa and early Meiji periods, numerous potters in the region began to manufacture teapots resembling Yūsetsu's, and the center of production of Banko wares shifted to the town of Yokkaichi, where they are still produced today.

Like Tokoname ware, Banko emulated Yixing stonewares, in this case a special type that featured overglaze enamel designs on bare clay. Yet the Yūsetsu and Yokkaichi Banko potters were not mere imitators but creative synthesizers of various styles. They drew inspiration from

79. CHRYSANTHEMUM-SHAPED TEAPOT
Sugie Jumon (1828–1897). Tojoname ware; unglazed burnished red stoneware. H: 7 cm. Tokoname City Folk Museum.

the delicate overglaze floral designs of Kyoto wares and devised original adaptations of literati motifs, sometimes decorating the surfaces of their pots with random impressions of seals. Banko ware was distinguished by its paper-thin white stoneware clay bodies modeled by hand, moldmade, or wheel thrown. Handles were patterned with elegant pierced designs (herame) terminating in dangling rings, and lids were adorned with knobs sculpted in the shape of jewels or flowers.

Yokkaichi's factories employed many people left impoverished and homeless by the natural disasters and political turmoil of the times. As early as 1859, Banko ware had become such a thriving industry that its products were sold abroad, with the finest of the pieces displayed at major international expositions in Europe and the United States (Morse 1901, 97; Schaap 1987, 95). The majority of domestic buyers for Banko ware were the throngs of travelers who passed through the towns where it was made along the Tōkaidō road between Kyoto and Tokyo. These patrons particularly enjoyed teapots exhibiting whimsical designs in unusual, often zoomorphic shapes with three-dimensional surface ornamentation, a style that Banko potters created in the third quarter of the nineteenth century. A group of Banko wares excavated from a Tokyo commoners' neighborhood reveals the wide range of popular Banko ware teapots produced for the mass market (fig. 80). Although they were mass produced, no two pieces appear to be identical. They date from the mid-Meiji period (1870s-1880s), the era of production of the best quality Banko wares, prior to 1889, when trains supplanted overland traffic and customers dwindled (Mizutani 1986; Mitsuoka 1981, 6: 76, 82–83, 129–133).

Other than ceramics, the most significant quantities of sencha utensils have been made by craftspeople specializing in metallurgy, working in bronze, pewter, silver, and even gold to create kettles, leaf tea containers, flower vases, and saucers for teacups. Unlike other pre-modern metal artisans, who specialized in traditional forms that were nearing obsolescence in the beginning of the Meiji period—mirrors, sword fittings, and cast bronze Buddhist sculptures—their patronage increased during this era in response to sencha's popularity. They took as models imported examples of similar objects from China: pewter leaf tea containers and saucers, ancient bronzes, and finely wrought silver kettles. Of these objects, only Chinese bronzes had a long history of appreciation in Japan among chanoyu and ikebana enthusiasts for whom artisans had been copying Yuan and Ming bronzes since the Muromachi period. Although bronzes routinely were created by casting (chukin), most of the sencha utensils made of other metals featured textures and designs created by meticulous hammering (tankin) and chasing (chokin) techniques.

80. GROUP OF BANKO WARE TEAPOTS
Excavated in a commoners' neighborhood at the Mukogaoka High School site, Bunkyō-ku, Tokyo, from the mid-late nineteenth century. Stoneware with assorted glazes. H: 9 cm (sight). Tokyo Municipal Government. Photo: P. Graham.

The first metalsmith to fashion metal kettles especially designed to heat water for sencha (ginbin) was Kata Ryūmon (1780–1841), better known by his studio names of Yasuhei or Ryūmondō. Not only was he a close friend of both Rai San'yō and Aoki Mokubei, he also became a disciple of Mokubei in pottery. Mokubei in turn had learned techniques for casting coins in his youth from Ryūmon's father, Ryūmondō I (1731–1798) (Mitsuoka 1990, 93). Ryūmon's official successor, Kata Yasunosuke (1796–1850), was also patronized by the literati crowd; he is known to have made bronze teapots and scholars' implements for Kumagai Naotaka of the Kyūkyodō. Another of the students in Ryūmon's atelier, Hata Zōroku (1823–1890), became the most famous metalworker of the Meiji period, noted for his studious analysis and replication of ancient Chinese bronzes (Museum of the Imperial Collections 1995, pls. 29, 30). Among his more opulent commissions for sencha use was a kettle dated to 1876, cast in solid gold and topped with two intertwined jade rings, with relief and incised taotie (mythic Chinese animal form) designs on the lid and shoulder reminiscent of ancient Chinese bronzes (fig. 81). His style, representative of the highest quality and character of sencha metalcrafts, has been perpetuated by followers and descendants, including Hata Zōroku IV (1898–1984). (Shufunotomosha 1981, 285, 358).

The tea scoop is another essential sencha utensil that has inspired the creativity of skilled studio artisans from the Meiji period to the present. It was originally made from a lengthwise section of bamboo in the shape of Chinese scholars' wrist rests, though smaller in proportion. Traditional bamboo tea scoops featured convex exteriors carved or incised with calligraphic inscriptions in Chinese, or designs of landscapes, figures, or plants and animals. These were often the work of seal carvers and sculptors such as Kanō Tessai (1845–1925), who created an image of Baisaō for Manpukuji's Baisadō (Shufunotomosha 1981, 427–428; Parker 1984), or netsuke carvers who were skilled at sculpting in miniature. During the late Meiji and Taishō periods, shapes of tea scoops became more elaborate and, as with netsuke, artisans devised them from many other materials, including wood, bone, silver, lacquer, and porcelain (Art Gallery of Greater Victoria 1981). Sometimes they were carved in fanciful shapes imitating Chinese zithers (qin), animals, or leaves, such as a stained ivory tea scoop in the shape of lotus leaf by one of the most respected netsuke carvers, Masatsugu Kaigyokusai (ca. 1813–1892) (fig. 82).

Yet another important category of crafts associated with sencha is

81. KETTLE—1876
Hata Zōroku (1823–1890). Gold with two intertwined jade rings on lid. H: 14.5 cm. Private collection, Japan. Photo: courtesy Yanagi Takashi.

woven bamboo basketry. Since sencha tea gatherings often featured flower arrangements within the tokonoma of the tearoom, as well as in separate areas devoted to displays of flowers and bonsai, their containers were in great demand. Symmetrical and finely woven Chinese baskets were preferred initially. Earlier, these had been appreciated by chanoyu masters such as Kobori Enshū (Fujioka 1973, fig. 144; Nakamura M. 1986, pls. 46, 48–51, 54–56, 58). Gradually, by the beginning of the Meiji period, native basketmakers began incorporating Chinese knotting techniques into original designs in response to requests from patrons.

Baskets in Chinese styles for sencha became a specialty of artisans who resided in Sakai, south of Osaka. Prior to the shogun Toyotomi Hideyoshi's rise to power in 1579, Sakai was actually a larger, more cosmopolitan city than Osaka. It had a long and rich history beginning in

82. SENCHA TEA SCOOP IN THE SHAPE OF A LOTUS LEAF
Masatsugu Kaigyokusai (ca. 1813–1892). Stained ivory. 16.1 cm. Saint Louis Art Museum, Museum Shop Fund.

the fifth century with the placement of numerous large burial mounds (*kofun*) in its vicinity. By the Muromachi period, Sakai had become Japan's largest autonomous city, a haven from fighting elsewhere, populated by merchants, traders, and intellectuals. Until the establishment of Nagasaki as the sole international port in the early seventeenth century, Sakai served as the main embarkation point for foreign trade missions. As a result, a thriving international community developed there, which included immigrants knowledgeable in foreign handicraft techniques, such as basketmaking, who passed down their skills to naturalized descendants.

The Chinese-style baskets made in Sakai are characterized by precision, detail, and symmetry. They belong to the most formal and conservative shin style of basket design that was codified in the early Shōwa period (Faulkner 1995, 91–93). Among the first basketmakers to work in this style was Hayakawa Shokosai I (1815–1897), who was also one the earliest to sign his work in emulation of similar practices by studio potters (Hasebe 1985, 19; McCallum 1988, 27–30). Another important basketmaker working in this tradition was Tanabe Chikuunsai I (1877–1937), who initiated a distinctive style inspired by hanging baskets he saw in paintings by the literati painter Yanagisawa Kien (Moroyama 1989).

Contemporaneous with Chikuunsai was Maeda Chikubōsai I (ca. 1872–1950), whose work is representative of the finest Chinese-style baskets these studio artists created. Chikubōsai I began studying bamboo weaving when he was fourteen, establishing his own atelier at the young age of seventeen. In 1922 he became famous after the British crown prince visited his studio and admired his work. A flower container dated 1940 is an impressive example of his oeuvre (fig. 83). Typical of his personal style, it combines fine weaving with boldly placed bamboo root handles. Chikubōsai also favored shapes that were allusions to objects made of other materials; in this case, his form was inspired by the shape of a boat. His son, Chikubōsai II (1917–2003), is considered one of the foremost basketmakers of his generation, though favoring a more modern interpretation of the traditional style (Hasebe 1985, 42).

Beginning around the time of World War II, changes to the organizational hierarchy of traditional craft industries deeply affected the public's perception of the leading artisans who created studio crafts. Wartime austerity programs limited the output of studio artisans, as their products were deemed luxury goods. To assuage fears that

83. FLOWER BASKET IN THE FORM OF A BOAT (FUNAGATA MORIHANA-KAGO)—1940
Maeda Chikubōsai I (ca. 1872-1950). Woven bamboo with bamboo rhizome handle. 26.7 x 26.7 x 54.5 cm. Saint Louis Art Museum, William K. Bixby Trust for Asian Art.

techniques and traditions were being lost, the government passed a Cultural Properties Protection Act in 1950 to help sustain high technical skill among artisans working at traditional crafts and to encourage public patronage. The accomplishments of selected craftspeople were subsequently exhibited and offered for sale in a newly instituted *Traditional Crafts Exhibition (Dentō Kōgeiten)*, held at Tokyo's Mitsukoshi Department Store annually since 1954, the same year the Japan Crafts Association (Nihon Kōgeikai) was formed. Artisans producing crafts for sencha were asked to join this group and other newly formed craft associations in order to reach patrons through officially sanctioned channels for disseminating crafts in contemporary Japan (Faulkner 1995, 11–15; Moeran 1982–1983).

While the finest craftspeople who continue to make accouterments for sencha show their creations in juried exhibitions sponsored by national craft associations, many are also affiliated with the National Japanese Sencha Crafts Association (Nihon Sencha Kōgei Kyōkai), established in 1987. Patronized by sencha participants and administered by the sencha association at Manpukuji, the group holds its major sales exhibition in conjunction with Manpukuji's annual sencha gathering, awarding prizes to outstanding works. This exhibit then circulates to selected cities at galleries in major department stores. Department stores also exhibit sencha crafts personally selected by tea masters of particular schools, who concurrently stage sencha demonstrations to promote the crafts and encourage interest in their schools. Like other craftspeople in contemporary Japan, the most prominent of the sencha utensil makers also hold one-person exhibitions in department store and private galleries.

Today, practitioners of the sencha tea ceremony form a thriving subculture within contemporary Japanese society, comprised of networks of antique dealers who specialize in sencha utensils and related literati arts, contemporary craftspeople, amateur and professional tea masters, tea manufacturers, confectioneries, scholars, and publishers. These groups play a major role in sustaining public interest in the arts of Tokugawa-period literati painting and calligraphy.

Conclusion

So completely has chanoyu come to dominate the world of tea in Japan that when people today think of a Japanese tea ceremony, they invariably think of chanoyu. Most, in Japan as well as the West, are unaware that an alternate tradition exists, or are only vaguely familiar with its history and practice. From the modern perspective, the notion that senchadō at one time surpassed chanoyu in popularity seems incredible. Chanoyu developed first, and it has been more successful in promoting its ideology and asserting its position as an essential Japanese art form. But sencha, which originated in opposition to chanoyu, and which has developed over time a complex relationship with the older tradition, has made significant contributions to Japanese culture and society.

When Baisaō first promulgated sencha, he stressed its spiritual ties to ancient Chinese sages as a means of protesting and coping with an intolerable political climate. Baisaō, celebrated for his untrammeled personality and unceremonious presentation of tea, became mythologized, admired rather than emulated, for his proclivities toward eccentricity could not be handed down from one generation to the next. Some would say that Baisaō's linkage of the drink with spirituality and self-cultivation became subsumed by the polluting and formalizing influences of chanoyu. Yet it is precisely these influences—the incorporation of chanoyu's emphasis on stylized etiquette and appreciation of utensils as treasured material possessions—that have enabled sencha to develop an identity of its own. The standardized procedures and objects for sencha are in large measure what have endeared it to its many followers and consequently allowed for its assimilation into Japanese culture. This assimilation is remarkable since initially, along with its role as a vehicle for achieving spiritual fulfillment, the drinking of sencha carried strong anti-establishment sociopolitical implications.

Sencha at once served as a symbol of rejection of both chanoyu and of the political status quo, and as an affirmation of deep respect for Chinese literati culture.

Despite this initial ideological rift, chanoyu exerted profound influence on sencha in numerous subtle and not-so-subtle ways. Unintentionally, the detractors of chanoyu who initiated the sencha tea ceremony created formalized alternate rituals that paralleled the forms they ostensibly sought to obliterate. Following similar tendencies in chanoyu circles, they venerated and copied Baisaō's utensils, for example. Chanoyu offered them models for organizing formalized schools and for creating standardized nomenclature of accouterments. Sencha also emulated chanoyu's many varieties of publications, which ranged from records of famous tea ceremonies and self-promoting histories to meticulous documents describing and illustrating intricate rules of etiquette.

What has continued to distinguish sencha from chanoyu, however, has been its clearly identifiable Sinicized canon of taste, defined in the appearance of its accessories and in the ambiance of its serving environments. Further, through veneration of the spirit of the sages of Chinese literati culture, sencha has successfully forged a distinct philosophical identity. Ultimately, the new canon of aesthetic taste and philosophical values identified with sencha incorporated and expanded upon, rather than rejected outright, ideas and forms associated with chanoyu. While their familiarity contributed to the ready acceptance of sencha among the Japanese populace, they also linked it irrevocably with chanoyu.

Although Chinese artifacts had been incorporated into chanoyu from its beginnings, the arts of China revered in sencha circles were not synonymous with those admired by chanoyu followers. They encompassed a broader range of Ming and Qing arts, especially those associated with the elite of Chinese society, such as literati painting and Yixing ware ceramics. Sencha, in its close association with the esteemed bunjin, has served as the main path by which Chinese literati ideals and artistic taste entered and moved to the forefront of the Japanese public's consciousness, though its followers often had conflicting motivations for their adoption. For some, particularly those who identified themselves as bunjin, the political agenda of Baisaō and his immediate followers remained valid, while for others sencha became a means of demonstrating proficiency in Chinese literati pastimes appreciated for their perceived moral and intellectual superiority. Thus, through sencha, appreciation for Chinese arts and Sinified-style arts produced in Japan became widely admired among the Japanese public.

The richness and diversity of sencha represent a startling expansion from its beginnings with Baisaō, who sought to introduce a philosophy along with a beverage to the populace of Kyoto. During the course of its evolution, sencha has both reflected and influenced broader cultural changes. The transformation from sencha as a simple beverage, to an emblem of the bunjin, to mass consumption accompanied by prescribed paraphernalia and set rules of conduct, and finally, a return to relative obscurity in the shadow of chanoyu, reveals much about the evolution of Japanese aesthetic taste, patterns of consumption, and the nation's complex and ever-changing relationship with China.

Ultimately, sencha arts and aesthetics reflect Chinese literati ideals filtered through the lenses of their Japanese practitioners' viewpoints and experiences. The embracing of sencha by followers from different backgrounds, holding a wide range of often conflicting ideologies, and the persistence of the tradition into contemporary culture reveal the Japanese society's success at metabolizing imported customs and integrating them into its cultural core. Furthermore, the proliferation of the relatively small schools of sencha that exist today reflects an important aspect of Japanese civilization, a predilection toward individuality and nonconformity within set parameters. Sencha is not a moribund ritual; rather, it has continued to mature and transform over time. In this it reflects a spirit that can be considered, at least in part, a legacy of its Chinese spiritual roots. Beyond its enduring popularity as a beverage, sencha has enriched the Japanese cultural landscape immeasurably with values and aesthetics that have inspired the creativity of Japanese writers, artists, and seekers of spiritual fulfillment for nearly three hundred years.

Notes

INTRODUCTION

1. On the meaning of these terms, see Cahill (1976, 9–12) and Yonezawa and Yoshizawa (1974, 129–141).

CHAPTER ONE

The Transmission of Chinese Tea Culture to Japan

1. Unless otherwise noted, information on the development of tea and tea utensils in Chinese history is derived from Chiu (1991) and Ayers (1991).
2. Translated into English by Francis Ross Carpenter in Lu (1974). For a concise summary of the text and biographical information on Lu Yu, see Sen (1977a).
3. Translation by Jonathan Chaves, in Addiss 1984, 120–121.
4. The latter edition of the book *Notes on Constructing Artificial Hills and Gardens (Tsukiyama niwa tsukuriden)*, 1859, illustrates a Japanese garden in Kamakura, the Gyokusentei, which was ostensibly modeled after a Tang dynasty garden where Lu Yu and Lu Tong enjoyed drinking tea. See Uehara (1989).
5. For excerpts from Eisai's treatise, see Tsunoda (1958, 237–240).
6. This scroll is known only through a number of Tokugawa-period copies. The original is attributed to Tosa Mitsunobu (1434–1525); see Mori T. (1985, 11–12, pl. 38).
7. For illustrations of the gongfucha brewing method, see Flagstaff House (1991, 359).
8. For a good discussion of wabicha and tea ceremony art in wabi taste, see Guth (1993, 54–60).
9. Ōba (1967, 688d) indicates that the *Eight Discourses on the Art of Living*, for example, had been imported to Japan in 1711. For an annotated list of selected Ming and Qing books on literati culture, with an emphasis on those relating to painting, see van Gulik (1958). For many of these, dates for Japanese reprints are listed.
10. Ōba (1967, 243b, 678c) has found two official records for the importation of the *Casual Expressions of Idle Feelings*, for 1711 and 1804.

CHAPTER TWO

The Reception of Chinese Material Culture in Tokugawa Japan

1. On clandestine importation of books, see Ōba (1980, 45–69) ; translated into English in Ōba (1995–1997). For a summary of Ōba's research in English, see Ōba (1988).
2. See Innes (1980, 328–332 and the table on p. 636) for documentation of the large numbers of Chinese ships that were refused entry into Nagasaki and thus became potential smugglers.
3. One catty is calculated as being equivalent to 1.325 pounds.
4. On the history of the school and its temple, see Backus (1974, 104–112, 123–125, 134–136). For an illustrated handscroll of a Confucian ceremony in 1729 and statues of Confucius and his disciples from the Owari Tokugawa family collection, see Shogun (1983, 179-180).
5. Few of these Confucian temples survive. One is discussed and illustrated in Mason (1993, 247–248).
6. Biographical information on Chu comes from Ching (1975) and Ching (1979).
7. On this book, see Ching (1975, 187). Tea is discussed in vol. 4.
8. Biographical information on Chen comes from Cort (1992, 145) and Addiss (1986, 13).
9. For illustrations of the temple, ceremonial utensils,

and a statue of Confucius used there, see Etchū and Ōto (1976, 109–111).

10. For sections of handscrolls of the Chinese compound attributed to Watanabe Shūseki and his followers owned by the Kobe Municipal Museum and the Nagasaki Prefectural Museum of Art, see Itabashi (1996, pls. 7-1–7-5). For excerpts from an eighteenth-century version in the British Museum, see Narazaki (1987, pls. 71, 72). For additional sections of the Nagasaki Prefectural Museum of Art scroll, see Plutschow (1983, 78–83). Kawahara Keiga (ca. 1786–1860), best known as a Nagasaki-school artist of Western subjects and styles, also painted similar scrolls of the Chinese quarter; see Etchū and Ōto (1976, 64).
11. Such a person, accompanied by an attendant carrying a parasol, is so labeled in the British Museum handscroll; see Narazaki (1987, pl. 73).
12. For a recently published facsimile edition of the *Saiyū ryodan*, see Shiba (1992). Chinese people and activities appear on pp. 112, 136.
13. Varieties of Chinese tea imported to Japan and utensils are recorded in Nakagawa C. (1966, 62: 3–7), where both sencha and oolong tea are mentioned, although the everyday tea preparation method described is for oolong tea prepared in individual lidded cups. Nakagawa C. (1966, 70: 66–68) illustrates a number of tea utensils, including a tea caddy; a charcoal brazier; a teapot, described as a tea bottle; a spouted pottery ewer for boiling medicine, which closely resembles later Japanese sencha pots for boiling water; and a lidded cup for steeping oolong tea, which according to Nakagawa C. (1966, 70: 96) was the only kind utilized by the Chinese.
14. Completed during the Bunka-Bunsei eras (1804–1830), this five-volume book was compiled by Tsuruta Akiyoshi and illustrated by Uchibashi Chikuun (reputedly a student of a famous visiting Chinese painter, Fei Hanyuan, who had made numerous visits to Nagasaki between 1734 and 1756). For reasons unknown, it was not published until 1931.
15. A woodblock illustration of the table setting for shippoku ryōri is illustrated in Etchū and Ōto (1976, pl. 246).
16. For general information on the influence of visiting Chinese artists on Japanese painters, see Addiss (1986) and Jansen (1992, 60–64).
17. The 1828 sencha treatise *Ryōzandō's Chats on Tea (Ryōzandō chawa)* quotes Sugai Baikan's descriptions of bunjin asobi in Nagasaki as occasions during which sencha was served.
18. The two best published extant daimyo collections are the Hosokawa collection (now housed at the Eisei Bunko, Tokyo) and the Owari Tokugawa collection, now in the Tokugawa Art Museum, Nagoya. Several recent international exhibitions have highlighted the Tokugawa collection. See, for example, Montreal (1989), esp. the chapter by Christine Guth (41–51). For scholars' paraphernalia from the Hosokawa collection, see Hosokawa (1978) and Hosokawa (1982).
19. On the Ashikaga shogunal collection catalogues, see Weigl (1980, 267–270), Nezu (1976), Shimizu and Wheelwright (1976, 223 n. 13), and Sen (1977a, vol. 2). On Ashikaga shogunal taste for karamono as represented in these catalogues, see Guth (1993, 46–54, 205 n. 4).
20. The shoin, literally "writing hall," originally referred to the study chamber in abbots' residences of Zen temples. It was here that early chanoyu tea ceremonies were held. By the late sixteenth century the term came to be applied to a set type of formal residential architecture that featured interiors having straw mat flooring (tatami); an alcove for displaying artworks, flower arrangements, and a hanging scroll (tokonoma); staggered shelves (*chigidana* or simply *tana*); a built-in writing desk low to the floor (*tsukeshōin*); sliding screens rather than the more old-fashioned fixed walls (*fusuma*); translucent white paper and lattice-covered windows (shoji); and sliding wooden shutters for the windows (*amado*).
21. For examples of these wares and a discussion of them within the broader context of Japanese taste in Chinese ceramics, see Hayashiya S. (1977) and Kyoto National Museum (1991). For a selection of these ceramics in the Idemitsu Museum of Arts, Tokyo, see Seattle (1988).
22. The play has been translated into English in Keene (1961, 57–131). On the relationship of the characters to those from life and knowledge of Confucian principles among Chikamatsu's audience, see Jansen (1992, 84–85) and Keene (1984, 130–134).
23. For information on the Sumiya in English, see Nishi and Hozumi (1985, 128–131) and Yasutaka (1989, 23–24).

CHAPTER THREE

Chinese Literati Ideals in the Formation of Appreciation for Sencha

1. For a complete catalogue of books Ingen brought to Japan, see Ingen Zenshi (1917). Among the various sixty-one secular books was Lu Yu's *Cha jing*.
2. Kanō Sansetsu (1589–1651), for example, depicted this theme in a pair of eight-fold screens now in the collection of Zuishinji, Kyoto. See Tokyo National Museum (1979, pl. 154).
3. Arthur Waley's free translation of Wang's preface is

published in Rawson (1992, 99–100). For another translation, see Lin (1961, 98–99).

4. The term "fucha" (C: bucha) seems to have entered the Japanese language in connection with Ōbaku. Standard dictionaries give its first appearance in the Ōbaku shingi. See Zengaku (1985, 1080) and Nihon Daijiten Kankōkai (1975, 17: 417).
5. For an English translation, see Baroni (1993, 318–340).
6. From vol. 3, p. 12.
7. For transcription and discussion of these, see Ōtsuki (1995–1996, pts. 5–8).
8. Enshin is the priest name of Akamatsu Norimura (1277–1350), a powerful samurai who was also a fervent Zen Buddhist.
9. The third shogun, Ashikaga Yoshimitsu (1358–1408), resided at Rokuonji (Deer Park), popularly known as the Kinkakuji (Golden Pavilion).
10. Wabi is here used as synonymous with chanoyu. Jōō is Takeno Jōō (1502–1555), and Shukō is Murata Shukō (died 1502). These two men, forerunners to Sen no Rikyū, are credited with the creation of the wabi aesthetic of chanoyu. Curiously, the author of this poem mentions these two figures by name and not Rikyū, whose fame, by the late seventeenth century, was actually greater.
11. On the meaning of this poem, see Ōtsuki (1995–1996, pts. 10–17).
12. This is recorded in the first true sencha treatise, *Chats on Tea by the Azure Harbor (Seiwan chawa)*, 1756, by Ōeda Ryūhō, and echoed by all later writers; see Hasegawa (1965, 87–88).
13. For illustrations of some of Ingen's personal possessions owned by Manpukuji, including sencha accouterments, see Gifu (1992, pls. 112–128) and Kyoto National Museum (1993, pls. 37–50). For several other sencha items purported to have been owned by Ingen and now in the Kagetsuan collection, see Tanaka (1973, 239, 248, 255).
14. Unless otherwise noted, biographical information on Jōzan comes from the sensitive portrayal of his life, cultural milieu, and artistic pursuits in Rimer (1991b). See also Anjō 2007.
15. The present appearance of Jōzan's home is somewhat different than what it was originally. See Suzuki H. (1991, 99–101).
16. Such towers were not uncommon in Japan; see Suzuki H. (1991, 100–101).
17. On fūryū in the context of the aesthetic preferences of famous chanoyu tea masters in the early eighteenth century, see Kramer (1985, 122). On the historical development of this term, see Ueda M. (1983). In Tokugawa-period popular culture, fūryū was similar in meaning to sui (elegance). For a discussion of fūryū in this latter sense, see Tsuji (1994).
18. Translated in Wilson (1991, 66–69).
19. For translations of these, see Wilson (1991, 206).
20. See translations in Chaves (1991, 43) and Watson (1990, 30).
21. See translations in Watson (1983, 32, 36).
22. The Kenzan scholar Richard Wilson (in private correspondence) indicates that he thinks Kenzan also drank the beverage.

CHAPTER FOUR

Sencha in the Eighteenth Century, under the Spell of Baisaō and Beyond

1. On elegance in Nankai's poetry, see Keene (1978, 542–543). For an English translation of Nankai's comments on ga and zoku, see Nakano (1989, 127–128).
2. On the influence of kyō and ki in eighteenth century Japanese visual arts, see Kanō (1990, 4–13). See also Brecher 2013.
3. Information presented here on Baisaō's well-documented life is culled from the following sources, all based on primary materials: Hasegawa (1965, 88–91), Tanimura (1983), and Waddell (1984), who has translated into English portions of the 1763 *Verses of the Old Tea Peddler (Baisaō gego)*.
4. For Rikunyo's biography and a selection of his poems translated into English, see Watson (1990, 37–61).
5. Translation by Norman Waddell, in Waddell 1984, 105–106. The translation has been modified from the earlier published version at the request of the translator.
6. Translation by Norman Waddell, in Waddell 1984, 98, from the *Verses of the Old Tea Peddler*.
7. Translation by Norman Waddell, in Waddell 1984, 110.
8. For the Jakuchū portrait and title page calligraphy, see Hickman and Sato (1989, 138–139).
9. A translation of this incident as recorded in the *Verses of the Old Tea Peddler* appears in Waddell (1984, 122–123). The utensils thought to have been burned are recorded in Saga (1983, 109), but the source for this list is not stated, nor is it known if it is complete.
10. Jakuchū paintings with Baisaō inscriptions include a *Rooster* in the collection of the Arthur M. Sackler Museum, Harvard University Art Museums, and *Chrysanthemum and a Rock*, at the Los Angeles County Museum of Art and published in Moss (1991, n.p.). A painting of *Crab and Bamboo* by Taiga inscribed with a poem by the eighty-two-year-old Baisaō is published in Tanaka (1973, 231).

11. Translation by Norman Waddell, in Waddell 1984, 120.
12. Of the numerous portraits of Baisaō by Jakuchū, the three most scholars agree are genuine, including the one illustrated here, are published in Shufunotomosha (1975, 67–69).
13. On kijin in the context of the *Kinsei kijin den*, see Takeuchi (1992, 123) and Brecher 2013. For English translations of Ban Kokei's introductions to these texts, see Marceau (1989, 206–209).
14. On Kenkadō's Seifūsha, see Tsukuda I. (1985, 120) and Tsukuda I. (1981, 486). Friends with whom he drank tea are recorded in his diary. For a modern printed, indexed edition of this document, see Mizuta (1972).
15. This text, one of ten ethical treatises that Ekken wrote for the general public, has been translated into English with sections on sencha identified as "green tea"; see Kaibara (1974, 81–83).
16. When this text was actually written remains unknown. It has been speculated to have been penned as early as the Kyōhō era (1716–1736); see Sen (1977a, 3: 490). For an annotated edition of *Talks on the Origin of Tea*, see Sen (1977a, 3: 397–497).
17. Brewing methods, as recorded in this and other Japanese sencha texts, are discussed in Hasegawa (1965, 98).
18. See poem vii in Waddell (1984, 102).
19. This entire album is illustrated in color in Shufunotomosha (1975, 9–11).
20. Many of these have been published in Saga (1983) and Shufunotomosha (1975).
21. For documentation, see Saga (1983, 21).
22. The preface to Ryūhō's 1756 book on sencha, *Chats on Tea by the Azure Harbor*, indicates that the manuscript for *Miscellaneous Records* was already in existence at that time, although the latter was not published until 1762.
23. This passage—"Hito no moteru chōdo ni te mo, sono hito no kokoro wa shiru mono nari. Zoku ni shite ga narazaru mono wa miru mo urusashi"—is from the introduction to the general section on scholars' utensils, which is the first section of volume 1. It is discussed in Takahashi H. (1988, 160–161).
24. On Ryūhō and his relationship with Tsuga Teishō, see Nakamura Y. (1961, 153–157).
25. On the *Drunken Words*, see Young (1982, 127, 157, n. 64).
26. Akinari's best-known work is *Tales of Moonlight and Rain (Ugetsu monogatari)*, a selection of supernatural stories. For biographical information on Akinari, see Young (1982) and Leon Zolbrod's commentary in Ueda (1977, 19–94).
27. For discussion of the *Miscellaneous Comments*, see Young (1982, 108–109).
28. The original reads "tenzuru wa ken, senzuru wa sei" and is discussed in Tsukuda I. (1985, 166–167).
29. Translation by Blake Morgan Young, in Young 1982, 109.
30. In private correspondence, the scholar Andrew Markus indicated that Ransui had an interest in gems, minerals, and rocks and was famous in his day for a translation of Chinese drama into Japanese in ca. 1804-1805. His brother Garekisha, also a monk, was a noted authority on sencha and Zen temple roof tiles.
31. For examples of his work, see Kyoto National Museum (1990, 188, figs. 26, 27).
32. Few Chinese books illustrated utensils, a notable exception being the Song treatise *Illustrated Notes on Tea Utensils* (C: *Chaju tuzan*). This book was included in the *Complete Collection of Tea Books*, well known in Japan and reprinted there just one year after publication of the *Woodblock Book on Boiled Tea*. The *Illustrated Notes* also was one of the Chinese books on tea appended to the first Japanese edition of the *Classic of Tea*, published in Japan in 1758.

CHAPTER FIVE

Bunjincha, Sencha of the Literati

1. For biographical information on San'yō, see Woodson (1983, 6–7) and Watson (1976, 121–170), which also includes translations of his kanshi and several prose essays. See also Shimamura 2022.
2. The fathers of both Shunkin and Hankō were more famous literati painters, Uragami Gyokudō (1745–1820) and Okada Beisanjin (1744–1820), respectively.
3. His art has been well published and researched; for a study in English, see Berry (1985).
4. For a better view of Baiitsu's inner study with a clearer picture of the utensils, see a handscroll by Tomioka Tessai dated 1917 in Tessai (1991, fig. 40, no. 16) or Graham (2003, fig. 5.7). Several of Baiitsu's Chinese utensils—an Yixing ware teapot, a pewter leaf tea container, and a pottery brazier—are in Japanese private collections. For the Yixing teapot, see Shufunotomosha (1981, 234).
5. Waka are five-line, thirty-one syllable poems in a form of literary Japanese found in Japan's earliest poetic anthologies of the eighth century. Often lyrical and sentimental in tone, they are the antithesis of poetry in Chinese. Kokugaku scholars helped revive interest in waka during the late Tokugawa period.
6. The other more elaborate version, dated to 1850, has a teapot atop a brazier beside a basket of charcoal.

See Nagoya City Museum (1981, pl. 115) or Nagoya (1998, fig. 89).
7. The National Japanese Sencha Association Library at Manpukuji has a photocopy of the original, which remains in the possession of a private collector.
8. Hagoromo must here refer to the crane robe (kakushō-e) that Chinese Daoists, Baisaō, and other Japanese eccentric intellectuals sometimes wore. It is an oblique reference to the ability of the tea to impart a sense of immortality to those who drank it. The story first appears in Takeda (1897, 6–7) and is repeated in Sugihara (1910, 716).
9. This gathering is discussed, in the context of Edo bunjincha, in Umezawa (1919, 822–824).
10. A gathering of sixteen Chinese literati that took place in the year 1086.
11. The first to be documented with a catalogue listing the exhibited items occurred in Takamatsu in 1793; see Yamanouchi (1981, 456–460).
12. In 1836, one year after his death, Chinese and Japanese paintings that had been owned by Chikuden were exhibited; see Kizaki (1929, 2: 491, 508–515). On exhibitions of Chinese paintings held to honor and memorialize Baiitsu, see Graham (1986) and Graham (1983, 106–116).
13. This reference to brewing tea in the snow is reminiscent of Ōbaku Ingen's poems on the theme of snow tea. The stone kettle refers to Yixing teapots, the surfaces of which resembled stone.
14. For the family's Chinese paintings, see Suzuki K. (1983, 4 : 475–505).
15. Participants included Ōkubo Shibutsu and Kikuchi Gozan, the writer Ōta Nanpo (1749–1823), and the literati painters Watanabe Kazan, Kameda Bōsai, and Haruki Nanmei, whose father, Nanko, had studied with Kimura Kenkadō. For references to mammoth gatherings sponsored or attended by these men, see Markus (1993, 137, 146–147, 152–153).
16. Among those pictured were Kazan's painting pupil Yamamoto Kinkoku (1811 1873), Tani Bunchō's pupils Takahisa Aigai (1796–1843) and Onishi Chinnen (1792–1851), and Chinzan's wife accompanied by the couple's two young children.
17. For a representative sampling of his wares, see Kawahara (1990, colorpls. 43–53, figs. 40–45).
18. For the letters, see Ishikawa J. (1979, 126–140).
19. On Mokubei's relationship with Chikuden and San'yō, see Sasaki (1982).
20. Translated into English in Chu (1910).
21. For illustrations from this album, see Ishikawa J. (1979, pls. 22–29, 53–65).
22. The extent of the import of Dehua wares to Japan in the Tokugawa period remains unclear, but implications are that trade was brisk; see Donnelly (1969, 122, 207, pl. c, fig. 61).
23. Mokubei verified the source of inspiration for his pot in his inscription on the accompanying box.
24. It is illustrated, along with its box inscribed by sencha luminaries, in Shufunotomosha (1975, 21).
25. One, a fresh water pot, is illustrated in Mitsuoka (1990, colorpl. 7).
26. Letters Mokubei wrote to friends Tanaka Kakuō and Tonomura Keiin, another Osaka merchant-patron, detail these events. See Wakimoto (1921, 195, letter no. 2 to Keiin) and Ishikawa J. (1979, 139, for a letter to Kakuō). I have made use of translations into English of these and other letters in an unpublished manuscript by John Teramoto.
27. For a shonzui-style dish attributed to Katō Tamikichi in the Freer Gallery of Art, Smithsonian Institution, Washington, D.C., see Cort (1992, 47 [colorpl.], 215).
28. For documents relating to the history of the Kameyama kiln, see Etchū (1968). See also illustrations in Mitsuoka (1981, 11: 75–77), Aichi (1991, pls. 152, 153), Ayers (1982, pl. 61e), Smith (1973, pls. 51–54), Jenyns (1965, 256–258, pl. 24a), Nagasaki City Museum (1995, pls. 9, 17), and Itabashi (1996, pls. 35, 37–44, 127–128).
29. For information on Itsuun and sencha, see Nagami (1927, 93), Nagasaki (1923, 364, 370), and Hayashi (1932). On Chikuden's involvement with the Kameyama kiln, see Berry (1985, 102, 174, nn. 155, 156).
30. See, for example, a sencha tea set with kanshi poetry by Nukina Kaioku in collaboration with the Kyoto potter Waki Kitei V (1808–1871) in Graham (1985b, 193, fig. 14).
31. For information on this kiln, see Shimonaka (1984, 108) or Mitsuoka (1981, 9: 135–136, pl. 256). The kiln specialized in porcelain with underglaze blue decoration; potters were recruited from Seto and painter-decorators came from Kyoto. It is unknown when production there ceased.

CHAPTER SIX

The Assimilation of Sencha into Japanese Society

1. For other examples of sencha utensils in the Sumiya collection, see Kawahara and Degawa (1993).
2. For a discussion of Rengetsu in the context of other women artists of the Tokugawa period, see Fister (1988, 144–146, 149–157) and the online materials for the 2023 "Her Brush" exhibition at the Denver Art Museum. https://her-brush.denartmus.org/.
3. For a detailed discussion of this manuscript and reproduction of all the illustrations, see Onchi (1983).

4. The following are the sencha tea masters included in the *Collection of Great Sencha Tea Masters of Naniwa* (with the main points from their accompanying biographies):
   - i. Nosato Baien: a friend of Tanaka Kakuō.
   - ii. Kondō Seiga: a post office proprietor who played No drums.
   - iii. Zōjuan Chizen: a Zen priest, collector of antiquities, and well-known connoisseur.
   - iv. Yasuda Roshu: a samurai who collected gourds.
   - v. Shinozaki Shōchiku: a samurai, famous as a Confucian scholar and calligrapher.
   - vi. Tonomura Rosai: a rice dealer who excelled at waka poetry and was known for having acquired a teapot once owned by Baisaō.
   - vii. Tanaka Kakuō: a sake merchant considered the third-generation successor to Baisaō's Way of sencha and the greatest sencha teacher of Osaka; he collected antique sencha utensils and held regular memorial services for Baisaō (monthly) and Lu Yu (annually).
   - viii. Sugimura Shōhakuan: an antique dealer, disciple of Tanaka Kakuō.
   - ix. Satake Jusen: a pottery disciple of Mokubei and Kiyomizu Rokubei and a student of sencha with Kakuō; he excelled at designing bonseki (miniature tray gardens).
   - x. Kishida Kiyū: a disciple of Ōbaku Monchū.
   - xi. Kimura Kenkadō: famous for his many friends and skilled at poetry and ink painting; he collected sencha utensils once owned by Baisaō.
   - xii. Okada Hankō: a famous painter of Osaka, son of Beisanjin; he was good at calligraphy and kanshi poetry.
   - xiii. Hiraoka Kajō: a moneylender.
   - xiv. Sachiko: the wife of Shinozaki Shōchiku.
   - xv. Baichūshi: a waka poet and disciple of Kakuō.
   - xvi. Yagi Sonsho: a painter and calligrapher, Confucian scholar, and inheritor of some of Baisaō's sencha utensils.
   - xvii. Hayashi Bairin: a participant in *kyogen* (comic No theater), an antique dealer, and a neighbor of Kakuō.
   - xviii. Kagawa Shūtetsu: an obstetrician who collected antiquities, porcelains decorated with landscapes, and unusual rocks; also known as a poet of kanshi and waka.
   - xix. Sen Jinshi: a poet who wrote haikai in the style of Bashō and studied sencha with Kakuō.
   - xx. Inoue Kakushū: a Shinto priest and fortune teller.
   - xxi. Abe Kenshū (Ryōzandō): a famous seal carver who was also a kanshi poet, calligrapher, and painter.
   - xxii. Kogetsu Yoshō: formerly a priest at Kyoto's Zen temple of Tenryūji who lived like a hermit.
5. Unless otherwise noted, biographical information on Kakuō is derived from Tanaka (1973, 315–321), a modern history of the Kagetsuan sencha tea school, authored by Tanaka Seiha, the fifth-generation iemoto. Whenever possible I have corroborated the facts therein with other primary sources.
6. This is an often repeated story that first appeared in two books published in 1823, *Collection of the Golden Brocade of Naniwa [Osaka] (Naniwa kinran shu)* and the *Continuing Record of Old Friends of Osaka*.
7. The "floating flowers" must refer to the brewing of the tea leaves. Yet this may also refer to the Lanting Gathering, where cups filled with wine floated in a stream.
8. A record of the utensils used at this gathering appears in Saeki (1940, 195–242).
9. Information on Kashin and his Ogawa school is based on personal interviews with the sixth head of the school, Ogawa Kōraku, and publications by him; see Shufunotomosha (1981, 412–413), Ogawa (1975a), and Ogawa (1986a, 34–35).
10. The 1909 copies of the *Record of a Boiled Tea Ceremony* contain numerous omissions of characters and mistakes in transcription; see Akai (1970). Courtier patrons of Ogawa Kashin included Takatsukasa Masamichi (1789–1868), Konoe Tadahiro (1808–1898), Horikawa Yasuchika, and Ichijō Tadaka, who was also a friend of Tanaka Kakuō.
11. For information on Yatsuhashi Baisa, see Kōdansha (1982, 44–46). His date of birth is here indicated to be 1760, but other sources state he was born in 1758 or 1759.
12. The sencha room contains thirteen mats and the study, four. For additional illustrations, see Kitao (1957, 40–63).
13. For information on the Kutani kilns of the late Tokugawa period, see Kaga (1984), Ishikawa (1975), and Komatsu (1974).
14. For works from this and other daimyo kilns of Wakayama, see Sasayama (1991, pls. 11–37).
15. For other examples of Kōtō wares, see Hikone (1988) and Sasayama (1991, pls. 38–53).

CHAPTER SEVEN

Sencha in Modern Japan

1. For information on Naitō Konan's attitude toward China and a general introduction to Meiji Sinology, see Fogel (1984). For broader overviews of various Japanese attitudes toward Asia and China in the early

Meiji period, see Jansen (1967), Keene (1971), and Tanaka S. (1993).

2. For others, see Fister (1988, 174–175).
3. Information on these two artists and their involvement with sencha comes from Ibara (1992), Kyoto Prefectural Library (1985), and Tessai (1991).
4. These included Yamanaka Shintenʼō (1832–1885) and two prominent women painters, Noguchi Shōhin and Okuhara Seiko (1837–1913). See Kido (1983–1986), Guth (1993, 30–35), and Guth (2006).
5. Translations and transcriptions of Chokunyū's accompanying text were provided by Philip Wu and Du Zhonggao.
6. Berry (1985, 246–247), Tsuchida (1973), and Murayama (1973). The *Binkaron* is an undated, handwritten manuscript discovered after Chikuden's death. According to Murayama, it appears to date from the Bunsei era (1818–1830).
7. For examples of some of these rooms, see Itō and Yokoyama (1983–1985, vols. 2, 3, and 6) and Kitao (1957). Well-known sencha aficionados included the Nihonga painter Hashimoto Kansetsu (1883–1945) from Kyoto and the Western-style sculptor Asakura Fumio (1883–1964) of Tokyo. Asakura's home and studio (constructed in 1936), which includes rooms designed in sencha taste, is now an easily accessible museum open to the public.
8. Records indicate that this particular example was once owned by the thirteenth abbot of Manpukuji, Jikuan Jōin (1699–1756).
9. Information on the history of the Ogawa school and this particular event was provided by Ogawa Koraku.
10. It is practically impossible to find written information on when the emergence of the many discrete schools for sencha occurred. The number of schools suggested as existing at this time comes from conversations with various sencha tea masters, whose families have been practicing the art for generations.
11. His father, a samurai in the service of the daimyo of Fukui, had relocated to Tokyo where he opened an antique shop and founded his own lineage of sencha inspired by the teaching of Baisaō.
12. For an example of a painting by Chikuun on a sencha theme, see Rogers (1997, 186).
13. For an admittedly incomplete list of sencha schools throughout Japan, see Shufunotomosha (1973, 302–309).
14. See, for example, teapots by Yamada Jōzan III (born 1924), illustrated in Wilson (1991, colorpl. 19). See also Aichi 2007.

GLOSSARY

Sencha Utensils

Although their forms are generally standardized, many sencha utensils are known by more than one name, some borrowed from chanoyu, some not. An asterisk (*) following a term indicates that the utensil is also used for chanoyu, although the actual appearance and corresponding function of the piece may be different. I have attempted to list first the most commonly used name, but this is not always possible, for which term employed depends upon various factors such as school affiliation and personal preference. Illustrations show most, but not all, of these utensils arranged for service, with some utensils appearing in more than one of the drawings. However, the drawings are not intended to convey the full extent of the diversity of utensil assemblages or the unique serving styles of sencha.

While most utensils are employed for all types of sencha service, some are used on special occasions, such as at nodate (informal, outdoor picnics), with gyokuro tea (which requires careful monitoring of water temperature), or in the two main types of tea preparation methods: sencha temae (when tea leaves are thrown directly into the kettle full of boiling water) and encha temae (when the tea leaves are placed in the teapot first, and hot water from the kettle is poured over them).

Useful sources for preparing this glossary were Tanaka (1973), Shufunotomosha (1988), and Zen Nihon Senchadō Renmei (1992). I have also relied upon the advice and assistance of Tsukuda Ikki of the Issa-an school, who supplied photographs that served as models for figures A and B. Figure C is based on my photograph of a sencha utensil arrangement of the Kagetsuan school.

Drawings are by David M. Dunfield

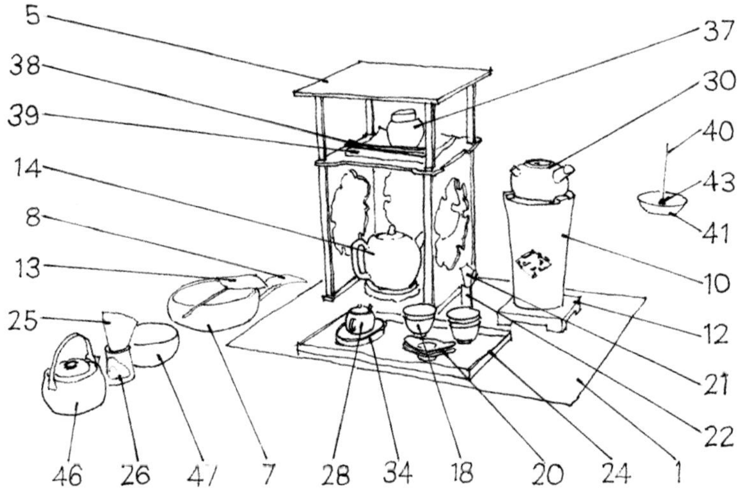

Chagu Joku	1.	Tea service mat (for placement underneath tea utensils and brazier)
Kikyoku	2.	Tea utensil cabinet
Teiran	3.	Tea utensil basket (used in nodate or outdoor service; not pictured)
Chabitsu/Toriire	4.	Lidded box for tea utensils (used in the most informal of tea ceremonies; not pictured)
Tana/Chaka/Meika	5.	Tea utensil stand
Robyō/Kekkai	6.	Hearth screen
Ufu/Sumikago*	7.	Charcoal basket
Habōki	8.	Feather broom (for dusting charcoal)
Hibashi*/Kakyō	9.	Charcoal tongs
Konro/Ryōro	10.	Tall, cylindrical pottery brazier
Hairo (Karo)/Binkake*	11.	Stout brazier of metal or pottery
Rodai/Roban/Roza	12.	Brazier stand
Rosen	13.	Brazier fan (used only with tall, cylindrical pottery brazier)
Suichū	14.	Fresh water ewer
Mizusashi*/Chūshi	15.	Fresh water bucket
Mizutsugi*	16.	Fresh water pot (for replenishing fresh water ewer or bucket; not pictured)
Hyōshaku	17.	Gourd water ladle (for use only with fresh water bucket)
Chawan*/Meiwan	18.	Teacups
Wantō	19.	Teacup storage container
Chataku*/Takusu	20.	Teacup saucers
Chakin*	21.	Teacup cleaning cloth
Chakinzutsu*/Kinzutsu (Kinto)	22.	Tube-shaped container for teacup cleaning cloth
Kinbako/Kingō	23.	Small lidded box for storing teacup cleaning cloth
Meibon/Tōsaibon	24.	Teacup tray
Bonkin	25.	Cloth to wipe the teacup tray

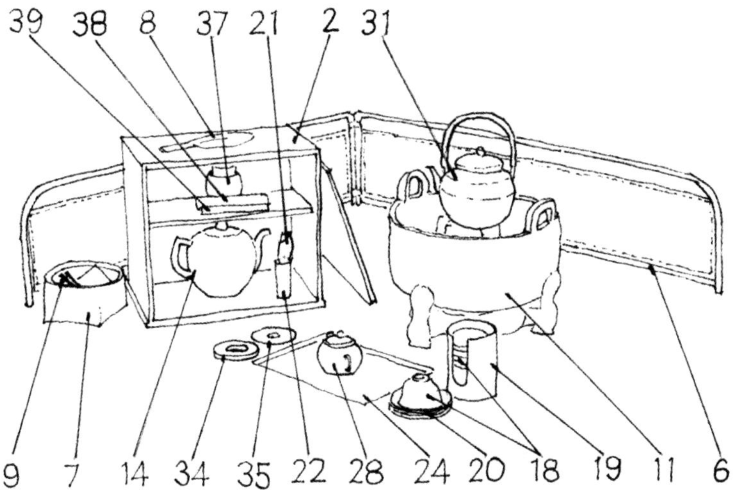

Bonkinzutsu	26.	Container for the cloth to wipe the teacup tray
Kyūsu/Kibishō/Kyūshō	27.	Side-handled teapot
Chachō/Chachū/Chahei	28.	Loop-handled teapot (used for serving gyokuro with encha temae)
Hōhin	29.	Handleless teapot (used only with gyokuro; not pictured)
Bōfura/Yuwakashi / Tōkan	30.	Pottery kettle (for boiling hot water on a brazier; term originally used interchangeably with others for teapot)
Ginbin/Bōfura / Yuwakashi	31.	Metal kettle (silver or gold; for boiling hot water on a stout brazier)
Tetsubin	32.	Iron kettle (for informal service, used only with stout brazier; not pictured)
Yusamashi (Yuzamashi)	33.	Water cooler (spouted vessel into which boiling water from the kettle is poured prior to being poured into the teapot; for use with encha temae and gyokuro; see fig. 78)
Bindai/Chōza	34.	Teapot stand
Binshō/Binshiki	35.	Kettle stand
Kayoi Bindai	36.	Small tray or basket (to place under teapot when passing it to guests; not pictured)
Chashinko/Chaire*/ Hachaki	37.	Leaf tea container (tea caddy)
Chagō (Sagō)/Charyō/ Chasoku/Senbai	38.	Tea scoop
Fukusa*	39.	Square of silk brocade or printed cotton cloth (for ceremonially wiping tea scoop and leaf tea container)
Senkō*	40.	Stick incense
Kōzara	41.	Stick incense saucer
Kōzutsu	42.	Stick incense container (not pictured)

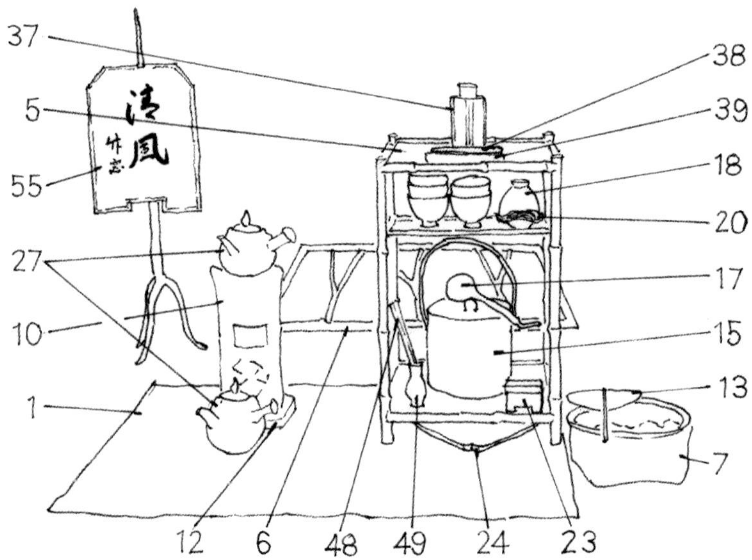

Kōza/Kōtate 43. Small support for lighted stick incense

Kōro* 44. Incense burner (not pictured)

Kōgō* 45. Incense box (see fig. 41, far right)

Senbin 46. Water pot (spouted vessel, often metal; containing clean water for rinsing utensils)

Nōo/Kensui* 47. Waste water bowl

Chahashi 48. Tea chopsticks (for removing used tea leaves from teapot)

Chohei/Hashitate 49. Tea chopsticks holder

Shiu/Chakotsu Ire 50. Lidded refuse bowl (for used tea leaves; not pictured)

Sōka/Bunjin Bana 51. Flower arrangement (see fig. 67)

Morimono 52. Arrangement of fruits and vegetables (not pictured)

Hanaire*/Kaki*/Hanaike* 53. Flower vase (see fig. 67 and fig. 59)

Bunbō Kazari* 54. Display of scholars' writing implements (see fig. 75)

Charen/Chahata 55. Tea ceremony banner

GLOSSARY

Characters

This list is limited to names of important people, books, tea terminology, and utensils relevant to the study of sencha in Japan. Chinese books published in Japan, citizens active in Japan, and appropriated Chinese terms are rendered in Japanese.

Abe Kenshū (Ryōzandō)	阿部絹洲（良山堂）
Aoki Mokubei	青木木米
Aoki Shukuya	青木夙夜
Asaka Tanpaku	安積澹泊
Baisanshu chafu ryaku	梅山種茶譜略
Baisaō	売茶翁
Baisaō chagu zu	売茶翁茶具図
Baisaō chaki zufu	売茶翁茶器図譜
Baisaō gego	売茶翁偈語
bancha	番茶
bindai	瓶台
binkake	瓶掛
Binkaron	瓶花論
binshiki	瓶敷
binshō	瓶床
bōfura	保夫良（ボーフラ）
Bokusekikyo sencha ketsu	木石居煎茶訣
bonkin	盆巾
bonkinzutsu	盆巾筒
bunbō kazari	文房飾り
Bunbō seiyaku zu	文房清約図
bunbōgu	文房具
bunga	文雅
bunjin asobi	文人遊び
bunjin bana	文人花
bunjin bokkyaku	文人墨客
bunjincha	文人茶
bunmei kaika	文明開化
Cha shi	茶史
chabitsu	茶櫃
chachō	茶銚
chachū	茶注
chagō	茶合
chagu joku	茶具褥
Chagu zufu	茶具図譜
chahashi	茶箸
chahata	茶旗
chahei	茶瓶
chaire	茶入れ
chajin	茶人
chaka	茶架
Chaka suigen	茶瘕酔言
chakai	茶会
chakin	茶巾
chakinzutsu	茶巾筒
chakotsu ire	茶骨入れ
Chakyō	茶経
Chakyō shōsetsu	茶経詳説
chanoyu	茶の湯
charen	茶帘
charyō	茶量
Charyō zusan	茶寮図賛
Chasetsu zufu	茶説図譜
chashinko	茶心壷
Chasho zenshū	茶書全集
chasoku	茶則

chataku	茶托
chatō	茶董
chawan	茶碗
Chikudensō chasetsu	竹田荘茶説
Chin Genpin	陳源贇
chohei	箸瓶
Chōkōen	釣耕園
chōza	銚座
chūshi	注子
Daichō Genkō	大潮元皓
Daiten Kenjō	大典顕常
dashicha	出し茶
Dazai Shundai	太宰春台
Dokugo	独語
Edo ryūkō ryōri tsū daizen	江戸流行料理通大全
Eicha shiroku	詠茶詩録
Eiraku Hozen	永楽保全
encha	淹茶
Fu Shizen	傅士然
fucha	普茶
fucha ryōri	普茶料理
fūga	風雅
Fukada Seiichi	深田精一
fukusa	袱紗
Fukuyama Chōgan	福山朝丸
fūro	風炉
fūryū	風流
Fūzoku monzen	風俗文撰
ga	雅
Gankyokō	巖居稿
Gayū manroku	雅遊漫録
Gekkai Genshō	月海元昭
Genryū chawa	源流茶話
Geppō Shinryō	月峯辰亮
Gettan Dōchō	月潭道澄
Gikō jihu fu	宜興磁壷譜
Gikōkan	宜興罐
ginbin	銀瓶
Gion Nankai	祇園南海
Goshin Genmyō	悟心元明
gyō	行
gyokuro	玉露
Gyokusentei	玉川庭
habōki	羽箒
hachaki	葉茶器
hairo (karo)	火炉
hanaike	花生
hanaire	花入
Hasegawa Shōshōkyo	長谷川瀟々居
hashitate	箸立
Hata Zōroku	秦蔵六
hibashi	火箸
hōcha	泡茶
Hōcha ketsu	泡茶訣
Hōcha ki	泡茶記
Hōcha shinsho sanshu	泡茶新書三種
Hōcha shōsho	泡茶樵書
hōhin	抱瓶
Honchō shokkan	本朝食鑑
hyōshaku	瓢杓
iemoto	家元
Iiyama Gihō	飯山義方
Ike Taiga	池大雅
Ingen	隠元
Ishikawa Jōzan	石川丈山
Itō Jakuchū	伊藤若冲
Ka Juhō	夏樹芳
Kagetsu	花月
Kagetsuan	花月庵
Kagetsuanryū hōshiki zufu sencha seiganki	花月庵流法式図譜煎茶清玩規
Kaibara Ekken	貝原益軒
kaki	花器
kakyō	火筴
Kameda Ryōrai	亀田綾瀬
karamono	唐物
Katayama Hokkai	片山北海
kayoi bindai	通瓶台
kazari	飾り
kekkai	結界
kencha	献茶
kensui	建水
ki	奇
kibishō	急尾焼
kijin	奇人

Kikuchi Gozan	菊地五山	kyūshō	急焼	Nanpōroku	南方録
kikyoku	器局	kyūsu	急須	Nihon Sencha Kōgei Kyōkai	日本煎茶工芸協会
Kimura Kenkadō	木村蒹葭堂	Lu Tong	盧仝	Nin'ami Dōhachi	仁阿弥道八
Kimura Kōyō	木村孔陽	Lu Yu	陸羽	nodate	野点
Kin Shikō	金士恒	Maeda Chikubōsai	前田竹房斎	nōo	納汚
kinbako	巾箱	Manpukuji	万福寺	Ōbaku	黄檗
kingō	巾盒	Masuyama Sessai	増山雪斎	Ōbaku shingi	黄檗清規
Kinryō Dōjin	金竜道人	matcha	抹茶	Ōbakusan	黄檗山
kinzutsu	巾筒	Meien hinmoku	茗讌品目	Ōeda Ryūhō	大枝流芳
Kitaōji Rosanjin	北大路魯山人	meika	茗架	Ogata Kenzan	尾形乾山
Kiyomizu Rokubei	清水六兵衛	Meiko zuroku	茗壷図録	Ogata Shūhei	尾形周平
Kiyota (or Seida) Tansō	清田儋叟	meiwan	茗碗	Ogawa Hisataka (Kairaku)	小川久敬(偕楽)
Kō Fuyō	高芙蓉	Minagawa Kien	皆川淇園	Ogawa Jijirō (Katei Kōraku)	小川治次郎(霞汀後楽)
Kō Yūgai	高遊外	Mitani Sōchin	三谷宗鎮	Ogawa Kashin	小川可進
Kōcha roku	考茶録	Miura Chikusen	三浦竹泉	Ogawa Kōraku (Narabayashi Tadao)	小川後楽(楢林忠男)
kōgō	香盒	mizusashi	水指	Ogawa Shin'an	小川信庵
konro	焜炉	mizutsugi	水次	Ogawa Shioko	小川塩子
Kōrakudō kissa ben	後楽堂喫茶弁	Monchū Jōfuku	聞中浄復	Ogawa Tamemi (Kiraku)	小川爲美(其楽)
kōro	香炉	Morikawa Kyoroku	森川許六	Oku Randen (Saburōbei)	奥蘭田(三郎兵衛)
kōsen	香煎	morimono	盛物	Ōkubo Shibutsu	大窪詩仏
kōtate	香立	Mujaku Dōchū	無著道忠	Okuda Eisen	奥田穎川
kōza	香座	Murase Kōtei	村瀬栲亭	Ōtagaki Rengetsu	大田垣蓮月
kōzara	香皿	Nagatani Sōen	永谷宗円	Ōsato Kōan (Yutaka)	大里浩庵(豊)
kōzutsu	香筒	Nakajima Rakusui	中島楽水	Rai San'yō	頼山陽
kucha	供茶	Nakajima Yōsuke	中島庸介	Rakurakutei	楽楽亭
Kutani Shōza	九谷庄三	Nanban	南蛮	Rikunyo	六如
kyō	狂	Naniwa fūryū hanjōki	浪華風流繁昌記	roban	炉坂
Kyūkyodō	鳩居堂	Naniwa sencha taijin shū	浪華煎茶大人集		

robyō	炉屏
rodai	炉台
rosen	炉扇
roza	炉座
ryōro	涼炉
Ryōzandō chawa	良山堂茶話
Ryū Genchō	劉源長
Ryūi hisho	竜威秘書
Ryūkatei Ransui	柳下亭嵐翠
Saeki Futoshi	佐伯太
Sakata Keizō	坂田圭蔵
Sakura Seidan (Seidanrō shujin)	桜青談（清談楼主人）
Sankatei	三華亭
Sanshi Suimeisho	山紫水明処
seifū	清風
Seifū sagen	清風瑣言
Seifū sencha yōran	清風煎茶要覧
Seifūryū hōcha shoshiki shōkai	清風流烹茶諸式詳解
Seigojō	清娯帖
Seiwan chakai zuroku	青湾茶会図録
Seiwan chawa	青湾茶話
Seiwan meien zushi	青湾茗醼図誌
seki	席
Sen Inzen	仙胤善
senbai	仙媒
senbin	洗瓶
sencha	煎茶
sencha hana	煎茶花
Sencha hayashi nan	煎茶早指南
Sencha ketsu	煎茶訣
Sencha kigen	煎茶綺言
Sencha ryakusetsu	煎茶略説
Sencha shiki	煎茶式
Sencha shōjutsu	煎茶小述
Sencha shōshū	煎茶小集
Sencha tebiki no tane	煎茶手引の種
senchadō	煎茶道
senji cha	煎じ茶
senji mono	煎じ物
senkō	線香
senten	煎点
shin	真
Shinakan	支那館
Shinozaki Sachiko	篠崎佐智子
Shinozaki Shōchiku	篠崎小竹
Shinsen sencha ichiran	新撰煎茶一覧
Shinzoku kibun	清俗紀聞
Shisendō	詩仙堂
shiu	滓盂
shogakai	書画会
Shōin rōjin zuiroku	松隠老人随録
Shū Kōki	周高起
Shu Ryūkyō	朱柳橋
Shu Shunsui	朱舜水
Shunsui Shushi danki	舜水朱氏談綺
sō	草
Sō Senshun	曾占春
Sōchoō	桑苧翁
sōka	挿花
Sugai Baikan	菅井梅関
Sugie Jumon	杉江寿門
suichū	水注
sumikago	炭篭
Sumiya	角屋
Tachi Ryūwan	館柳湾
takusu	托子
tana	棚
Tanaka Akihito	田中香坡
Tanaka Fūtani	田中楓谷
Tanaka Issō	田中一窓
Tanaka Kakuō	田中鶴翁
Tanaka Seiha	田中青坡
Tanaka Tokuō	田中徳川翁
Tanomura Chikuden	田能村竹田
Tanomura Chokunyū	田能村直入
teiran	提藍
temae	手前
tencha	点茶
tetsubin	鉄瓶
Tetsusō chafu	鉄荘茶譜
tōcha	闘茶
Tōen	東園
Tōgyū Baisa	東牛売茶

tōkan	湯罐
Tokutomi Sohō	徳富蘇峰
Tomioka Tessai	富岡鉄斎
toriire	取入れ
tōsaibon	都載盆
Tōto Utaguchi	東都歌口
Totoki Baigai	十時梅崖
Tsubaki Chinzan	椿椿山
Tsuga Teishō	都賀庭鐘
Tsukamoto Yasushi	塚本靖
Tsukiyama niwa tsukuriden kōhen	築山庭造伝後編
tsusen shiki	通仙式
Tsusentei	通仙亭
Tsūzoku sencha hōshiki	通俗煎茶法式
Ueda Akinari	上田秋成
ufu	烏府
Uno Meika	宇野明霞
Uragami Shunkin	浦上春琴
ūroncha	烏竜茶
wabicha	詫び茶
Wakan chashi	和漢茶誌
wantō	碗筒
Watanabe Kazan	渡辺崋山
Yabunouchi Chikushin	藪内竹心
Yamamoto Baiitsu	山本梅逸
Yamamoto Chikuun	山本竹雲
Yamamoto Tokujun	山本徳潤
Yamanaka Kichirōbei (Shunkōdō)	山中吉郎兵衛（春篁堂）
Yaozentei	八百善亭
Yatsuhashi Baisa	八橋売茶
Yixing	宜興
Yōjōkun	養生訓
Yōsen	葉雋
Yōsen meiko kei	陽羨茗壷系
Yotsugashira	四柱
Yukawa Gen'yō	湯川玄洋
yusamashi	湯冷
Yusei	喩政
yuwakashi	湯沸
Zen Nihon Senchadō Renmeikai	全日本煎茶道連盟会
Zenrin shōkisen	禅林象器箋
zoku	俗
zokujincha	俗人茶

Bibliography

Annotated Bibliography of Selected Premodern Japanese Texts on Sencha

Texts are listed chronologically. All attempts were made to examine original editions or at least to read them in modern printed versions, although those are scarce for books on sencha. Several of the books were totally inaccessible; in those instances reliance on information from other scholars is indicated by an asterisk (*) at the beginning of the entry. Citations are to reprints, facsimile editions, or English translations of the texts. Major Chinese tea texts are discussed and reproduced in facsimile in Nunome (1987). For short descriptions of a larger selection of books on sencha, see Tsukuda I. (1981), Shufunotomosha (1976, 200-213), and Fumoto (2019).

***Honchō shokkan (Compendium of Food from Our Time)*, 1692. 12 volumes. Sencha is described as a popular morning beverage among the women of Edo.

Gankyokō (Manuscript of the Rock Dweller), preface dated 1703. 6 volumes. By Gettan Dōchō. Contains a long, historical poem about sencha, titled *Sencha uta.*

Yōjōkun (Precepts on Health Care), 1713. 1 volume. By Kaibara Ekken. One of the *Ekken jukun (Ten Primers of Ekken)*. Sencha is recommended for good health (Kaibara 1974).

Wakan chashi (Documents on Tea in China and Japan), 1728. 3 volumes. By Mitani Sōchin. The first chanoyu text to emphasize the history of tea in China.

Genryū chawa (Talks on the Origin of Tea), published in 1745 but perhaps written as early as the Kyōhō era (1716-1736). 1 volume. By Yabunouchi Chikushin. Surveys the history of tea in China and Japan (Sen 1977a, vol. 3).

Baisanshu chafu ryaku (A Collection of Tea Documents from the Plum Mountain), 1748; expanded edition published 1838. 1 volume. By Baisaō. Presents Baisaō's views on tea (Hayashiya, Yokoi, and Narabayashi 1972, 59–67; Shufunotomosha 1975).

Seiwan chawa (Chats on Tea by the Azure Harbor), 1756; reprinted as *Sencha shiyō shū (Collected Essentials on Sencha)*, 1913. 2 volumes. By Ōeda Ryūhō. Preface by Tsuga Teishō. The first treatise on a sencha tea ceremony (Hayashiya, Yokoi, and Narabayashi 1972, 69–152).

***Chatō (Tea Treatises)*, 1758. 1 volume. By Xia Shufang (J: Ka Juhō). Preface by Kiyota Tansō. Published in Kyoto; the first Japanese edition of the Chinese book *Chadong (Tea Treatises)* of circa 1610.

Chakyō (Classic of Tea), 1758. 2 volumes. By Lu Yu. The first Japanese reprint of the *Cha jing (Classic of Tea)*, based on a Ming edition that included several other Chinese tea books.

Gayū manroku (Miscellaneous Records of Elegant Pastimes), 1762. 7 volumes. By Ōeda Ryūhō. Preface by Tsuga Teishō. Describes various Chinese literati pastimes and related material culture.

Baisaō gego (Verses of the Old Tea Peddler), 1763. 1 volume. By Baisaō. Compiled by Kinryū Dōjin and others. Preface by Kinryū Dōjin. Biography by Daiten Kenjō. Portrait of Baisaō by Itō Jakuchū. Title calligraphy by Ike Taiga. Afterword by Daichō Genkō. The main source of information about Baisaō's life, poetry, and philosophy (partially translated in Waddell 1984; Shufunotomosha 1975).

Sencha ketsu (Secrets of Steeped Tea), 1764; reprinted in Edo by Iiyama Gihō, 1838. 1 volume. By Ye Zhuan (J: Yōsen). Edited by Daiten Kenjō. Published by Kimura Kenkadō. The first Japanese edition of the Chinese treatise *Jiancha jue (Secrets of Steeped Tea).*

Chakyō shōsetsu (Detailed Explanation of the Classic of Tea), 1774. 2 volumes. By Daiten Kenjō. The first Japanese vernacular translation of Lu Yu's tea treatise.

***Kōcha roku (Record of Tea Investigation)*, 1779. Inner title: *Sencha hayashi nan (Quick Guide to Sencha).* 1 volume. By Tōto Utaguchi. Sencha in Edo is discussed.

Seifū sagen (Miscellaneous Comments on the Way of Pure Elegance), 1794. 2 volumes. By Ueda Akinari. Preface by Murase Kōtei. A bestseller in its day, this book helped propel widespread popularity of sencha (Iwahashi 1918, 2: 479–502; Hayashiya, Yokoi, and Narabayashi 1972, 153–210).

Sencha ryakusetsu (Detailed Record of Sencha), 1798. 1 volume. By Nakajima Rakusui. Preface by Kikuchi Gozan. Published by Maekawa Zenbei. A Japanese translation of the Chinese text *Jiancha jue (Secrets of Steeped Tea)*, by Ye Zhuan, with supplemental information on sencha in Japan.

Shinzoku kibun (Record of Chinese Customs), 1799. 6 volumes. By Nakagawa Chuei. The lifestyles and material culture of Chinese residents in Nagasaki are discussed (Nakagawa C. 1966).

Cha shi (History of Tea), 1801. 2 volumes. By Liu Yuanzhang (J: Ryū Genchō). Preface by Totoki Baigai. The first Japanese edition of the important Chinese tea compendium *Cha shi (History of Tea)*, of circa 1675.

Sencha hayashi nan (Quick Guide to Sencha), 1802. 1 volume. By Ryūkatei Ransui. Explains sencha in simple terms, with names of utensils borrowed from chanoyu (Hayashiya, Yokoi, and Narabayashi 1972, 223–258).

Hōcha shōsho (Woodblock Book on Boiled Tea), 1803. 1 volume. By Sō Senshun. Tea and utensils are explained in the first part of this book; in the second part, *Charyō zusan (Notes on a Tea Gathering)*, by Ōkubo Shibutsu, utensils used at a specific gathering are described.

Chasho zenshū (Complete Collection of Tea Books), 1804. 3 volumes. Edited by Yu Zheng (J: Yusei). Preface by Minagawa Kien. The first reprint in Japan of the Ming (1613) compendium *Chashu quanji (Complete Collection of Tea Books)*.

Sencha shiki (Sencha Techniques), 1804. 1 volume. By Masuyama Sessai. How to host a sencha gathering in the style of the Chinese literati.

Chaka suigen (Drunken Words of a Tea Addict), begun 1806, completed circa 1807. 1 volume. By Ueda Akinari. The author's personal ruminations on sencha and its underlying philosophy of purity in the manner of the Chinese literati (Nakamura Y. 1961, 219–249).

**Encha shiki (Techniques of Encha)*, 1819. 1 volume. By Master Shitekika. A sencha manual for the less educated, sencha is presented in terms of chanoyu rules of etiquette.

Baisaō chaki zufu (Pictorial Record of Baisaō's Tea Utensils), 1823. 1 volume. By Kimura Kenkadō. Published and appended posthumously by Kenkadō's son, Kōyō. Illustrations by Aoki Shukuya. A printed album, with supplementary information, of Kenkadō's sketchbook *Baisaō chagu zu (Illustrations of Baisaō's Tea Utensils)* (Shufunotomosha 1975, 9–11). A 1924 edition of 300 copies was published in memory of Tanaka Kakuō.

Ryōzandō chawa (Ryōzandō's Chats on Tea), preface dated 1824, published 1828, reprinted 1919. 2 volumes. By Abe Kenshū (Ryōzandō). An important source for understanding bunjincha in the early nineteenth century.

Hōcha ketsu (Chats on Boiling Tea), 1829. 1 volume. By Tanomura Chikuden. Written in kanbun, this book discusses sencha growing, processing, and utensils; republished as volume 3 of Chikuden's 1831 compendium *Hōcha shinsho sanshu (A Collection of Three New Books on Boiling Tea)*, with a preface by Zhu Liuqiao (Shu Ryūkyō).

Chagu zufu (Pictorial Album of Tea Utensils), 1829. Inner title: *Sekisansai chagu zufu (Sekisansai's Pictorial Album of Tea Utensils)*. 1 volume. A Chinese text, abridged and adapted by Tanomura Chikuden for a Japanese audience. The original Chinese author, Old Man Sangzhu (J: Sōchoō), wrote a five-part text on tea, *Chaju tupu (Pictorial Album of Tea Utensils)*. A Chinese merchant in Nagasaki, Fu Shiran (J: Fu Shizen), reduced the text to two volumes. Chikuden's text is based on a one-volume abridgement by another Chinese merchant, Xian Yinshan (J: Sen Inzen). Chikuden also republished this as volume 1 of his 1831 compendium, *Hōcha shinsho sanshu (A Collection of Three New Books on Boiling Tea)*. It contains extensive examples of Chinese sencha utensils and other ceramic utensils for rice, wine, and food. The 1831 edition has a preface by the Chinese merchant Zhu Liuqiao (J: Shu Ryūkyō). This book was also published in a different 1831 compendium (reprinted in 1870) by Chikuden, *Chasetsu zufu (Illustrated Discussion about Tea)*, together with his *Chikudensō chasetsu (Discussion on Tea by Chikuden)*. Chikuden's *Hōcha ketsu (Chats on Boiling Tea)* and *Chagu zufu (Pictorial Album of Tea Utensils)* were reprinted together in 1850 with an introduction by Shinozaki Shōchiku.

Chikudensō chasetsu (Discussion on Tea by Chikuden), 1831. 1 volume. By Tanomura Chikuden. A Japanese vernacular edition of Chikuden's book *Hōcha ketsu (Chats on Boiling Tea)* with different illustrations. It was published together with *Chagu zufu (Pictorial Album of Tea Utensils)* in 1831 in the *Chasetsu zufu (Illustrated Discussion about Tea)*. This book was also printed together with *Hōcha ketsu (Chats on Boiling Tea)* and *Chagu zufu (Pictorial Album of Tea Utensils)* as volume 2 of Chikuden's 1831 compendium, *Hōcha shinsho sanshu (A Collection of Three New Books on Boiling Tea)*. The *Hōcha shinsho sanshu* and the *Chasetsu zufu* contain prefaces by Rai San'yō copied by his pupil Gotō Shōin.

Seifūryū hōcha shoshiki shōkai (A Detailed Explanation of the Elegant Commodity of Boiled Tea), a manuscript written sometime during the Tenpō era (1830–1844) of the Tokugawa period. 7 volumes. By Tanaka Kakuō. Three slightly dissimilar copies exist. Procedures for preparing sencha in a variety of settings are explained, using assorted utensils according to rules borrowed from chanoyu.

**Sencha shōjutsu (Small Book about Sencha)*, 1834. 1 volume. Inner title: *Sencha tsū (Understanding Sencha)*. By Yamamoto Tokujun. Written in vernacular Japanese, this is a general book about the history of tea and utensils for sencha.

Naniwa sencha taijin shū (Collection of Great Sencha Tea Masters of Naniwa [Osaka]), 1835. 1 volume. By Ōsato Kōan. An illustrated handwritten manuscript, unpublished. Short biographies and illustrations of twenty-two sencha tea masters of Osaka from various walks of life are included (Onchi 1983).

Sencha shōshū (A Small Sencha Gathering), 1838; reprinted in an accordion-folded album, 1916. 1 volume. Illustrations by Tsubaki Chinzan. Title calligraphy by Tachi Ryūwan. Preface by Kameda Ryōrai. Epilogue by Iiyama Gihō. A pictorial record of a sencha gathering in Edo.

**Eicha shiroku (Written Record of Poems on Tea)*, 1839. 1 volume. Edited by Tachi Ryūwan. Preface by Kameda Ryōrai. Epilogue by Iiyama Gihō. A collection of Chinese poems about tea from the Tang through the Ming dynasties.

Seigojō (*Album of pure entertainment*) 1844. By Yamamoto Baiitsu. Manuscript (not printed) album with sixteen illustrations (see Aichi 2016 and Fukunaga 2019).

Shinsen sencha ichiran (New Selections of Sencha at a Glance), 1847. 1 volume. By Sakura Seidan (Seidanrō shujin). A pocket-sized guide to sencha, intended for the general public.

Sencha tebiki no tane (Concise Guide to Sencha), 1848. 1 volume. By Yamamoto Tokujun. Illustrations by Katsushika Ōi. A popular, pocket-sized manual for sencha, very similar to the *Shinsen sencha ichiran (New Selections of Sencha at a Glance)*.

Bokusekikyo sencha ketsu (Secrets of Steeped Tea by Bokusekikyo), 1849. 2 volumes. By Fukada Seiichi. Explains the essential points of bunjincha and distinguishes it from sencha as practiced by plebeians, described as zokujincha (Hayashiya, Yokoi, and Narabayashi 1972, 259–270).

Seifū sencha yōran (Outline of the Pure Spirit of Sencha), 1851. 1 volume. By Tōen. Another pocket-sized guide based on the *Shinsen sencha ichiran (New Selections of Sencha at a Glance)* and the *Sencha tebiki no tane (Concise Guide to Sencha)*.

**Hōcha ki (Record of a Boiled Tea Ceremony)*, 1851. By Ogawa Kashin. Survives only in manuscript copies of the Meiji period dated 1909. An illustrated record of a tea ceremony hosted by the author at Kōdaiji in Kyoto.

Meien hinmoku (A list of items for a tea gathering), 1852. By Yamamoto Baiitsu. Published on the occasion of his 70th birthday. A landmark publication in the history of sencha books in that it illustrates the appearance and arrangement of objects at sencha gatherings (Fukunaga 2019. Digitized at https://kokusho.nijl.ac.jp/biblio/100288261/20?ln=ja)

Kōrakudō kissa ben (Kōrakudō's Talks on Tea Drinking), 1857, reprinted 1879. 1 volume. By Ogawa Kashin. Preface by Horikawa Yasuchika. A detailed explanation of sencha preparation based on Kashin's philosophy (Hayashiya, Yokoi, and Narabayashi 1972, 271–295).

Sencha kigen (Elegant Sayings about Sencha), 1857 (volume 1), 1858 (volume 2), reprinted in 1871. 2 volumes. By Tōgyū Baisa. Extremely influential in the late Tokugawa and early Meiji periods, this book presents an extensive history of the sencha tradition. It was the first to include Ishikawa Jōzan in the lineage of sencha tea masters.

Seiwan chakai zuroku (Pictorial Record of the Azure Sea Tea Gathering), 1863. 3 volumes. By Tanomura Chokunyū. The first detailed record of a sencha gathering, this book became the model for many that followed. It recorded the people, artifacts, and events connected with two gatherings in Osaka in 1862 and 1863.

Tetsusō chafu (Tessai's Tea Records), 1867. 2 volumes. By Tomioka Tessai. The first volume of this book, *Gikō jihu fu (Record of Clay Pots of Yixing)* is an illustrated connoisseurship study of Yixing ware teapots. It includes a translation into Japanese of the earliest known treatise on Yixing wares in China, the *Yangxian minghu xi (An Account of the Teapots of Yangxian*; J: *Yosen meiko kei*) by Zhou Gaoqi (J: Shū Kōki), written during the Wanli era (1573–1620) of the Ming dynasty. In the second volume, *Bunbō seiyaku zu (Sketches of Pure Scholar's Accouterments)*, the proper atmosphere in which to enjoy sencha is illustrated and described.

Seiwan meien zushi (Pictorial Record of Famous Utensils Used at the Azure Sea Tea Gathering), 1875. 4 volumes. By Yamanaka Kichirōbei (Shunkōdō). Illustrations by Tanomura Chokunyū. An illustrated connoisseurship study, the first of its kind, of the Chinese utensils used in a sencha gathering. The names of owners are provided and assemblages of utensils are shown.

Meiko zuroku (C: *Ming hu tu lu*; *Pictorial Record of Famous Teapots*), 1876. 2 volumes. By Oku Randen (Saburōbei). Thirty-two teapots, mostly Yixing wares, owned by the author and his friends are illustrated and described (Chinese reprint in Huang and Deng 1963).

Secondary Sources

Entries preceded by * mark publications that post-date the 1998 edition of this book.

Abiko, Bonnie F. 1982. "Watanabe Kazan: The Man and His Times." Ph.D. diss., Princeton University.

Addiss, Stephen. 1978. *Ōbaku: Zen Painting and Calligraphy*. Lawrence: Spencer Museum of Art, University of Kansas.

———. 1982. "Japanese Literati Artists of the Meiji Period." In *Essays on Japanese Art Presented to Jack Hillier*, edited by Matthi Forrer, 10–23. London: Robert G. Sawers.

———. 1984. *The World of Kameda Bōsai*. New Orleans: New Orleans Museum of Art; Lawrence: University Press of Kansas.

———, ed . 1986. *Japanese Quest for a New Vision: The Impact of Visiting Chinese Painters, 1600–1900*. Lawrence: Spencer Museum of Art, University of Kansas.

———. 1989. *The Art of Zen: Paintings and Calligraphy by Japanese Monks, 1600–1925*. New York: Harry N. Abrams.

Aichi. 1991. *Tokubetsuten, Edo jidai o kazaru oniwayaki to goyōgama no sekai* (Special exhibition of the world of garden potteries and daimyo-sponsored kilns that embellished the Edo period). Aichi: Aichi Ken Tōji Shiryōkan [Aichi Prefectural Ceramic Museum].

*———. 2000. *Sencha to yakimono: Edo Meiji no Chūgoku shumi* (Sencha and ceramics: Chinese pastimes in the Edo and Meiji periods). Aichi: Aichi-ken Tōji Bijutsukan [Aichi Prefectural Ceramic Museum].

*———. 2007. *Sencha tōgei no bi to dentō: ningen kokuhō sandai Yamada Jōzan e no michi: shūki tokubetsu kikakuten = Tradition and beauty of ceramic art 'sencha': living national treasure, Yamada Jozan III, and the development of tea vessels: special exhibition*. Aichi: Aichi-ken Tōji Bijutsukan [Aichi Prefectural Ceramic Museum].

*———. 2016. *Yamamoto Baiitsu to Owari Mikawa no bunjin bunka = Literati Painter Yamamoto Baiitsu and Bunjin Culture in Owari Province and Mikawa Province*. Aichi: Aichi-ken Tōji Bijutsukan [Aichi Prefectural Ceramic Museum].

Akai Tatsurō. 1970. "Kaei yōnen sencha kaiki, Hōchaki" (A record of a boiled tea ceremony from Kaei 4). *Geinōshi kenkyū* (History of the performing arts) 13 (October): 49–54.

Anjō. 1991. *Tokubetsuten, Bunjin, Ishikawa Jōzan no sekai* (Special exhibition on the literati, the world of Ishikawa Jōzan). Anjō: Anjō-shi Rekishi Hakubutsukan [Anjō Municipal Museum of History].

———. 2007. *Sencha no Sekai: Tokubetsuten Ishikawa Jōzan no kokoro* (The world of sencha: special exhibition on the heart of Ishikawa Jōzan). Anjō: Anjō-shi Rekishi Hakubutsukan [Anjō Municipal Museum of History].

Aoyama Kiyoshi, ed. 1986. *Senchadō bijutsu taikan* (Compendium of the arts of sencha). Tokyo: Fujin Gahosha.

*Arapova. 2015. Arapova, T. and A. A. Egorova. *"Sosud vechnoi radosti": iaponskie miniatiurnye chainiki dlia chaia Sentia v sobranii Ermitazha: katalog vystavki = A Vessel of Eternal Joy: Japanese Miniature Teapots for Sencha Tea from the Hermitage Collection*. St. Petersburg, Russia: Izdatel'stvo Gosudarstvennogo Ėrmitazha. (Text in Russian with English summary).

Art Gallery of Greater Victoria. 1981. *Japanese Sen Cha Ceremony Utensils*. Victoria: Art Gallery of Greater Victoria.

Arts, P. L. W. 1988. *Tetsubin: A Japanese Waterkettle*. Groningen: Geldermalsen Publications.

Ayers, John. 1982. *The Baur Collection, Geneva: Japanese Ceramics*. Geneva: Collections Baur.

———. 1991. "From Cauldron to Teapot: The Evolution of Ceramic Tea Vessels in China." In *Chinese Ceramic Tea Vessels: The K. S. Lo Collection, Flagstaff House Museum of Tea Ware*, 60–78. Hong Kong: Chinese Museum of Hong Kong.

Backus, Robert L. 1974. "The Relationship of Confucianism to the Tokugawa Bakufu as Revealed in the Kansai Educational Reforms." *Harvard Journal of Asiatic Studies* 34: 97–162.

Baekeland, Frederick, and Robert Moes. 1993. *Modern Japanese Ceramics in American Collections*. New York: Japan Society.

Baroni, Helen Josephine. 1993. "Buddhism in Early Tokugawa Japan: The Case of Ōbaku Zen and the Monk Tetsugen Dōkō." Ph.D. diss., Columbia University.

Bartholomew, Terese Tse. 1977. *I-hsing Ware*. New York: China House Gallery.

*Beerens, Anna. 2006. *Friends, Acquaintances, Pupils, and Patrons: Japanese Intellectual Life in the Late Eighteenth Century: A Prosopographical Approach*. Leiden, The Netherlands: Leiden University Press.

Berry, Paul. 1985. "Tanomura Chikuden, 1777–1835: Man amidst the Mountains." Ph.D. diss., University of Michigan.

*Bincsik, Mónika and Moroyama Masanori. 2017 *Japanese Bamboo Art: The Abbey Collection*. New York:

The Metropolitan Museum of Art Bulletin, spring 2017.

*———. 2019. *Take kōgei meihinte: Nyū Yōku no Abī ko-rekushon: Metoroporitan Bijutsukan shozō = Japanese Bamboo Art from New York: The Abbey Collection: Gifts to the Metropolitan Museum of Art*. Tokyo: NHK Promotions.

Blofeld, John. 1985. *The Chinese Art of Tea*. Boston: Shambhala.

Bodart-Bailey, Beatrice. 1993. "The Persecution of Confucianism in Early Tokugawa Japan." *Monumenta Nipponica* 48, 3 (autumn): 293–314.

Bourdieu, Pierre. 1984. *Distinction: A Social Critique of the Judgement of Taste*. Cambridge: Harvard University Press.

*Brecher, W. Puck. 2013. *The Aesthetics of Strangeness: Eccentricity and Madness in Early Modern Japan*. Honolulu: University of Hawai'i Press.

Bring, Mitchell, and Josse Wayembergh. 1981. *Japanese Gardens: Design and Meaning*. New York: McGraw-Hill.

Brown, Kendall H. 1997. *The Politics of Reclusion: Painting and Power in Momoyama Japan*. Honolulu: University of Hawai'i Press.

BSN Niigata. 1983. *Chadō ten, sencha* (Tea ceremony exhibition, sencha). Niigata: BSN Niigata Bijutsukan [BSN Niigata Museum of Art].

*Bunjinga Kenkyūkai. 2015. *Yamamoto Baitsu Meien hinmoku no sekai: Baisaryu iemoto yusenkutsu kaiso 100 shunen kinengo* (The world of Yamamoto Baiitsu's catalogue of famous utensils). Tokorozawa: Bunjinga Kenkyukai; Tokyo: Kyuko Shoin (Hatsubai).

*Bunjinga Kenkyūkai. 2008. *Seigojō: Baiitsu no chakaiseki zuan* (Album of pure entertainment: the layout of Baiitsu's tea gathering environments). Tokyo: Bunjinga Kenkyūkai.

Cahill, James. 1976. *Scholar Painters of Japan: The Nanga School*. New York: Asia Society.

Cardeiro, C. Philip. 1989. *Japanese Hirado Porcelain, 1640–1909*. Monterey, Calif.: Art Asia Museum.

Chang, Ho-chin. 1970. "The Chinese Community of Nagasaki in the First Century of the Tokugawa Period (1603–1688)." Ph.D. diss., St. John's University.

Chaves, Jonathan. 1991. "Jōzan and Poetry." In *Shisendō Hall of the Poetry Immortals*, by J. Thomas Rimer et al., 27–78. New York: Weatherhill.

Ching, Julia. 1975. "Chu Shun-shui, 1600–82: A Chinese Confucian Scholar in Tokugawa Japan." *Monumenta Nipponica* 30, 2 (summer): 177–191.

———. 1979. "The Practical Learning of Chu Shun-shui (1600–1682)." In *Principle and Practicality: Essays in Neo-Confucianism and Practical Learning*, edited by William Theodore de Bary and Irene Bloom, 189–229. New York: Columbia University Press.

Chiu, Simon K. S. 1991. "The History of Tea and Tea-making in China as Recorded in Texts, Paintings, and Artefacts." In *Chinese Ceramic Tea Vessels: The K. S. Lo Collection, Flagstaff House Museum of Tea Ware*, 26–43. Hong Kong: Hong Kong Museum of Art.

Chu, Yen. 1910. *Description of Chinese Pottery and Porcelain, Being a Translation of the T'ao Shuo*. Edited by Stephen W. Bushell. Reprint, London: Oxford University Press, 1977.

Clunas, Craig. 1991. *Superfluous Things: Material Culture and Social Status in Early Modern China*. Urbana and Chicago: University of Illinois Press

Collcutt, Martin. 1981. *Five Mountains: The Rinzai Zen Monastic Institution in Medieval Japan*. Cambridge: Harvard University Press.

Conant, Ellen P., et al. 1995. *Nihonga, Transcending the Past: Japanese-Syle Painting, 1868–1968*. Saint Louis: Saint Louis Art Museum.

Cooper, Michael. 1989. "The Early Europeans and Tea." In *Tea in Japan: Essays on the History of Chanoyu*, edited by Paul Varley and Kumakura Isao, 101–133. Honolulu: University of Hawai'i Press.

Cort, Louise Allison. 1979. *Shigaraki, Potters' Valley*. Tokyo: Kōdansha.

———. 1992. *Seto and Mino Ceramics*. Washington, D.C.: Freer Gallery of Art, Smithsonian Institution.

de Bary, William Theodore. 1979. "Sagehood as a Secular and Spiritual Ideal." In *Principle and Practicality: Essays in Neo-Confucianism and Practical Learning*, edited by William Theodore de Bary and Irene Bloom, 127–188. New York: Columbia University Press.

Donnelly, P.J. 1969. *Blanc de Chine: The Porcelain of Tehua in Fukien*. London: Faber and Faber.

Dore, Ronald P. 1965. *Education in Tokugawa Japan*. Berkeley: University of California Press.

*Earle, Joe. 2017. *Baskets: Masterpieces of Japanese Bamboo Art, 1850-2015*. Hong Kong: Stark Studios Ltd.

Etchū Tetsuya. 1968. "Kameyama yaki bunsho ko" (Study of documents pertaining to the Kameyama pottery kiln). *Nagasaki Shiritsu Hakubutsukan kanpo* 9: 21–27.

Etchū Tetsuya and Ōto Yoshihisa, eds. 1976. *Nagasaki, Yokohama*. Vol. 25 of *Edo jidai zushi* (Pictorial record of the Edo era). Tokyo: Chikuma Shobo.

*Farris, William Wayne. 2019. *A Bowl for a Coin: A Commodity History of Japanese Tea*. Honolulu: University of Hawai'i Press.

Faulkner, Rupert. 1995. *Japanese Studio Crafts: Tradition and the Avant-Garde*. Philadelphia: University of Pennsylvania Press.

*Feltens, Frank, ed. 2023. *Japan in the Age of Modernization: The Arts of Ōtagaki Rengetsu and Tomioka Tessai.* Washington, D.C. Smithsonian Scholarly Press.

Finn, Dallas. 1995. *Meiji Revisited: The Sites of Victorian Japan*. New York: Weatherhill.

*Fischer, Felice with Kyoko Kinoshita. 2007. *Ike Taiga and Tokuyama Gyokuran: Japanese Masters of the Brush.* Philadelphia: Philadelphia Museum of Art.

Fister, Patricia. 1988. *Japanese Women Artists, 1600–1900.* Lawrence: Helen Foresman Spencer Museum of Art, University of Kansas.

Flagstaff House. 1991. *Chinese Ceramic Tea Vessels: The K. S. Lo Collection, Flagstaff House Museum of Tea Ware.* Hong Kong: Hong Kong Museum of Art.

Fogel, Joshua A. 1984. *Politics and Sinology: The Case of Naitō Konan (1866–1934)*. Cambridge: Council on East Asian Studies, Harvard University Press.

———. 1996. *The Literature of Travel in the Japanese Rediscovery of China, 1862–1945*. Stanford: Stanford University Press.

Fujioka, Ryōichi. 1973. *Tea Ceremony Utensils*. Translated by Louise Allison Cort. New York: Weatherhill/Shibundō.

*Fukunaga, Ai. 2019. "Scholar's Utopia: Rethinking the Display for Sencha in the Late Edo period." *Andon* 107: 3-14.

*———. 2021. "British Collecting of Ceramics for Tea Gatherings from Meiji Japan: British Museum and Maidstone Museum Collections." PhD. thesis. SOAS University of London.

Fukuyama Chōgan. 1933. *Baisaō*. Nagoya: Shorin-kichūdō.

*Fumoto Kazuyoshi. 2000. "Sencha kūkan: sono bunken-shiteki tokushitsu (the atmosphere of sencha, special characteristics of its cultural history). In *Chashitsu, Roji*, edited by Nakamura Toshinori. *Chadōgaku taikei* 6. Kyoto: Tankōsha, 205–54.

*Fumoto Kazuyoshi, Hitsumoto Satoko, and Hamada Shinichi. 2019. "Senchakai zuroku no shoshiteki kōsai" (Consideration of the bibliography of illustrated books of the green tea ceremony). *Journal of Architecture and Planning*, Architectural Institute of Japan, 84/755: 209-219 (January). https://www.jstage.jst.go.jp/article/aija/84/755/84_209/_article/-char/ja/

*Funasaka Fumiko. 2003. "Tachi Ryūwan to *sencha* no shiyu" (The advocates of sencha tea in Edo: Tachi Ryūwan and his friends). *Nomura bijutsukan kenkyū kiyō* 12: 1-28.

*———. 2015. "Koishi Genzui hitsu sencha kaiki: Gochiku saryō chagu mokuorku" (Record of a *sencha* tea gathering: Gochiku saryō catalogue of tea utensils). *Journal of Chanoyu* 233: 53–73.

Gardner Museum. 1993. "Competition and Collaboration: Hereditary Schools in Japanese Culture." In *Fenway Court*. Boston: Isabella Stewart Gardner Museum.

Gifu. 1992. *Ōbaku: Zen to geijutsu* (Ōbaku: Zen and art). Gifu: Gifu-shi Rekishi Hakubutsukan [Gifu Municipal Museum of History].

Graham, Patricia J. 1983. "Yamamoto Baiitsu: His Life, Literati Pursuits, and Related Paintings." Ph.D. diss., University of Kansas.

———. 1984. "Nanga Painters of Nagoya." *Orientations* 15, 10 (October): 34–48.

———. 1985a. "Japan through an Artist's Eyes: The True-View Pictures of Yamamoto Baiitsu." *Orientations* 16, 2 (February): 12–27.

———. 1985b. "Sencha and Its Contribution to the Spread of Chinese Literati Culture in Edo Period Japan." *Oriental Art*, n.s., 31, 2 (summer): 186–195.

———. 1986. "Yamamoto Baiitsu no Chūgokuga kenkyū" (Yamamoto Baiitsu's study of Chinese painting). *Kobijutsu* 80 (autumn): 62–75.

———. 1990. "Lifestyles of Scholar-Painters in Edo Japan." *Bulletin of the Cleveland Museum of Art* 77, 7 (September): 262–283.

———. 1991. "On the Development of an Architectural Setting for the Sencha Tea Ceremony." *Orientations* 22, 9 (September): 65–75.

———. 1991–1992. "A Heterodox Painting of Shussan Shaka in Late Tokugawa Japan." *Artibus Asiae* 51, 3/4: 275–292; 52, 1/2: 131–145.

———. 1993a. "Documents and Monuments in the History of the Sencha Tea Ceremony in Japan." *Kansai Daigaku Tōzai Gakujutsu kenkyū kiyō* (Proceedings of the Institute of Oriental and Occidental Studies, Kansai University) 26 (March): 51–67.

———. 1993b. "Edo jidai ni okeru sencha bijutsu to Chūgoku bunjin kyōmi" (Arts for senchadō and Chinese literati taste in Edo-period Japan). In *Nihon bijutsushi no sumiyaku* (Currents in Japanese art history, festschrift for Professor Tsuji Nobuo of Tokyo University), 860–880. Tokyo: Pelican Press.

———. 1999. "Japanese Appreciation of Chinese Flower Baskets." In *Japanese Bamboo Baskets: Masterworks of Form and Texture, from the Collection of Lloyd Cotsen.* Los Angeles: Cotsen Occasional Press, 60-83.

*———. 2003. "*Karamono* for *Sencha*, Transformations in the Taste for Chinese Art." In *Japanese Tea Culture: Art, History, and Practice,* edited by Morgan Pitelka. London: Routledge-Curzon Press, 110-136.

*———. 2007a. *Faith and Power in Japanese Buddhist Art, 1600-2005*. Honolulu, University of Hawai'i Press, 2007.

*———. 2007b. "Ōtagaki Rengetsu and the Japanese Tea Ceremony." In *Black Robe, White Mist: The Art of the Japanese Buddhist Nun* Ōtagaki *Rengetsu*. Canberra: National Gallery of Australia, 63-68.

*———. 2009. "Dissention in the World of Tea: The Fashion for *Sencha* and Chinese Culture in Early Modern Japan." In *Steeped in History: The Art of Tea*, edited by Beatrice Hohenegger. Los Angeles: Fowler Museum at UCLA, 90-105.

*———. 2014. "Ōbaku and Sencha." In *Eat This and Drink Some Tea: Huangbo / Obaku Crosscultural Zen Calligraphy*, edited by Paul Moss. London, Sydney L. Moss, Ltd., 44-54.

*———. 2017. "The Importance of Imports: Ingen's Chinese Material Culture at Manpukuji." In *Zen and Material Culture*, edited by Pamela Winfield and Steven Heine. Oxford University Press. 137-163.

*———. 2023. "Obaku and Sencha (Huangbo and Tea-making)—Second Lecture of 'Huangbo Lecture Series." *Journal of Studies on Fujianese Entrepreneurs Culture Supplement 2023 Special Issue Huangbo (Ōbaku) Studies* (translated into Chinese by Jia Guangzuo, Pi Jinling, Chen Zhiqi): 96-109.

*Graham, Patricia J. and Frank Chance. 2021. "Japanese Literati Painting and Calligraphy." *Oxford Bibliographies* online. https://www.oxfordbibliographies.com/display/document/obo-9780199920105/obo-9780199920105-0163.xml?rskey=BLRS8Q&result=1&q=literati+paint%E2%80%A6#firstMatch

*Griffiths, John C. 2007. *Tea: The Drink That Changed the World*. London: Andre Deutsch.

Guth, Christine M.E. 1989. "The Tokugawa as Patrons and Collectors of Painting." In *The Tokugawa Collection: Japan of the Shoguns*, 41–51. Montreal: Montreal Museum of Fine Arts.

———. 1993. *Art, Tea, and Industry: Masuda Takashi and the Mitsui Circle*. Princeton: Princeton University Press.

*———. 2006. "Meiji Response to *Bunjinga*." In *Challenging the Past and Present: The Metamorphosis of Nineteenth-Century Japanese Art*, edited by Ellen P. Conant. Honolulu: University of Hawaii Press, 177-196.

Harada, Hiroji. 1993. "Nagasaki and Chinese Culture: An Introductory Sketch." *Crossroads: A Journal of Nagasaki History and Culture* 1 (summer): 19–33.

Hasebe Mitsuhiko et al. 1985. *Take no kōgei: kindai ni okeru tenkai* (Modern bamboo craft: developments in the modern era). Tokyo: Tokyo Kokuritsu Kindai Bijutsukan, Kōgeikan.

Hasegawa Shōshōkyo. 1965. *Sencha shi* (Sencha records). Reprint, Tokyo: Heibonsha.

Hashimoto, Fumio. 1981. *Architecture in the Shoin Style: Japanese Feudal Residences*. Translated by H. Mack Horton. Tokyo: Kōdansha and Shibundō.

Hayashi Genkichi. 1932. "Kameyama-yaki to Kinoshita Itsuun" (Kameyama ware and Kinoshita Itsuun). *Nagasaki dansō* (Random thoughts on Nagasaki) 10 (May): 34–37.

Hayashiya, Seizo, et al. 1977. *Chinese Ceramics from Japanese Collections: T'ang through Ming Dynasties*. New York: Asia Society and Weatherhill.

Hayashiya Tatsusaburō. 1978. *Bakumatsu bunka no kenkyū* (Research on the culture of the late Edo period). Tokyo: Iwanami Shoten.

Hayashiya Tatsusaburō, Yokoi Kiyoshi, and Narabayashi Tadao, eds. 1972. *Nihon no chasho* (Japanese books on tea). Vol. 2. Tōyōbunko, 206. Tokyo: Heibonsha.

Heibonsha. 1992. *Chanoyu kaiga shiryō shūsei* (Compilation of reference pictures on chanoyu). Tokyo: Heibonsha.

Hickman, Money L., and Yasuhiro Sato. 1989. *The Paintings of Jakuchū*. Tokyo: Agency for Cultural Affairs; New York: Asia Society Galleries; Los Angeles: Los Angeles County Museum of Art.

Hikone. 1988. *Kōtōyaki*. Hikone: Hikone-jō Hakubutsukan [Hikone Castle Museum].

Ho, Wai-kam, et al. 1980. *Eight Dynasties of Chinese Painting: The Collections of the Nelson Gallery-Atkins Museum, Kansas City, and the Cleveland Museum of Art*. Cleveland: Cleveland Museum of Art.

Hosokawa Morisada, ed. 1978. *Eisei Bunko meihin sen, bungu* (Selected treasures of the Eisei Bunko: scholars' utensils). Tokyo: Mokujisha.

———. 1982. *Ittoku roku* (Record of merits: scholars' paraphernalia). Tokyo: Chūōkōronsha.

Hosono, Masanobu. 1978. *Nagasaki Prints and Early Copperplates*. Translated by Lloyd R. Craighill. Tokyo: Kōdansha.

Huang Binhong and Deng Shi, eds. 1963. *Mei shu cong shu* (Collection of printed books on art). 1st ed. Vol. 23, 67–124. Taipei: Guangwenshu Chuban She. Reprinted in Deng Shi and Huang Binhong, eds., *Zhongguo gudai mei shu cong shu* (Collection of ancient Chinese books on art), vol. 12. Beijing: Guojiwenhua Chuban She, 1993.

Ibara. 1992. *Tanomura Chokunyū to Mori Roppo*. Ibara: Ibara-shi Denchū Bijutsukan [Ibara Municipal Denchū Museum of Art].

Ingen Zenshi. 1917. "Ingen Zenshi no yuisho mokuroku" (Catalogue of Master Ingen's books). *Zenshū* 264 (March): 21–25.

Innes, Robert LeRoy. 1980. "The Door Ajar: Japan's Foreign Trade in the Seventeenth Century." Ph.D. diss., University of Michigan.

Iruma. 1995. *Sencha no sekai* (The world of sencha). Iruma: Iruma-shi Hakubutsukan [Iruma City Museum].

*———. 2001. *Tokubetsuten "sencha" denrai: Baisaō to bunjincha no jidai* (Special exhibition on the origin of sencha: the era of Baisaō and literati tea). Iruma: Iruma-shi Hakubutsukan [Iruma City Museum].

Ishikawa. 1975. *Yoshidayagama meihinten zuroku* (Exhibition catalogue of famous works of the Yoshidaya kiln). Kanazawa: Ishikawa Kenritsu Bijutsukan [Ishikawa Prefectural Art Museum].

Ishikawa Jun et al., eds. 1979. *Mokubei*. Vol. 16 of *Bunjinga suihei* (The essence of literati painting). Tokyo: Chūōkōronsha.

Itabashi. 1996. *Nagasaki tōjin bōeki to senchadō* (The Nagasaki China trade and the sencha tea ceremony). Tokyo: Itabashi Kuritsu Kyōdō Shiryōkan [Itabashi Ward Museum of Folklore].

Itō Teiji and Yokoyama Tadashi, eds. 1983–1985. Gendai wafu kenchiku shū (Compilation of modern Japanese-style architecture). 7 vols. Tokyo: Kōdansha.

Iwahashi Koyata, ed. 1918. *Ueda Akinari zenshū* (Collected works of Ueda Akinari). 2 vols. Tokyo: Kokusho Kankōkai.

Iwao, Seiichi. 1976. "Japanese Foreign Trade in the Sixteenth and Seventeenth Centuries." *Acta Asiatica* 30: 1–18.

Jansen, Marius B. 1967. "Japanese Views of China during the Meiji Period." In *Approaches to Modern Chinese History*, edited by Albert Feuerwerker et al., 163–189. Berkeley: University of California Press.

———. 1992. *China in the Tokugawa World*. Cambridge: Harvard University Press.

Jenyns, Soame. 1965. *Japanese Porcelain*. London: Faber and Faber.

Kadoyama Shigeru. 1988. *Ocha to bunka* (Tea and culture). Vol. 3 of *Nihon no ocha* (Tea of Japan). Tokyo: Gyōsei.

Kaempfer, Engelbert. 1906. *The History of Japan: Together with a Description of the Kingdom of Siam, 1690–1692*. Translated by J . G. Scheuchzer. 3 vols. Glasgow: James MacLehose and Sons.

Kaga. 1984. *Enuma Kutani aka-e saibyō no sekai ten zuroku* (Exhibition catalogue of fine overglaze red enamel painting of Enuma Kutani). Kanazawa: Kaga-shi Bijutsukan [Kaga Municipal Museum of Art].

*Kageyama Sumio and Funasaka Fumiko. 2007. *Bunjin to sencha: Koishi Genzui to sono shūhen* (Literati and sencha: Koishi Genzui and his circle). Kobe: Kōbe Daigaku Bunjin Kenkyūkai.

Kaibara Ekken. 1974. *Yōjōkun: Japanese Secret of Good Health*. Translated by Kunihiro Masao. Tokyo: Tokuma Shoten.

*Kameda-Madar, Kazuko. 2022. *Imagery of the Orchid Pavilion Gathering: Visualizing Tokugawa Cultural Networks*. Leiden and Boston: Brill.

Kanematsu Rōmon. 1910. *Chikutō to Baiitsu* (Chikutō and Baiitsu). Tokyo: Gahōsha.

Kanō Hiroyuki. 1990. "Juhasseki to iu jidai" (The era of the eighteenth century). In *Tokubetsu tenrankai: juhasseki no Nihon no bijutsu, kattō suru biishiki* (Special exhibition: Japanese art in the eighteenth century, conflicting aesthetics), 4–13 . Kyoto: Kyoto Kokuritsu Hakubutsukan [Kyoto National Museum].

Kateigahō. 1982. *Meihin senchaki* (Famous examples of sencha utensils). Tokyo: Kateigahō.

Kawahara Masahiko. 1985. *Eisen, Mokubei, Dōhachi* (Potters Eisen, Mokubei, and Dōhachi). Vol. 227 of *Nihon no bijutsu* (Arts of Japan). Tokyo: Shibundō.

———. 1990. *Kyōyaki* (Kyoto ware). Vol. 26 of *Nihon tōji taikei* (Compendium of Japanese ceramics). Tokyo: Heibonsha.

Kawahara Masahiko and Degawa Tetsurō. 1993. "Sumiya shozōhin zuhan mokuroku (tōji hen)" (Catalogue of the Sumiya collection, ceramics). *Sumiya kenkyū* 4: 1–41.

Keene, Donald, trans. 1961. *Four Major Plays of Chikamatsu*. New York: Columbia University Press.

———. 1971. "The Sino-Japanese War of 1894–95 and Its Cultural Effects in Japan." Chap. 4 in *Tradition and Modernization in Japanese Culture*, edited by Donald H. Shivley, 121–175. Princeton: Princeton University Press.

———. 1978. *World within Walls: Japanese Literature of the Pre-Modern Era, 1600–1867*. Tokyo: Tuttle.

———. 1984. "Characteristic Responses to Confucianism in Tokugawa Literature." In *Confucianism and Tokugawa Culture*, edited by Peter Nosco, 120–137. Princeton: Princeton University Press.

———. 1985. "The Survival of Chinese Literary Traditions in the Meiji Era." In *Papers of the [1979] International Symposium on Sino-Japanese Cultural Interchange*, 75–90. Hong Kong: Institute of Chinese Studies, Chinese University of Hong Kong.

Kido, Takayoshi. 1983–1986. *The Diary of Kido Takayoshi*. Translated by Sidney Devere Brown and Akiko Hirota. 3 vols. Tokyo: University of Tokyo Press.

Kitao Harumichi, ed. 1957. *Sencha shitsu* (Sencha rooms). *Kenchiku shashin bunko* 60 (Library of architectural photographs, 60). Tokyo: Shōkokusha.

Kizaki Kōshō. 1929. *Daifūryū Tanomura Chikuden* (The great elegant Tanomura Chikuden). 8 vols. Tokyo: Minyūsha.

*Kobayashi and Nelson. 2005. Kobayashi, Tadashi and Julie Nelson Davis. "The Floating World in Light and Shadow: Ukiyo-e Paintings by Hokusai's Daughter Oi." In *Hokusai and his Age: Ukiyo-e Painting, Printmaking and Book Illustration in Late Edo Japan*, edited by John T. Carpenter. Amsterdam: Hotei Publishing.

Kōdansha. 1982. *Dentō to bi* (Tradition and beauty). Vol. 1 of *Zusetsu, Sencha* (Pictorial history of sencha). Tokyo: Kōdansha.

Komatsu. 1974. *Onogama ten* (Exhibition of works of the Ono kiln). Komatsu: Komatsu Shiritsu Hakubutsukan [Komatsu Municipal Museum].

*Komazawa. 2023. *Ōbaku Zen to Sencha: Ōbaku sanpitsu no bokuseki to sencha dōgu* (Ōbaku Zen and sencha: The three brushes of Ōbaku and sencha utensils). Tokyo: Komazawa Daigaku Zen Bunka Rekishi Hakubutsukan [The Museum of Zen Culture and History, Komazawa University]. 20-page downloadable leaflet https://www.komazawa-u.ac.jp/facilities/museum/overview/exhibition-room/2023/0414-14049.html

Kramer, Robert. 1985. "The Tea Cult in History." Ph.D. diss., University of Chicago.

Kuck, Loraine. 1980. *The World of the Japanese Garden*. New York: Weatherhill.

Kumakura Isao. 1976. "Sencha shi jokō, Nihon to Chōsen" (Introductory research on the history of sencha, Japan and Korea). *Fuzoku* (Customs) 4, 3 (May): 12–19.

———. 1980. *Kindai chadōshi no kenkyū* (Research on the recent history of the tea ceremony). Tokyo: Nihon Hōsō Shuppan Kyōkai.

Kyoto. 1973. Kyoto City. *Dentō no teichaku* (The establishment of traditions). Vol. 6 of *Kyoto no rekishi* (History of Kyoto). Kyoto: Gakugei Shorin.

Kyoto Municipal Museum. 1985. *Seitan 150 nen kinen Tomioka Tessai ten* (An exhibition of Tomioka Tessai in commemoration of the 150th anniversary of his birth). Kyoto: Kyoto-shi Bijutsukan [Kyoto Municipal Museum of Art].

Kyoto National Museum. 1990. *Tokubetsu tenrankai: juhasseki no Nihon no bijutsu, kattō suru biishiki* (Special exhibition: Japanese art in the eighteenth century, conflicting aesthetics). Kyoto: Kyoto Kokuritsu Hakubutsukan [Kyoto National Museum].

———. 1991. *Nihonjin ga kononda Chūgoku tōji* (Chinese ceramics admired by the Japanese people). Kyoto: Kyoto Kokuritsu Hakubutsukan [Kyoto National Museum].

———. 1993. *Ōbaku no bijutsu* (Ōbaku art). Kyoto: Kyoto Kokuritsu Hakubutsukan [Kyoto National Museum].

Kyoto Prefectural Library. 1984. *Ōtagaki Rengetsu: Bakumatsu jōryū kajin no shoga to tōgei* (Ōtagaki Rengetsu: the painting, calligraphy, and pottery of a female poet of the Bakumatsu era). Kyoto: Kyoto Furitsu Sōgō Shiryōkan [Kyoto Prefectural Library].

———. 1985. *Tanomura Chokunyū to Tomioka Tessai: sono gagyō to nanga no kiseki* (Tanomura Chokunyū and Tomioka Tessai: their painting achievements and their position in nanga). Kyoto: Kyoto Furitsu Sōgō Shiryōkan [Kyoto Prefectural Library].

*Lai, Yu-chih. 2012. "Tea and the Art Market in Sino-Japanese Exchanges of the Late Nineteenth Century: Sencha and the *Seiwan meien zushi*." In *The Role of Japan in Modern Chinese Art*, edited by Joshua A. Fogel. Berkeley: University of California Press, 2012.

Lawrence, Louis. 1997. *Hirado: Prince of Porcelains*. Chicago: Art Media Resources.

Lin, Yutang. 1961. *The Importance of Understanding: Translations from the Chinese*. Cleveland and New York: World Publishing Company.

Lo, K. S. 1986. *The Stonewares of Xixing*. Hong Kong: Sotheby's and Hong Kong University Press.

Lu, Yū. 1974. *The Classic of Tea*. Translated by Francis Ross Carpenter. Boston: Little, Brown and Company.

Maeda Toshiko. 1979. *Rengetsu*. Vol. 11 of *Bunjin shofu* (Literati-style calligraphy). Kyoto: Tankōsha.

*Maezaki, Shinya. 2009. "Qing-style Porcelain in Meiji Japan: The Ceramic Art of Seifū Yohei III." PhD. thesis. SOAS University of London.

*Maezaki, Shinya and Sinéad Vilbar. 2023. *Colors of Kyoto: The Seifū Yohei Ceramic Studio*. Cleveland: The Cleveland Museum of Art in association with D Giles Limited.

*Mair, Victor H. and Erling Ho. 2009. *The True History of Tea*. New York: Thames & Hudson.

Marceau, Lawrence Edward. 1989. "Literati Consciousness in Early Modern Japan: Takebe Ayatari and the Bunjin." Ph.D. diss., Harvard University.

Markus, Andrew. 1993. "Shogakai: Celebrity Banquets of the Late Edo Period." *Harvard Journal of Asiatic Studies* 53, 1: 135–167.

Maruyama, Masao. 1974. *Studies in the Intellectual History of Tokugawa Japan*. Princeton: Princeton University Press; Tokyo: Tokyo University Press.

Mason, Penelope. 1993. *History of Japanese Art*. New York: Harry N. Abrams.

McCallum, Toshiko M. 1988. *Containing Beauty: Japanese Bamboo Flower Baskets*. Los Angeles: UCLA Museum of Cultural History.

*Mikasa, Princess Akiko of. 2009. "Collecting and displaying 'Japan' in Victorian Britain: the case of the British Museum." PhD thesis. University of Oxford.

Miller, Alan L. 1971. "Ritsuryō Japan: The State as Liturgical Community." *History of Religions* 11, 1 (August): 98–121.

Mitchell, C.H. 1972. *The Illustrated Books of the Nanga, Maruyama, Shijo, and Other Related Schools of Japan: A Biobibliography*. Los Angeles: Dawson's Book Shop.

Mitsuoka Tadanari. 1975. *Himeji hanyō Tōzanyaki* (The Himeji fief kiln Tōzan ware). Tokyo: Kōbijutsu Kōgei Kabushiki Kaisha.

———, ed. 1981. *Nihon yakimono shūsei* (Compilation of Japanese ceramics). 12 vols. Tokyo: Heibonsha.

———. 1990. *Mokubei*. Vol. 25 of *Nihon tōji taikei* (Compendium of Japanese ceramics). Tokyo: Heibonsha.

Mizuta Toshihisa, ed. 1972. *Kenkadō nikki*. Osaka: Kenkadō Nikki Kankōkai.

Mizutani Hidezo. 1986. "Bankōyaki no senchaki" (Banko ware sencha utensils). In *Edo no dezain* (Edo designs), 104–107. Vol. 9 of *Kōtō* (Antiques). Tokyo: Yomiuri Shinbunsha.

Mody, N.H.N. 1969. *A Collection of Nagasaki Colour Prints and Paintings*. Tokyo and Rutland, Vt.: Tuttle.

Moeran, Brian. 1982–1983. "A Survey of Modern Japanese Pottery." *Ceramics Monthly* 30, 8 (October): 30–32; 30, 9 (November): 44–46; 30, 10 (December): 32–34; 31, 1 (January): 54–57.

Montreal. 1989. *The Tokugawa Collection: Japan of the Shoguns*. Montreal: Montreal Museum of Fine Arts.

Mori Senzō. 1939. "Baiitsu to Shibutsu." *Gasetsu* 32 (August): 749–759. Reprinted in *Mori Senzō Chosakushū* (Complete works of Mori Senzō), vol. 4, 230–243. Tokyo: Chūōkōronsha, 1971.

Mori Tōru. 1985. "Shokunin utaawase-e ni tsuite" (On paintings of poetry competitions with figures representing different occupations). *Kobijutsu* 74 (April): 6–12.

*Moriya Masaji. 2000. "Seiwanhi to Seiwan Chakai" (The Blue Sea Memorial and the Blue Sea Tea Gathering). *Osaka no rekishi to bunkazai* 6: 13–20.

Moroyama Masanori. 1989. "Chikukōgei kindaika no shokō: kindai Tanabe Chikuunsai ron" (The dawn of modern bamboo crafts: an essay on Tanabe Chikuunsai I). *Tokyo Kokuritsu Kindai Bijutsukan kenkyūkiyo* (Bulletin of the National Museum of Modern Art) 2: 33–51, 86–88.

Morse, Edward S. 1901. *Catalogue of the Morse Collection of Japanese Pottery*. Boston: Museum of Fine Arts.

Moss, Paul. 1991. *Autumn Guests: Edo Period Painting and Lacquer*. London: Sydney L. Moss.

Mujaku Dōchū. 1909. *Zenrin shōkisen* (Zen notes on objects in the world). Reprint, Tokyo: Sanbō Shoin, 1981.

Murai Yasuhiko. 1980. *Chanoyu jinbutsu-shi* (Records of tea masters). Tokyo: Kadokawa Shoten.

———. 1989. "The Development of Chanoyu: Before Rikyu." In *Tea in Japan: Essays on the History of Chanoyu*, edited by Paul Varley and Kumakura Isao, 3–32. Honolulu: University of Hawai'i Press.

Murayama Yoshihiro. 1973. "Tanomura Chikuden no Binkaron" (The treatise on flower arranging by Tanomura Chikuden). *Chūgoku koten kenkyū* 19 (June): 62–63.

Museum of the Imperial Collections. 1995. *Meiji bijutsu saiken I, Meiji bijutsukai to Nihon kinkōkyōkai no jidai* (Reappraisal of Meiji period art. I, The era of the Meiji art association and the Japanese metalworkers guild). Tokyo: Kunaichō Sannomaru Shozōkan [Museum of the Imperial Collections].

Nagami Tokutarō. 1927. *Nagasaki no bijutsu-shi* (History of art in Nagasaki). Reprint, Kyoto: Rinsen Shoten, 1974.

Nagasaki. 1923. *Fūzoku ben* (Volume on manners and customs). Vol. 8 of *Nagasaki-shi shi* (History of Nagasaki city). Nagasaki: Nagasaki Shiyakusho [Nagasaki City Hall].

Nagasaki City Museum. 1995. *Nagasaki Shiritsu Hakubutsukan shiryō zuroku IV* (Catalogue 4 of materials in the Nagasaki City Museum). Nagasaki: Nagasaki Shiritsu Hakubutsukan [Nagasaki City Museum].

Nagoya City Museum. 1981. *Owari no kaiga-shi, nanga* (The history of painting in Owari, nanga). Nagoya: Nagoya-shi Hakubutsukan [Nagoya City Museum].

*———. 1998. *Nangakka Yamamoto Baiitsu* (Literati painter Yamamoto Baiitsu). Nagoya: Nagoya-shi Hakubutsukan [Nagoya City Museum].

Nakagawa Chuei. 1966. *Shinzoku kibun* (Record of Chinese customs). Edited by Sun Boshun and Muramatsu Kazuya. *Tōyō bunko*, 62 and 70. Tokyo: Heibonsha.

Nakagawa Tokuuemon. 1989. *Sumiya annai ki* (Guide to the Sumiya). Kyoto: Sumiya Bungeisha.

Nakai, Kate Wildman. 1980. "The Naturalization of Confucianism in Tokugawa Japan: The Problem of Sinocentrism." *Harvard Journal of Asiatic Studies* 40, 1: 157–199.

Nakajima Yōsuke. 1943. *Senchadō* (The Way of sencha). Kyoto: Taigadō.

Nakamura Masao et al., eds. 1986. *Chadōgu 1* (Tea utensils, part 1). Vol. 10 of *Chadō shukin* (Tapestry of tea). Tokyo: Shōgakkan.

———. 1987. *Zashiki to roji* (Rooms and gardens). Vol. 7 of *Chadō shukin* (Tapestry of tea). Tokyo: Shōgakkan.

Nakamura Yukihiko. 1961. *Kinsei sakka kenkyū* (Research on writers of the early modern era). Tokyo: Sanichi Shobō.

Nakano, Mitsuyoshi. 1989. "The Role of Traditional Aesthetics." In *Eighteenth-Century Japan: Culture and Society*, edited by C. Andrew Gerstle, 124–131. Sydney: Allen and Unwin.

Nakanodō Kazunobu. 1981. "Edo kōki no kyōyaki" (Kyoto ceramics of the late Edo period). In *Kyoto*, 108–118. Vol. 5 of *Nihon yakimono shūsei* (Compilation of Japanese ceramics), edited by Mitsuoka Tadanari. Tokyo: Heibonsha.

Narabayashi Tadao. 1971. *Sencha no sekai* (The world of sencha). Tokyo: Tokuma Shoten.

Narazaki Muneshige, ed. 1987. *Hizō ukiyo-e taikei, Daiei Hakubutsukan I* (Compendium of Ukiyo-e masterpieces in the British Museum, 1). Tokyo: Kōdansha.

Natsume, Sōseki. 1968. *The Three Cornered World*. Translated by Alan Turney and Peter Owen. Tokyo: Tuttle.

Nezu. 1976. *Higashiyama gyomotsu: zakkashitsuin ni kanshin shiryō o chūshun ni* (Artworks commissioned for Higashiyama rulers: centering on documents concerning miscellaneous dwellings). Tokyo: Nezu Bijutsukan and Tokugawa Bijutsukan [Nezu Art Museum and Tokugawa Art Museum].

Nihon Daijiten Kankōkai. 1975. Nihon Daijiten Kankōkai. *Nihon kokugo daijiten* (Complete dictionary of the Japanese national language). 20 vols. Tokyo: Shōgakkan.

Nishi, Kazuo, and Kazuo Hozumi. 1985. *What Is Japanese Architecture?* Translated by H. Mack Horton. Tokyo: Kōdansha.

Nishiyama Matsunosuke et al., eds. 1984. *Edogaku jiten* (Dictionary of learning in Edo). Tokyo: Kobundō.

Nitta Kiyoharu. 1990. *Kyūsu no miryoku* (The charm of teapots). Tokyo: Kōgei Shuppan.

*Nomura Bijutsukan. 2007. *Nomura bijutsukan kenkyū kiyō. Tokushū sencha* (Special issue on *sencha* of the Nomura Art Museum research bulletin) 16. (Issue includes ten articles by Japanese scholars on various aspects of *sencha* and its arts).

Nunome Chōfu, ed. 1987. *Chūgoku chasho zenshū* (Complete collection of Chinese books on tea). 2 vols. Tokyo: Kyūko Shoin.

Ōba Osamu. 1967. *Edo jidai ni okeru karafune mochiwatashi sho no kenkyū* (A study of books imported to Japan on Chinese vessels during the Edo period). Osaka: Kansai University Institute of Oriental and Occidental Studies.

———. 1980. *Edo jida no Nichū hiwa* (The secret history of Sino-Japanese relations in the Edo period). Tōhō Sensho, 5. Tokyo: Tōhō Shoten.

———. 1984. *Edō jidai ni okeru Chūgoku bunka juyō no kenkyū* (A study of the reception of Chinese culture in the Edo period). Kyoto: Dōhosha.

———. 1988. "Nagasaki and the Importation of Chinese Books to Japan in the Edo Period." Translated by Joshua A. Fogel. *Sino-Japanese Studies Newsletter* 1, 1 (November): 24–32.

———. 1990. *Hakuen kinenkai setsuritsu sanjūshūnen Hakuen Shoin ten* (Exhibition of works related to the Hakuen Shoin in association with the thirtieth anniversary memorial service). Osaka: Kansai University Institute of Oriental and Occidental Studies.

———. 1995-1997. "Sino-Japanese Relations in the Edo Period." Translated by Joshua A. Fogel. *Sino-Japanese Studies* 8, 1 (October): 40–52; 8, 2 (May): 50–61; 9, 1 (October): 56–74; 9, 2 (April): 3–12; 10, 1 (October): 33–55.

*———. 2012. Joshua Fogel translator. *Books and Boats: Sino-Japanese Relations and Cultural Transmission in the Eighteenth and Nineteenth Centuries*. Portland: MerwinAsia.

Ogawa Kōraku. 1975a. "Ogawaryū sencha no rekishi 2" (Sencha of the Ogawa school, part 2). *Ogawaryū sencha* (Ogawa school sencha) 4 (summer): 6–12.

———. 1975b. "Tamekazuō kanreki chakai zuroku maki o miru" (Examination of the handscroll, illustrated record of the tea gathering in honor of Old Man Tamekazu's sixty-first birthday). *Ogawaryū sencha* 4 (summer): 30–35; 5 (autumn): 49–52.

———. 1982. *Ogawa Kōraku no sencha no miryoku* (The charm of sencha according to Ogawa Kōraku). Vol. 3 of *Kurashi no sekkei, dentō shirizu* (Traditional life series, plan for living). Tokyo: Chūōkōronsha.

———. 1986a. *Sencha ki no kiso chishiki* (Basic knowledge of sencha utensils). Kyoto: Mitsumura Suikō Shoin.

———. 1986b. *Sencha seki no hana* (Flower arrangements for sencha rooms). *Karaa bukkusu* 708 (Books in color series, 708). Osaka: Hoikusha.

*———. 2013. " 'Sencha-teki' to iu koto" (Sencha-like words). *Kagudōgu shitsunai shi*. 5 (May): 14–37.

*———. 2000. "Nihon no senchadō to chugoku rekidai no cha" (Japan's senchadō and tea in successive generations in China). In *Tōyō no cha* (Tea of the Orient), edited by Takahashi Tadahiko. Kyoto: Tankosha.

Okakura, Kakuzo. 1903. *The Ideals of the East, with Special Reference to the Art of Japan*. London: John Murray.

———. 1906. *The Book of Tea*. New York: Fox, Duffield and Company.

Onchi Keiko et al. 1983. "Jinbutsu-shi ni shu: Naniwa sencha taijinshū, Naniwa sanjuroku kajin" (Two types of records about people: a collection of great sencha tea masters of Naniwa [Osaka] and thirty-six beautiful women of Naniwa [Osaka]). *Osaka Furitsu Nakanoshima Toshokan kiyō* 19 (March): 37–55.

O'Neill, P. G. 1984. "Organization and Authority in the Traditional Arts." *Modern Asian Studies* 18, 4: 631–645.

Osaka. 1997. *Bunjin no akogare, seifu no kokoro: sencha, bi to sono katachi* (Sencha: Its beauty and spirit, seeking after seifu; the purity of mind like a bracing breeze). Osaka: Osaka Shiritsu Bijutsukan [Osaka Municipal Museum of Art].

Ōtsuki Mikio. 1995–1996. "Sencha shi shōyō" (Ramblings on the history of sencha). An ongoing series in the journal *Senchadō*, published by the Zen Nihon Senchadō Renmeikai. Part 1, no. 453 (May): 22–23; part 5, no. 457 (September): 14–15; part 6, no. 458 (October): 16–17; part 7, no. 459 (November): 18–19; part 8, no. 460 (December): 20–21; part 10, no. 462 (February): 26–27; part 11, no. 463 (March): 28–29; part 12, no. 464 (April): 22–23; part 13, no. 465 (May): 22–23; part 14, no. 466 (June), 26–27; part 15, no. 467 (July): 22–23; part 16, no. 468 (August): 36–37; part 17, no. 469 (September): 12–13.

———. 1996. "Ōbakusan no kaisō to sencha" (The establishment of Mount Ōbaku and sencha). In *Nagasaki Tōjin bōeki to senchadō* (The Nagasaki China trade and the sencha tea ceremony), 104–111. Tokyo: Itabashi Kuritsu Sōgō Shiryōkan [Itabashi Ward Museum of Folklore].

*———. 2004. *Sencha bunka kō: bunjincha no keifu* (Notes on sencha culture: the genealogy of literati tea). Kyoto: Shibunkaku.

*———. 2013. *Baisaō gego: yaku chū* (Verses of the Old Tea Peddler: translation notes). Uji-shi: Zen Nihon Senchado Renmei.

Parker, William, and Betty Parker. 1984. "Kanō Tessai and His Last Apprentice." *Arts of Asia* 14, 2 (March–April): 72–81.

Pierson, John D. 1980. *Tokutomi Sohō, 1863–1957: A Journalist for Modern Japan*. Princeton: Princeton University Press.

Plutschow, Herbert E. 1983. Historical Nagasaki. Tokyo: Japan Times.

———. 1986. *Historical Chanoyu*. Tokyo: Japan Times.

Pollack, David. 1986. *The Fracture of Meaning: Japan's Synthesis of China from the Eighth through the Eighteenth Centuries*. Princeton: Princeton University Press.

Pollard, Clare. 1989. "The Influence of Sencha and the Literati Movement on Kyoto Ceramics in the Late Edo Period." Tripos diss., Cambridge University.

Rawson, Jessica, ed. 1992. *The British Museum Book of Chinese Art*. New York: Thames and Hudson.

Rimer, J. Thomas. 1991a. "Ishikawa Jōzan." In *Shisendō: Hall of the Poetry Immortals*, by J. Thomas Rimer et al., 3–26. New York: Weatherhill.

Rimer, J . Thomas, et al. 1991b. *Shisendō: Hall of the Poetry Immortals*. New York: Weatherhill.

*Roddy, Stephen J. 2015. "In Praise of Jeweled Streams: 'Ugetsu monogatari,' Nativism, and Tea." *Japanese Language and Literature* 49/1 (April): 1-29.

Rogers, Howard. 1985. "Beyond Deep Waters." *Sophia International Review* 7: 15–37.

———. 1997. "Visions of Man in Chinese Art, with Selected Japanese Paintings." *Kaikodo Journal* 3 (Spring).

Saeki Futoshi. 1940. *Sencha temae* (Sencha serving procedures). Vol. 9 of *Chadōbunko* (Books on the tea ceremony). Reprint, Kyoto: Kawahara Shoten, 1967 and 1986.

Saga. 1983. *Baisaō*. Saga: Saga Kenritsu Hakubutsukan [Saga Prefectural Museum].

Saionji Ayumi. 1980. *Sencha no dōgu* (Sencha utensils). Tokyo: Yūzankaku.

Sakai Keiji. 1987. *Ōita Kenritsu Geijutsukaikan shozō Chikuden nikki ni miru Tanomura Chikuden to Kagetsuan Kakuō no deai* (Records of meetings between Tanomura Chikuden and Kagetsuan Kakuō as seen in the Chikuden diary owned by the Ōita Prefecture Art Hall). Osaka: Kagetsuan.

Sakata Keizō. 1917. *Kagetsuanryū hōshiki zufu sencha seiganki* (An illustrated book of rules for the pure enjoyment of sencha according to methods of the Kagetsuan school). Reprint, Osaka: Shōsendō, 1922.

———. 1927. *Tsūzoku sencha hōshiki* (Popular methods of preparation for sencha). 1927. Reprint, Osaka: Maeda Bunshindō, 1929.

Sasaki Gōzō. 1982. "Mokubei to Chikuden" (Mokubei and Chikuden). *Kōbijutsu* 64 (October): 4–7.

Sasayama. 1988. *Ōchiyama yaki fukkō kinen, Ōchiyama meihinten zuroku* (Catalogue of an exhibition of Ochiyama ware commemorating the restoration of interest in Ochiyama ware). Sasayama: Sasayama Rekishi Bijutsukan [Sasayama Museum of History and Art].

———. 1991. *Nikon no hanyō jiki* (Porcelains from official daimyo-sponsored kilns). Sasayama: Sasayama Rekishi Bijutsukan [Sasayama Museum of History and Art].

Schaap, Robert, ed. 1987. *Meiji: Japanese Art in Transition*. Leiden: Society for Japanese Arts and Crafts.

Screech, Timon. 1993. "The Strangest Place in Edo: The Temple of the Five Hundred Arhats." *Monumenta Nipponica* 48, 4 (winter): 407–428.

———. 1996. *The Western Scientific Gaze and Popular Imagery in Later Edo Japan: The Lens within the Heart*. New York: Cambridge University Press.

Seattle. 1988. *In Pursuit of the Dragon: Traditions and Transitions in Ming Ceramics*. Seattle: Seattle Art Museum.

*Seikadō Bunko Art Museum. 1998. *Senchagu meihin ten* = Art of "Sencha"—selected from the Seikadō collection. Tokyo: Seikado Bunkō Bijutsukan [Seikado Bunko Art Museum].

*———. 2015. *Sencha dōgu kanshō no tebiki* (Guide to appreciating *sencha* utensils). Tokyo: Seikado Bunkō Bijutsukan [Seikadō Bunko Art Museum].

Sen Sōshitsu, ed. 1977a. *Chadō koten zenshū* (Complete collection of old texts on the tea ceremony). Vols. 2 and 3. Kyoto: Tankosha.

———. 1977b. "The Classic of Tea, the Ch'a Ching of Lu Yu." *Chanoyu Quarterly* 19: 5–6.

Sendai. 1994. *Kōko no gajin Sugai Baikan* (The noble painter Sugai Baikan). Sendai: Sendaishi Hakubutsukan [Sendai City Museum].

Shiba Kōkan, 1992. *Edo, Nagasaki-e kikō, Saiyū ryodan* (Illustrated travelogue of Edo and Nagasaki, the journey to the West). Tokyo: Kokusho Kankōkai.

*Shimamura Yukitada. 2022. *Rai San'yō to sencha: kinsei kōki no bunjin no shumi to sono seishinsei ni kansuru shiron* (Rai San'yō and Sencha: An essay on the pastimes and spirituality of literati in the early modern period). Tokyo: Kasama Shoin.

Shimizu, Yoshiaki, and Carolyn Wheelwright, eds.1976. *Japanese Ink Paintings from American Collections: The Muromachi Period, An Exhibition in Honor of Shūjirō Shimada*. Princeton: Princeton University Art Museum and Princeton University Press.

Shimonaka Kunihiko, ed. 1984. *Yakimono no jiten* (Ceramics dictionary). Tokyo: Heibonsha.

Shogun Age Executive Committee. 1983. *The Shogun Age Exhibition*. Tokyo: Tokugawa Art Museum.

Shufunotomosha. 1973. *Sencha zensho* (Complete book of sencha). Tokyo: Shufunotomosha.

———. 1975. *Baisaō shūsei* (Collected records of Baisaō). Tokyo: Shufunotomosha.

———. 1976. *Zoku sencha zensho* (The second series of the complete book of sencha). Tokyo: Shufunotomosha.

———. 1981. *Gendai senchadō jiten* (Dictionary of modern sencha). Tokyo: Shufunotomosha.

———. 1988. *Sencha no yōgo shū* (Glossary of terminology on sencha). Vol. 13 of *Chanoyu annai shiriizu* (Guide to chanoyu). Tokyo: Shufunotomosha.

Singer, Robert T., and Hollis Goodall. 1997. *Hirado Porcelain of Japan from the Kurtzman Family Collection*. Los Angeles: Los Angeles County Museum of Art.

Smith, Lawrence. 1973. "Japanese Porcelain in the First Half of the Nineteenth Century." *Transactions of the Oriental Ceramic Society* 39: 43–82.

Sugihara Izan, ed. 1910. *Nihon shoga jinmei jiten* (Dictionary of Japanese painters and calligraphers). Reprint, Tokyo: Nihon Tosho Sentaa, 1978.

*Surak, Kristin. 2013. *Making Tea, Making Japan: Cultural Nationalism in Practice*. Stanford, CA: Stanford University Press.

Suzuki, Hiroyuki. 1991. "The Garden of the Shisendō: Its *Genius Loci*." In *Shisendō: Hall of the Poetry Immortals*, by J . Thomas Rimer et al., 91–110. New York: Weatherhill.

Suzuki Kei, comp. 1983. *Chūgoku kaiga sōgō zuroku* (Comprehensive illustrated catalogue of Chinese paintings). 5 vols. Tokyo: University of Tokyo Press.

Takahashi Hiromi. 1988. *Kyoto geien no nettowaaku* (Networks of art and literary circles of Kyoto). Tokyo: Pelican Press.

Takahashi, Tadahiko. 1992. "White Tea: Tea in the Song Dynasty." *Chanoyu Quarterly* 69: 33–42.

Takakusa Junjirō and Watanabe Kaigyoku, eds. 1924–1935. *Taishō shinshō daizōkyō* (The new Taishō-period compilation of the Tripitaka). 100 vols. Tokyo: Taishō Issaikyō Kankōkai.

Takeda Shinken. 1897. "Yamamoto Baiitsu koto" (Notes on Yamamoto Baiitsu). *Kaiga sōshi* 130.

Taketani Chōjirō. 1977. *Chikuden-sō shiyū garoku yakkai* (Annotated translation of Chikudensō's record of painting by teachers and friends). Tokyo: Chikuma Shoin.

Takeuchi, Melinda. 1983. "Ike Taiga: A Biographical Study." *Harvard Journal of Asiatic Studies* 43, 1: 141–186.

———. 1992. *Taiga's True Views: The Language of Landscape Painting in Eighteenth-Century Japan*. Stanford: Stanford University Press.

Tanaka Seiha. 1973. *Sencha Kagetsuan* (Kagetsuan-school sencha). Tokyo: Shufunotomosha.

Tanaka, Stefan. 1993. *Japan's Orient: Rendering Pasts into History*. Berkeley: University of California Press.

Tanihata, Akio. 1984. "Tea and Kyoto Ceramics in the Late Edo Period." Translated by Richard Wilson. *Chanoyu Quarterly* 39: 7–27.

Tanimura Tameumi. 1983. "Baisaō nenpo" (Chronology of Baisaō's Life). In *Baisaō*, 86–99. Saga: Saga Kenritsu Hakubutsukan [Saga Prefectural Museum].

Tessai Art Museum. 1991. *Tessai to sencha no sekai* (Tessai and the world of sencha). Takarazuka: Kiyoshikōjin Seichōji Tessai Bijutsukan.

Toby, Ronald P. 1991. *State and Diplomacy in Early Modern Japan: Asia in the Development of the Tokugawa Bakufu*. Stanford: Stanford University Press.

Tokoname. 1986. *Kin Shikō ten* (Exhibition on Jin Shiheng). Tokoname: Tokoname-shi Minzoku Shiryōkan [Tokoname City Folk Museum].

Tokyo National Museum. 1979. *Tokubetsu ten: Kanō-ha no kaiga* (Special exhibition: paintings of the Kanō school). Tokyo: Tokyo Kokuritsu Hakubutsukan [Tokyo National Museum].

Totman, Conrad. 1993. *Early Modern Japan*. Berkeley: University of California Press.

Tsuchida Kenjirō. 1973. "Tanomura Chikuden no Binkaron" (Treatise on Flower Arranging). *Chūgoku koten kenkyū* 19 (June): 64–78.

Tsuji, Nobuo. 1994. "Ornament (Kazari): An Approach to Japanese Culture." *Archives of Asian Art* 47: 35–45.

Tsukiyama 1989. *Tsukiyama niwa tsukuriden (kōhen) kaisetsu* (Explanation of the latter edition of the notes on constructing artificial hills and gardens). Typeset modern edition edited by Uehara Keiji, Tokyo: Kajima Shoten, 1989.

Tsukuda Ichiyū. 1972. *Sencha nyūmon* (Introduction to sencha). Osaka: Naniwasha.

Tsukuda Ikki. 1981. "Sencha no shomotsu" (Sencha books). In *Gendai senchadō jiten* (Dictionary of modern sencha), 479–487. Tokyo: Shufunotomo.

———. 1985. *Sencha no tabi: bunjin no sokusei o honete* (Travels with sencha: visiting the footsteps of the literati). Osaka: Osaka Shoseki.

*———. 2013. "Sencha no rinen to hyōgen" (Sencha philosophy and expression). In *Kōza Nihon chanoyu zenshi 3. Kindai*, edited by Chanoyu Bunka Gakkai. Kyoto: Shibunkaku, 211–241.

Tsunoda, Ryusaku, et al. 1958. *Sources of the Japanese Tradition*. Vol. 1. New York: Columbia University Press.

Tucker, Mary Evelyn. 1989. *Moral and Spiritual Cultivation in Japanese Neo-Confucianism: The Life and Thought of Kaibara Ekken (1630–1714)*. Albany: State University of New York Press.

Ueda, Akinari. 1977. *Ugetsu monogatari: Tales of Moonlight and Rain*. Translated by Leon Zolbrod. Tokyo: Tuttle.

Ueda, Makoto. 1983. "Fūryū." In *The Encyclopedia of Japan*, 2: 374. Tokyo: Kōdansha.

Uehara Keiji, ed. 1989. *Tsukiyama niwa tsukuriden (kōhen) kaisetsu* (Explanation of the latter edition of notes on constructing artificial hills and gardens). Tokyo: Kajima Shoten.

Ukers, William H. 1935. *All About Tea*. 2 vols. New York: Tea and Coffee Trade Journal.

Umezawa Seiichi. 1919. *Nihon nanga-shi* (History of Japanese literati painting). Tokyo: Nanyōdō.

van Gulik, R. H. 1958. *Chinese Pictorial Art as Viewed by the Connoisseur*. Orientale Roma Series, 19. Rome: Instituto Italiano per il Medio ed Estremo Oriente.

Varley, Paul. 1989. "Chanoyu: From the Genroku Epoch to Modern Times." In *Tea in Japan: Essays on the History of Chanoyu*, edited by Paul Varley and Kumakura Isao, 161–194. Honolulu: University of Hawaii Press.

Waddell, Norman. 1984. "The Old Tea Seller: The Life and Poetry of Baisaō." *Eastern Buddhist* 17, 2 (autumn): 93–123.

*———. 2008. *The Old Tea Seller: Baisaō—Life and Zen Poetry in 18th Century Kyoto*. Berkeley, CA: Counterpoint; Distributed by Publishers Group West.

Wakimoto Sokurō. 1921. *Heian meitōden Mokubei* (Record of the great Kyoto potter, Mokubei). Kyoto: Rakutōkai.

Watson, Burton. 1976. *Poetry and Prose in Chinese by Japanese Writers of the Later Period*. Vol. 2 of *Japanese Literature in Chinese*. New York: Columbia University Press.

———. 1990. *Kanshi: The Poetry of Ishikawa Jōzan and Other Edo-Period Poets*. San Francisco: North Point Press.

Watson, Burton, trans. 1983. *Grass Hill: Poems and Prose by the Japanese Monk Gensei*. New York: Columbia University Press.

Watt, James C. Y. 1987. "The Literati Environment." In *The Chinese Scholar's Studio: Artistic Life in the Late Ming Period*, edited by Chu-tsing Li and James C.Y. Watt, 1–13. New York: Asia Society and Thames and Hudson.

Weigl, Gail Capitol. 1980. "The Reception of Chinese Painting Models in Muromachi Japan." *Monumenta Nipponica* 36, 3 (autumn): 259–272.

Wilson, Richard. 1989. "The Tea Ceremony: Art and Etiquette for the Tokugawa Era." In *The Tokugawa Collection: Japan of the Shoguns*, 63–74. Montreal: Montreal Museum of Fine Arts.

Wilson, Richard L. 1991. *The Art of Ogata Kenzan: Persona and Production in Japanese Ceramics*. New York: Weatherhill.

Woodson, Yoko. 1983. "Traveling Bunjin Painters and Their Patrons: Economic Life Style and Art of Rai Sanyo and Tanomura Chikuden." Ph.D. diss., University of California, Berkeley.

*Wu, Jiang. 2015. *Leaving for the Rising Sun: Chinese Master Yinyuan and the Authenticity Crisis in Early Modern East Asia*. New York: Oxford University Press.

Wu Zhiho. 1990. *Ming Qing shidai fanzha shenghuo* (The life of tea drinking in the Ming and Qing dynasties). Taipei: Boyuan Chuban You Xian Gong Si.

Wylie, Hugh. 1991. "Nanga Painting Treatises of Nineteenth-Century Japan: Translations, Commentary, and Analysis." Ph.D. diss., University of Kansas.

Xu Xianyao, ed. 1990. *Zhongguo cha shu ti yao* (Summary of Chinese books on tea). Taipei: Boyuan Chuban You Xian Gong Si.

Yamada Tōzan. 1986. "Tokoname to senchaki" (Tokoname and sencha utensils). In *Edo no dezain* (Edo designs), 108–111. Vol. 9 of Kōtō (Antiques). Tokyo: Yomiuri Shinbunsha.

Yamamoto Noritsuna. 1983. *Nagasaki tōjin yashiki* (The Chinese community at Nagasaki). Tokyo: Kenkosha.

Yamanouchi Chōzō. 1981. *Nihon nanga shi* (History of literati painting in Japan). Tokyo: Rurishobō.

Yanai Kenji. 1973. *Gairai bunka to Kyūshū* (Overseas culture and Kyūshū). Vol. 2 of *Kyūshū bunka ronshū* (Collected discussions on Kyūshū culture). Tokyo: Heibonsha.

Yasutaka, Teruoka. 1989. "The Pleasure Quarters and Tokugawa Culture." In *Eighteenth-Century Japan: Culture and Society*, edited by C. Andrew Gerstle, 3–32. Sydney: Allen and Unwin.

Yokoyama Tadashi. 1987. "Bunjin no konomi to sono kukan" (Scholars' pastimes and their environments). In *Zashiki to roji* (Rooms and gardens), edited by Nakamura Masao et al., 252–262. Vol. 7 of *Chadō shukin* (Tapestry of tea). Tokyo: Shōgakkan.

Yonezawa, Yoshiho, and Chu Yoshizawa. 1974. *Japanese Painting in the Literati Style*. Translated by Betty Iverson Monroe. Tokyo: Weatherhill/Heibonsha.

Yoshikawa, Kōjirō. 1983. *Jinsai, Sorai, Norinaga: Three Classical Philologists of Mid-Tokugawa Japan*. Tokyo: Tōhō Gakkai.

Young, Blake Morgan. 1982. *Ueda Akinari*. Vancouver: University of British Columbia Press.

Yukawa Gen'yō. 1930. *Kinsei gajinden* (Biographies of elegant people of the early modern era). 3 vols. Tokyo: Hyōden.

Zen Nihon Senchadō Renmei. 1992. National Japanese Sencha Association. *Sencha: dōgu to shitsurai* (Sencha: tea utensils and their arrangement). Tokyo: Fujin Gahōsha.

Zengaku Daijiten Hensanjo. 1985. *Shinpan Zengaku daijiten* (New edition of the complete dictionary of Zen Buddhism). Tokyo: Taishukan.

*Zhang, Lawrence. 2016. "A Foreign Infusion: The Forgotten Legacy of Japanese Chadō on Modern Chinese Tea Arts." *Gastronomica: Rescuing Taste from the Nation: Oceans, Borders, and Culinary Flows*. Special Issue of *The Journal of Critical Food Studies*. 16/1: 53-62.

Index

Page numbers in *italic* refer to illustrations.

About the Author

PATRICIA J. GRAHAM, a former professor and museum curator, is an independent scholar based in Boulder County, Colorado, affiliated with the University of Kansas Center for East Asian Studies as a Research Associate, and a certified appraiser of East Asian art. Among her many other publications are two books: *Japanese Design: An Illustrated Guide to Art, Architecture and Aesthetics in Japan* (Tuttle, 2021) and *Faith and Power in Japanese Buddhist Art, 1600–2005* (University of Hawai'i Press, 2007).

Floating World Editions

Floating World Editions publishes books that contribute to a deeper understanding of Asian cultures. Editorial supervision: Ray Furse. Additional editorial support: David Dunfield, Stuart Katz, Janet Chen, and Mary Mortensen. Revised book and cover design: Michelle Landry. Printing and binding: 1010 Printing International Limited. The typefaces used are Minion Pro, Avenir, and Kozuka Gothic.